The Modern Contest

THE MODERN CONTEST

A Systemic Guide to the Pattern That Connects

Individual Psychotherapy, Family Therapy, Group Work, Teaching, Organizational Life and Large-Scale Social Problems

James P. Gustafson, M.D.

AND

Lowell W. Cooper, Ph.D.

W•W•NORTON & COMPANY   NEW YORK•LONDON

Permission to reprint quotations:
Morris, W., & Morris, M. (1971). *Morris dictionary of word and phrase origins* (pp. 583–584). New York: Harper & Row, Publishers, Inc. Reprinted with permission of publisher. Gass, W. H. (1988). The polemical philosopher (pp. 35–41). February 4, 1988. Reprinted with permission from *The New York Review of Books*. Copyright © 1988 Nyrev, Inc. Bourdieu, P. (1984). *Distinction. A social critique of the judgment of taste* (p. 33). Cambridge: Harvard University Press. Reprinted with permission from the publisher. Copyright © 1984 by the President and Fellows of Harvard College and Routledge & Kegan Paul Ltd. Havens, L. L. (1986). *Making contact* (p. 114). Cambridge: Harvard University Press. Reprinted with permission from the publisher. Copyright © 1984 by the President and Fellows of Harvard College. Leopold, A. (1949). *A Sand county Almanac* (p. 41). New York: Oxford University Press. Reprinted with permission from the publisher. Auerbach, R. (1986). Celtics. Madison, Wisconsin: *The Capital Times*, May 13, 1986. Reprinted by permission of *The Capital Times*. Galbraith, J. K. (1983). *The anatomy of power* (p. 41). Boston: Houghton Mifflin Company. Copyright © 1983 by John Kenneth Galbraith. Reprinted by permission of Houghton Mifflin Company. Terkel, S. (1972). *Working*. New York: 1972. Copyright Pantheon Books, a Division of Random House, Inc. Reprinted by permission of the publisher. Voltaire (1759). *Candide*. Translation copyright 1947 by John Butt. New York: Viking Penguin. Reprinted with permission. Brodsky, J. (1986). *Less than one: Selected essays*. New York: Farrar, Straus & Giroux. Gogol, N. (1842). *Dead Souls* (p. 10). Translation copyright David Magarshack, 1961. New York: Viking Penguin. St. Exupery A. de (1943). *The little prince*. Translated from the French by Katherine Woods. New York: Harcourt, Brace, Jovanovich. Reprinted with permission. Bloch, M. (1953). *The historian's craft*, translated by Peter Putnam. New York: Alfred A. Knopf, Inc. Reprinted by permission of the publisher. Selvini Palazzoli, M. (1985). The problem of the sibling as referring person (pp. 21–34). *Journal of Marital and Family Therapy*, Vol. 11, Number 1. Copyright 1985. Reprinted with permission from American Association for Marriage and Family Therapy. Kuhn, T. S. (1970). *Criticism and the growth of knowledge*. Cambridge, England: Cambridge University Press. Laing, R. D. (1959). *The divided self*. London: Tavistock Press. Reprinted with permission from the publisher. Kreeger, L. (Ed.) (1975). *The large group, dynamics and therapy*. London: Constable & Company, Ltd. Reprinted with permission from American Association for Marriage and Family Therapy. Marks, I. (1987). *Fear, phobias, and rituals*. New York: Oxford University Press. Reprinted with permission from the publisher. Foucault, M. (1980). *Power/Knowledge. Selected interviews and other writings* (1972–77). C. Gordon (Ed.). New York. Copyright © 1980 by The Harvester Press. Reprinted by permission of Pantheon Books, a Division of Random House, Inc. Balint, M. (1954). Method and technique in the teaching of medical psychology. II. Training general practitioners in psychotherapy. *British Journal of Medical Psychology, 27*, (pp. 37–41). London: British Psychological Society. Reprinted with permission of The British Psychological Society and Enid Balint. Lowell, R. (1985). Epilogue. In H. Vendler (Ed.), *The Harvard book of contemporary American poetry* (p. 112). Copyright © Farrar, Straus and Giroux, Inc. Reprinted with permission. Lifton, R. J. (1986). *The Nazi doctors*. New York: Basic Books. Machiavelli, N. *The prince and the discourses* (pp. 54–55, 65), translated by Luigi Ricci, revised by E. R. P. Vincent (OUP 1935). New York: Modern Library, Oxford University

Continued on page 243 which constitutes an extension of the copyright page

Printed in the United States of America.

First Edition.

Library of Congress Cataloging-in-Publication Data

Gustafson, James Paul.
  The modern contest : a systemic guide to the pattern that connects individual psychotherapy, family therapy, group work, teaching, organizational life, and large scale social problems / James P. Gustafson and Lowell W. Cooper.
      p.   cm.
  Includes bibliographical references.
  1. Success — Psychological aspects.   2. Competition (Psychology)
3. Psychotherapy.   4. Success — Social aspects.   5. Competition
(Psychology) — Social aspects.   6. Psychotherapy — Social aspects.
I. Cooper, Lowell W.   II. Title.
BF687.S8087 1990   302′.14 – dc20   89-38930

ISBN 0-393-70080-1

W. W. Norton & Company, Inc., 500 Fifth Avenue, New York, N.Y. 10110
W. W. Norton & Company Ltd., 37 Great Russell Street, London WC1B 3NU

1 2 3 4 5 6 7 8 9 0

To our parents,
Jane and Paul Gustafson
and Florence and Irving Cooper,
To our wives,
Ruth Gustafson and Susan Laughlin,
To our children,
Ian, Caitlin and Karin,
Michael, Cora and Rose.

Contents

PART I

Taking Our Bearings

Because the modern contest continually confuses help (and taking fierce advantage), loyalty is the best introduction, readiness for sudden change is the best policy, and meeting crude challenges cheerfully is the least troublesome for our friends.

PART II

Organizing

The best strategy for organizing groups is building alliances with others (Us) to engage with a common antagonist (Them, It), while watching for mimicry of loyalty.

The challenge can be won today as it was won yesterday if the field stays the same, but most modern fields of contest are continually altered by larger fields that surround them and take over (eventually), by smaller fields which burst open into the one in question (suddenly), for which we can prepare ourselves.

PART III

Reading Situations

Clarity can be gained and renewed by getting outside the cloud of a pattern:

by looking for its edge, by assuming it will envelop us, by changing vantage points.

The zeal, hope or confidence of any group depends upon readiness, not only for victory, but for nothing happening, for take over, for delayed disadvantages glossed over in the deal, since we live in a (not so) polite Darwinian world where territory (almost always) comes first.

PART IV

Moving Freely

Signs of entrapment can be recognized in oneself, in the group, in the surrounding envelope, allowing smooth, accented or abrupt transitions.

Entry and exit from groups depend upon mastery of the grammar of cages.

PART V

Counterposing

Many situations become workable when posed in a different time: in the past, in the present, in the future, after the lull, in the other half of the loop, in the simultaneous past and future.

Any territory will be invaded by three kinds of armies of contest: the armies of the oblivious who have something they are authorized to check; the armies of the desperate who must have their fortunes improved or else become lost; the armies of the overpowering who can clear the room. Each ought to get a different kind of counterproposal.

PART VI

Complex Counterposing

All complex proposals have to secure what is invaluable in a line of work while taking new adaptive forms.

11. Gathering Strength   155

   If war has been mastered as contest, then contest can be mastered by backing
   off from such fields into the inner, more protected compartments of civility,
   play and solitude, where maps can be redrawn, before winning and losing
   must be resumed.

PART VII

Taking Our Bearings

12. An Attitude for All Seasons   171

   Winning can be kept in perspective by listening to the audience that matters
   to you; lasting can be sustained by clear distinction between mistakes and
   larger purposes; and vigor can choose its own battles.

NOTES

Acknowledgments

W<small>E THANK THE</small> teachers, colleagues, friends, students and patients who have helped us along in our twenty years of delving into the troubles and triumphs of groups. We thank especially: Lars Lofgren and Margaret Rioch for getting us underway; Karl Tomm and Robin Skynner for helping us turn the systemic corner which changed our seeing altogether; our loyal readers and critics, Mike Moran, Kathleen Levenick, Mike Wood, Myron Sharaf, Les Havens, Claudia Bell, Verneice Thompson and Robin Fine; Dee Jones and Linda Ward for expert, faithful help with the manuscript; and Susan Barrows for her editorial insistence on clarity as the measure of thinking and writing.

Introduction

THIS IS A BOOK of systemic strategy for understanding our powers in the modern contest: the common pattern that connects individual psychotherapy, family therapy, group work, teaching, organizational life and large-scale social problems. The *modern contest* decides winning and losing very fast, continually evolves into new forms and confuses help (with fierce taking of advantage). Although rivals may resort to literal destruction of their opponents, they usually seek to *disqualify* them from the field of the contest. We propose a series of *postures* for meeting the challenge of any given case: slower and more complex to allow preparing for situations from a calm distance, fast and instinctive for action up close, then slower and more complex again for calm counterposing before second chances are taken.

Systemic thinking, borrowed from biology (Bateson, 1972, 1979; Maturana and Varela, 1980), has been surprisingly useful in handling problems in the field of family therapy (e.g., Selvini Palazzoli, 1988; Selvini Palazzoli, Boscolo, Cecchin, and Prata, 1978; Selvini Palazzoli, Cirillo, Selvini, and Sorrentino, 1989; White, 1983, 1984, 1988). From our experience we know that it makes a difference as well for neighboring fields—smaller like individual psychotherapy, larger like group work, teaching, organizational life and large-scale social problems. But why? For a long while, we did not understand why comparable strategies worked well from very small-scale to very large-scale social situations, until we saw the common structure of the modern contest, the pattern that connects (Bateson, 1979) them all.

We propose strategy for defending all of these causes as a single subject for systemic clinicians. We believe this subject will also interest broadly educated readers who must find their own way in this polite Darwinian world, as well as thoughtful students of the human condition who seek to place their focal academic interest upon the broad canvas of this surprising landscape.

What is this modern contest which is held everywhere? We see three structural constants. The first is that winning and losing are usually decided very fast. The second is that every fast contest is undergoing an evolution of what bears upon its play, which only slower consideration will notice. The third is that most contests have cooperative angles. We may discover friends to keep forever in mean situations, but typically it is very difficult to tell the proportion of help (and taking fierce advantage). How then do we play fast while taking our time to see what takes time to unfold?

Within the practical disciplines where we propose to be of help, there is so much that is hidden from view. We see but the small arcs of larger circles, loops and tangles (Gustafson, 1986). We are often asked to tie up a loose end, but then find ourselves tied into a huge, larger problem that was hidden in other compartments. Our reputations depend upon skill in taking up these questions of our patients, students and clients, but our lasting depends upon knowing something about the formidable pattern that is likely to be connected to the question.

A contemporary children's tale called *Doctor De Soto* (Steig, 1981) illustrates the usual subtlety we'll need for "meeting the challenge of the individual case" (Winnicott, 1965). Doctor De Soto is a mouse dentist who is moved by the suffering of a fox to remove his rotten, ailing tooth. Under the ether, the fox mumbled:

> "How I love them raw . . . with just a pinch of salt, and
> a . . . dry . . . white wine."
> They could guess what he was dreaming about. Mrs. De Soto
> handed her husband a pole to keep the fox's mouth open.
>   . . .
> "He didn't know what he was saying," said Mrs. De Soto. "Why
> should he harm us? We're helping him."
> "Because he's a fox!" said Doctor De Soto. "They're wicked,
> wicked creatures."

Doctor De Soto is more alert than his wife, who has been overly domesticated by her concept of a dentist's duty. Doctor De Soto plans not only to put in the new tooth for the fox but also to glue his mouth shut!

This introduces the kind of complexity necessary to all of us to last in this surprising landscape. Any simplicity of image, such as the image of the duty of a dentist to take out a rotten tooth, is apt to be one-third right, one-third dangerous and one-third undecidable. There are always other considerations, such as how not to be swallowed by the patient, how to get paid, how to get the patient to take care of his own teeth, and so forth. This is the usual "overcomplexity syndrome" (Botez, 1983) of any modern territory. Any improvement along one line of consideration may bring about worsening, reversals or even catastrophe along other lines of consideration. Forrester (1971) summarizes three striking characteristics of overcomplex situations: (1) "pressure relief" is usually counterproductive; (2) the obvious "points of influence or control" are usually counterproductive; (3) "short-term control" usually degrades the long-run control.

Thus, Dr. De Soto will jeopardize both himself and long-run control of the fox's illness by relieving pressure alone, however obvious the appeal of this point of control. Cleverly, he locates another point of control:

> The fox caressed the new tooth with his tongue.
> "My, it feels good," he thought. "I really shouldn't
> eat them. On the other hand, how can I resist."
>
> "We're not finished," said Doctor De Soto, holding up a large
> jug. "I have here a remarkable preparation developed only
> recently by my wife and me. With just one application, you can
> be rid of toothaches forever. How would you like to be the
> first one to receive this unique treatment?"
>
> "I certainly would!" the fox declared. He hated any kind of
> personal pain.
>
> "You will never have to see us again." said Dr. De Soto.
> "No one will see you again," said the fox to himself.

And thus the doctor utilizes this *second* control point to glue the fox's teeth together.

We are not recommending deceit as a general countermeasure for deceit in our patients, students and clients. We are not suggesting that the usual situation threatens us with being eaten. The usual danger is of being *disqualified* as a psychotherapist, teacher or consultant, and the usual countermeasure depends upon *seeing* the disqualification coming before it's too late. The time for reply is usually short.

The following could have happened to anyone in any profession: A doctor had an insecure medical student working with him in his general practice. The student seemed slow and reluctant. While he never quite objected to anything about the doctor's methods, he would often bring up doubts, such as "Do you really think five minutes is enough for a patient?" or ask questions for which there could be no satisfaction given, such as "How do you deal with the angry patient?" The student unsettled the doctor by disqualifying him at every turn.

But the doctor was so eager to be of help to the medical student that he took the doubting and general questioning at face value. All he knew was that he was failing to get much across. He dimly looked forward to the student's moving on. He underestimated what was now well underway.

The suddenness of the doctor's undoing gave him little chance. One day in the clinic, the medical student presented the patient he had just seen for the doctor's review. The student described an attorney who was failing to gain a practice and who was resorting to drink. The student spoke with contempt.

The doctor could no longer contain his temper, angrily telling the student he would be useless to the man with that kind of attitude. He fairly shouted. When he called the student in the very next day to talk over the unfortunate yelling, the student seemed to be interested in mending the relationship. At the end of the hour of discussion, the medical student told the doctor he had already made arrangements to be placed elsewhere with another doctor in general practice.

Since the doctor was my patient in individual psychotherapy, I heard about it the following week. He had been made to feel small, which, as Sullivan (1954, p. 234) wrote, leaves an open and lasting wound. He had also been embarrassed before the medical school. He felt helpless and angry.

He felt much better right away when I told him that this happens to all of us: The insecure student had diverted the doctor from the student's great weaknesses of knowledge by doubting the knowledge of the doctor. Once drawn into long explanations which were never quite satisfactory, the doctor was disqualified in countless minor ways in the student's mind, which the doctor could never quite ascertain but which dimly upset him. Once drawn in and rankled, he was eventually going to lose his temper and disqualify himself altogether. What had seemed to the doctor to be a helping relationship was seen too late to be a hostile contest.

The doctor was relieved to hear how this worked. He saw that doubting could be differently managed, so he would not be drawn into a losing struggle. He was even more delighted with his own discovery, which followed this lesson from me: He said that his wife got to him just like the student.

The doctor was unprepared for the world of the modern contest, because his idealizing family picture of how the world works had little to do with how it actually works (as with his student and his wife). Then, too, he had been selectively inattentive (Sullivan, 1956, Chapter 3) for the huge difference between the two pictures: He was simply amazed that these disqualifications kept happening over and over again. The more extensive and clear my map of the modern contest was, the more sharply could I show him that his family map was way off (it also had its virtues!). When his inadequate reckoning was taken into account, what happened to him was not amazing at all.

But how are we to have such perceptiveness about this surprising landscape, yet come to the point? How, like Dr. De Soto, to look over various fields, in various time frames, from various distances?

In general, simple dichotomies like *yes* and *no, go* and *stop, look* and *don't look* are very fast, while complex calculations are slower and risk too much uncertainty, openness and vulnerability of deep commitments. How then to have the advantages of simplicity *and* complexity? Our reply is to propose a simple *sequence of postures* to adopt as we move *towards* an unknown social landscape. The postures at a distance allow slower consideration, while those closer allow sudden moves. This sequence allows for: " . . . ignorance . . . that failure is possible, that second chances are desirable (so don't risk everything on the first chance)" (Berry, 1982).

We begin and end from the far distance in Chapters 1 and 12, so the book comes full circle. We come a little closer in Chapters 2 and 3, preparing to engage from a posture of organizing; yet closer in Chapters 4 and 5, from a posture for reading unfolding situations; closest in Chapters 6 and 7, concerning the posture for (suddenly) moving freely. Then we begin backing away again, in Chapters 8 and 9, into the posture of counterposing (after initial skirmishes); in Chapters 10 and 11, farther yet, in the posture for complex counterposing; finally we stand way back in Chapters 12 and 1, even to begin over. The even-numbered chapters (2, 4, 6, 8, 10, 12) have been written by Dr. Cooper, while the odd-numbered chapters (Introduction, 1, 3, 5, 7, 9, 11) have been written by Dr. Gustafson, but all the chapters are based on 20 years of discussions between us. The Notes at the conclusion of the book are important because they allow us to map out more extensively many different routes into this surprising landscape to meet the different needs of our diverse readers.

We apologize for the difficulties of the subject, even when we have taken pains to let simplicity shine through. Skill in modern contest is won by those who accept the difficulties and learn from them.

PART I

Taking Our Bearings

1. *The Modern Territory*

I COME UP AGAINST the modern territory at the end of my street every morning when I meet the rush of auto traffic on my bicycle. What occurs there is what occurs to my patients, students, and clients all day. But how we handle that recurrent modern event makes all the difference.

We may arrive there at the intersection of streets and be amazed that half of the drivers sail right through the stop signs and nearly run over anyone in the crosswalks. Riding further down the hill, we may be amazed again to find the stoplight red half of the time, robbing us of our precious momentum on the bicycle. Finally, arriving at work, we may be amazed to find a bevy of people flying about just like the cars sailing through the intersection, just as frustrated as the cyclist stopped by the red light.

If we just run naively into such a modern world, the results are going to be bad. We are going to be angry continually, and then we are going to find some small territory which we can defend without being harassed. Then we will be pretty shut down. The same will be true of our patients, our students, and our clients. This is what comes of looking at a small arc of a huge pattern: There is little you can do about it, you are continually amazed at how it keeps going wrong, and you eventually give up in favor of "little localized powers, and little narrow streaks of knowledge" (Holmes, 1858, p. 8); you also end up with too much resentment.[1]

There is another way to approach the end of my street, the stoplight down the hill, and bevy at the department. This is to see each well in advance of its coming, as just small arcs of a much larger pattern which connects the entire modern world. In other words, I can anticipate the struggle for position at the intersection and laugh; I can look for the light at the top of the hill and time my arrival at the bottom so I conserve my momentum through a green light; and I can learn the laws of swarming at the department.

Now if I take this longer view, I am going to be in a much abler position to help my patients, students, and clients, who all suffer from variants of struggling with loose ends of the modern contest. Some have the hurry-up strategy about 20 different ventures, while delaying as long as possible how they feel about anything (Freud, 1909; Bateson, 1971). Some give themselves away to others much too much, and then are surprised at the lack of return (Jacobson, 1953; Brenman, 1952; Porter, 1935). Some are very skeptical of everything and are left out of everything (Havens, 1986). Ordinarily, these are family strategies, passed from grandparents, to parents, to children. That they work poorly seems not to matter (the developmental difficulty is successfully denied [Robin Skynner, 1987]). The Russian writer, Gogol (1842), became preoccupied with this tendency of mankind to repeat over generations the very same fates:

. . . he was puzzled by man's perverse habit of straying from the road which lay wide open before him and which, if he followed it, would lead him to "a magnificent palace fit for an emperor to live in," and of preferring instead to follow all sorts of will-o'-the-wisps to the abyss and then asking himself in horror, Which is the right road? Which is the way out? Still more puzzling was the amazing way in which every generation laughed at the mistakes of its forebears and in the end followed a path that led to the same abyss. (p. 10)

In general, these familial strategies have *some* success, just enough to get the next generation started down the same road. After all, hurrying people can be useful for a while, as can people who give too much, and skeptics can make good auditors. It takes the long view to see that these strategies work poorly farther down the road, sacrificing objective self-possession of competence in the endless struggles of the hierarchy (Hesse, 1943) as well as subjective self-possession of feeling, desire and imagination (Mann, unpublished).

We propose a long view of the different variations of the modern contest for the reader to help himself or herself, and his or her patients, students, and clients.[2] If we are to overcome the fate of family strategy built into us, we must know broadly what we can reliably depend upon in the modern territory.

We suggest three broad strategies, which allow us to take our bearings accurately from very small- to very large-scale events. These strategies accept the way in which human beings group together in this period of our history. There are great advantages to moving with the swarm if we can keep our distance as well.

The first strategy recognizes that only insiders are well provided for. Therefore, we propose loyalty as the soundest introduction to any organization, from the family to the large-scale political group. The second strategy recognizes that help to insiders is often mixed up with fierce competition for places. Therefore, we propose keeping in mind a huge picture of the modern territory in three panels: the left panel is the territory of civility, where help is likely to be reliable; the right panel is the territory of outright contest where ferocity is relatively unchecked; the center panel is the confusing territory of the modern contest, where help is usually proposed (and fierce advantage usually taken). The third strategy recognizes the popular insistence that everyone participate in a positive way. Therefore, we propose to meet crude tests cheerfully, to diversify so that losses can be taken more lightly, and to recognize persons as more than the parts they are obliged to play.

We believe in the defense of local diversity (Vendler, 1985), which utilizes talent, form, sincerity and moral purpose to translate local struggles into wider interests.[3] Here it is our purpose to show what form to depend upon in the modern territory, whether it is to further the cause of individual patients, families, groups, teaching, organizations or large-scale social movements. The modern contest is so powerful that we derive great advantages from working with it, rather than against it.

FAMILY VIRTUE

The cardinal virtue in and for a family is loyalty. The inside version of this loyalty is being there to meet the needs of family members, without undue intrusion. The outside version is battling for the family's fortunes in the world.

Any outsiders, such as a family therapy team, will be welcomed only insofar as they can show this same loyalty to the family, temporarily becoming extended family. Showing loyalty to a family is more than a matter of the right words, more than so-called "positive connotation" (Selvini Palazzoli et al., 1978), although this important surface must be gotten right. Loyalty to their cause will also be conveyed by warmth, tact, consideration, one's very bearing toward them as a person who respects them (Stierlin and Weber, 1989). They can tell if they are being looked after well. They can also tell if they are being given a hard time where that is necessary for them to get better.

The family virtues are also very important in the less private helping realms of teaching, participant observation of groups, therapeutic groups, and organizational and political life.[4] In these realms, the great concern is to have a place, to be part of the action (Bourdieu, 1984, pp. 32–34) — in other words, to be an insider. Players who are encouraging in stance are less likely to arouse fear of abandonment. Players who are familiar in outline are less likely to arouse fear of intrusion associated with strangers (Balint, 1954). No one wants to be left out. No one wants to lose his place.

Yet this helping realm is not just helping. It is also harsh, in that some will win places while others will be replaced. Winners and losers are continually being selected in teaching situations, in participant observation groups, in therapeutic groups, and in organizations (Herndon, 1965; Mann, 1975), and in politics. This ambiguity between the helping/hurting possibilities of the helping realm is hard to face. Mostly it is not faced, but even forcefully denied.

Several extremely important devices of modern social organizations handle the two contradictory faces of helping groups: the cooperative face and the face of harsh competition for places. All of these devices locate the cooperative face in the familiar, encouraging inside, or backstage, and the face of harsh competition outside in the world external to the group. In other words, all these devices create *us* and *them* (see Chapter 2).

There are countless versions of this arrangement in the modern world, from the Jets and Sharks of *West Side Story* (Bernstein, 1957) to the capitalists and the communists on the world stage. Every such world, small or large, is evoked by its generative language (Freire, 1970). Take the loose alliances of used car salesmen:

Every trade has its own private language or jargon, whose chief purpose is to permit workers in the trade to converse with each other without an outsider's knowing what they are talking about. For example, if you hear one salesman talking to another refer to a used car as a *load*, an *orphan* or *a dog*—watch out. . . . If you are a *flea* or a *murderer*—a person who bargains shrewdly and demands top value—you will be sure to check the *grippers* (brakes), the *juice box* (batteries), the *glimmers* (headlights) and the *mill* (engine). Unless you have a large family you won't be interested in a *moose* (very large car). And while you're checking it over, take a good look at the *snortpipe* (exhaust) for signs of wear and, especially if you live in the North, you'll want to ask about the *slushers* (chains) and *liquor* (antifreeze). (Morris and Morris, 1971, pp. 583–584)

The insider to used car selling has the privilege of understanding the code of mutual help and warning, while the outsider is suitably bewildered, which is a great disadvantage. He will be compromised and used as much as possible in the taking of profit.

All businesses, bureaucracies and disciplines provide the same advantages to insiders over outsiders. This is why most of us will give our eyeteeth to become qualified. This symbolic capital (Bourdieu, 1977, 1984) is equally or more important than literal capital because it is a promise on the future which can be redeemed as needed. This symbolic capital comes in two forms. One is the certified competence or qualification, which gives a person the right to work as a member of a business, bureaucracy or discipline and take its rewards. The second is cultural capital, which takes the form of social distinctions that get the individual included in the social arrangements which are complementary to the working arrangements. Few want to miss the social connections or the advantages of being well placed at work. The two go together.[5]

This is the chief strategy in the modern world for being helped by the so-called helping organizations. You will get the cooperative face if you can place yourself as an insider by qualification and taste. The harsh face of competition will be turned upon the outsiders. You will find this strategy succeeds everywhere, from the smallest to the largest places, from teaching situations to large organizations: Act friendly in the familiar and encouraging ways, pass the tests, and share the same pleasures. This is how the family virtues carry over into the great helping realms of the modern world.

THE CENTER PANEL OF THE MODERN WORLD

This loyalty will get you in on the action (Bourdieu, 1984), but it will not allow you to last. You will get in trouble because the inside action is not all helpful to you; rather, it is often hostile. The face of cooperation is difficult to tell from the face of harsh competition after all.

Some of the difficulty comes from outright evil, which may always put on the clothes of helpers (Brodsky, 1986). We will all have the misfortune of falling prey to these people to some, hopefully lesser, extent. Machiavelli could be said to have charted their modern course. In *The Prince* (1527) he shows them how to rely upon the simple images of loyalty versus disloyalty. Machiavelli's leading idea is that you have only to *seem* to be what is wanted and then to proceed to do *whatever* you want on other levels:

A prince must take great care that nothing goes out of his mouth which is not full of the above-named five qualities, and, to see and hear him, he should seem to be all mercy, faith, integrity, humanity and religion. And nothing is more necessary than to seem to have this last quality, for men in general judge more by the eyes than by the hands. . . . (p. 65)

This idea is so deeply accepted nowadays that candidates for president are discussed by media commentators not in terms of their policies, but in terms of whether or not they look "presidential." The leader of the U.S.S.R. understands this idea so well that he need only talk like an American, dress like an American, and act like an American to impress Wyoming Republicans that he is a "forthright man, who will not beat around the bush." Indeed, Gorbachev boldly states that his policy is intended to deprive us of an enemy. This is quite an understatement. He not only gets out of the clothes of the enemy, but he also puts on the clothes of our business *and* faith. Our own Secretary of State catches onto this when he says, "The Russians are coming our way. They're singing out of our hymnbook" (Wisconsin State Journal, May 16, 1989).

When we are concerned about minimum defense, we must recall just what can be put over on us by men with such a thorough grasp of seeming to be what the vulgar image calls for. The answer is that *anything* can be put over, helpful or harmful. Gorbachev is probably putting over a huge business deal which is probably to our advantage. He badly needs our goods and we badly need his markets. Other skilled tacticians have had far worse purposes. But both good and bad rely on the same clothes and take the same precautions. Machiavelli wrote: " . . . whenever one does not attack the property or honour of the generality of men, they will live contented . . . " (p. 66). Therefore, thinking this through, he proposes:

. . . men must be either caressed or else annihilated; they will revenge themselves for small injuries, but cannot do so for great ones; the injury therefore that we do to a man must be such that we need not fear his revenge . . . those who are injured, remaining poor and scattered, can never be any harm to him, and all the others . . .

are fearful of offending lest they should be treated like those who have been disposed. . . . (p. 9)

Minimum defense is to be ready for such invaders from all sides, on all levels, for this is modern predatory strategy.

While we must be ready for these invaders, ordinarily this is not going to be our chief difficulty in defending our causes. Our trouble is more deeply structured. I can explain the confusion by proposing a huge canvas divided into three panels, upon which the action of the modern world would be painted.

In the left panel, we see the civility of reliable help afforded even to complete strangers:

In complex societies, A is helped by X,Y,Z—total strangers (e.g., firemen, hospital orderlies, etc.). A pays, of course, but what A pays is minute, compared with what he receives. What A receives is the cumulated labor and skill of strangers, most of whom are dead. (Tuan, 1985)

Teachers, doctors, coaches, scientists, engineers, secretaries, firemen and hospital orderlies: helpers of all kinds, battlers of all kinds, who can be counted on to do their best for you. Often, this comes from professional honor, but it may come from civic pride or religious duty.

In the right panel, we see the armies of outright contest, for whom victory is everything: in business, in sport, in politics, in whatever. Love is not absent, but it is put in its place in the shape of dedication to the contest—showing grace, charisma, or authority to move along the cause. Insofar as the contest is respected, these armies of contest will abide by the rules, but this is always uncertain. All too often, they will revert to outright war, which suspends the rules to go for the kill. This becomes tempting when a chief competitor can be driven from the field (Foucault, 1980). Thus, the sport becomes dirty, destroying playing careers and professional careers, entire businesses and departments, even entire peoples and countries.

The center panel is ambiguous. The onlooker is unable to tell whether the businesses, bureaucracies, and disciplines in the center panel are out to help or out to win. Are they using their full ferocity to help? Are they out to win at all costs, utilizing the charms of love ever so stealthily? The onlooker may also see a procession moving across the three panels. If in the fortunate family (the left panel) the child is loved but obliged to accept discipline, then in the marketplace (on the right) he accepts discipline to win the best he can over his rivals, while smoothing the way with the graces. Notice the inversion of virtues: discipline in the service of love in the protected, civil or family compartment; love in the service of prevailing over others in the less protected compartment of the contest. The virtues are the same but in reversed priority. This similarity of virtues is what allows a child to switch compartments, from the family to the marketplace. He simply switches the order of his virtues. Of course, there is usually a *series* of compartments—

from kindergarten to the rough athletic contest to the do-or-die of winning a post in a firm — allowing children gradually to shift the balance between love and discipline, winning and love, learning to live with ferocity more and more. The child moves from the left panel, through the center panel, to the right panel, in growing up to a rough world. He or she also learns to slip back into the center or left as needed.

The center panel is where most of the difficult practical problems of our various trades lie. Often, we cannot tell if teaching is intended to put students farther ahead or load them down. Often, group therapy and the study of group relations seems dedicated to helping, equally often to choosing winners and losers. Family therapy is described equally in the language of help or tricking. Organizations have also these two faces. The great problems of the planet, like nuclear war, famine and pollution, slide between cooperation and defection among the parties involved.

Without the center panel, there could be a clear boundary between civility and contest. In the Middle Ages, the world was divided, at least theoretically, between the church and the princes, the armies of the Black and the Red. But as Bosch shows in his unforgettable painting of the Temptation of St. Anthony, these two realms could be utterly confused in practice. Help could be thoroughly perverted into exploitation. In the early 19th century, the world was still divided between the Black and the Red. But as Stendhal (1830) shows in his novel, there was little difference between them. Thus, the problems of the helping trades that we face today are very old confusions between help and taking advantage.

The modern world is even more confusing than a Bosch painting in the center panel.[6] This is because the language of helping has become the prevailing discourse of the world, while at the same time the action is more and more organized as winning and losing. It is no accident that a conversation with a used car salesman will always begin with, "Can I help you?" Nearly every group or organization in America introduces itself by an offer to help. Always the guise of the family is adopted. When Governor Dukakis explained to the Democratic Convention that we are all immigrants in the same boat, who have the common cause of an extended family, who will all benefit from his election, he was simply utilizing the language of the family to win a ferocious contest for taking the helm of the country. This is the parlance of every business, political party, university or school. President Bush proposes a "kinder, gentler nation" to the very people who have seen him conduct one of the meanest of campaigns. Even the Army, Navy and the Air Force are out to help us "be all that we can be."[7]

This has been the overwhelming drift of the modern world since the two world wars. The commercial contest seems to be taking over all compartments of the world. The great benefit has been that the commercial contest has replaced outright war. The great hazard has been the buying and selling of more protected spaces — civil, playful and religious:

At one time, in Western Europe, when Church and State were still important rivals, the cultural life of the people . . . was in the keeping of the Church. . . . In the United States . . . the separation of the two powers . . . has permitted commercial interests to take over culture and determine values, successfully invading and subverting both politics and religion. It is what capitalism has come to signify. Politics and religion (as well as art) are simply business by other means. (Gass, 1988)

We could go even farther, with Foucault (1980), and suggest that business is covert war: the war by other means which we call the modern contest, which invades, judges and snares politics, culture (art and science), play, and love (innermost being).[8]

In sum, there is an overwhelming tendency for the most external of perspectives, namely war, to collapse upon more internal perspectives, in the modified guise of business. Virtually any situation in the social landscape can suddenly turn into a struggle between us and them.[9]

Recently, when I posed this problem to some British colleagues, one of them sat up very keenly to tell me just how shocking and swift these collapses may arrive. She had been consulting to a high government task force about one of Britain's major social problems, which has aroused great concern among diverse political groups. So long as the discussion proceeded with fervor, cooperation was complete, but as soon as the chairperson wrote up the report of the task force, the alliance fell to pieces because of fierce territorial interests.

Awareness of the three panels of the modern world can keep us ready for these drastic changes in the weather, which occur across the entire scope of the social world, from these large political events to middle-sized teaching events to the microcosm of the family. If you see only concern, be prepared for periods of ferocious competition. If you see only savagery, be looking for a shift to concern. Most of the time, look for some confusion of the two extremes. Friendly classes will get mean. Cruel families can be merciful.

Just how different a group can look from one time to another is simply astonishing. In contemporary chaos theory (Gleick, 1988, pp. 92–94) there is a rule of thumb about these patterns in physical systems which fits the world of social systems just as well. Mandelbrot called this the Joseph and Noah principle: If the weather is now harsh, look for it to stay harsh; but if it is harsh, it will also be likely to turn suddenly (when it turns) into a great improvement. Who could have imagined the difference between the cold war of the early Reagan years and the current glasnost? Conversely, how well a class or a family therapy may go for a while, only to be completely disqualifying one fine day! This is a way of saying that fortune, good and bad, seems to come in bunches. When I start making errors in tennis, I tend to make them for a while. When I am consulting splendidly in a group relations conference, I tell myself: Enjoy it, the weather will soon turn.

Yet we must also remember that the periodicity of social systems can be very extended. Entire sectors of society may be blessed, or impossible, for a hundred years:

Partly, for this reason, the period of Walpole and the Pitts was the heyday of unchallenged abuses in all forms of corporate life. Holders of ecclesiastical, academic, charitable, and scholastic endowments had no fear of inquiry or reform. Schoolmasters could draw their salaries without keeping school. Universities could sell degrees without holding examinations or giving instruction. Parliamentary boroughs and municipal obligarchies could be as corrupt and ridiculous as they liked; it was enough that they were old. "Whatever is is right — if it can show a charter" seems the watchword of the Eighteenth Century. (Trevelyan, 1942, p. 378)

The challenge is to decide which systems have a likely hundred-year history of decline and which are relatively capable of transformation. It is foolish to fight a glacier, when systems amenable to change can be tackled vigorously. A region, a department, or a family may decline, having little readiness for change, having alternatives much too weak to arouse. When such is the case, a person would be well advised to put her genius into other compartments.[10]

MEETING THE CHALLENGE OF THE CASE

Let us conclude our argument. First we proposed that the friendly face of cooperation will be elicited in the world by the family virtue of loyalty. Second we proposed that loyalty is very dangerous in the long run, if one does not anticipate evil outfitted in the clothes of the good or contest taking over help in the center panel of the modern world. Now, thirdly, we suggest to our readers that they play naively and simply and straightforwardly (that is, positively), while utilizing knowledge of the complications in such play.

Most people do not want to take any distance upon their engagement with the world. They just want to play their part, defend it, and hope for the best. For most people, it is better to *feel* secure than to study the extent to which it may or may not be the case (Sullivan, 1954, 1956; Gustafson, 1986, Chapter 5). Sullivan called this posture the method of "selective inattention" or of "security operations." Reich (1935; Gustafson, 1986, Chapter 3; Bourdieu, 1977, pp. 94–95) called this posture the constant bodily attitude. In general, people are steadied by being encouraged and by finding the world familiar — by pretending that their niche in the world is more or less like the family. They insist upon getting on with the game, as positively as possible:

The desire to enter into the game, identifying with the characters' joys and sufferings, worrying about their fate, espousing their hopes and ideals, living their life, is based on a form of *investment*, a sort of deliberate "naivety", ingenuousness, good-natured credulity ("We're all here to enjoy ourselves") which tends to accept formal experiments and specifically artistic effects *only to the extent that they can be forgot-*

forgotten and do not get in the way of the substance of the work. (Bourdieu, 1984, p. 33)

This popular insistence on the positive (for fitting in) has several implications for the conduct of individual and family therapy, teaching, group work, and organizational life.

The first is to accept that most contests will be decided by crude tests, no matter at what level or scale we find them. An individual patient will test his doctor by whether his chief complaint is improved, worse or the same, no matter how interested the doctor may be in related findings. Family members will judge in numerous contradictory ways, as will a group of students (what is good for one is bad for another). An organization is apt to judge by the bottom line. Large-scale politics is about competing versions of us against them, such as the New Frontier or anti-communism. We call cheerful acceptance of crude tests "meeting the challenge of the case" (Winnicott, 1965). We expect no appeal to a higher level (only privately).

In this respect, we emulate the Japanese, who are probably the most successful country in recent rounds of the modern contest on the global scale. They have struck the right attitude for modern contesting:

The Japanese discovered a very distressing statistic: Americans have won 143 Nobel prizes, Japanese 5. Rather than accuse the Swedish Academy of racism, the Japanese are putting the blame on their own educational and scientific institutions. They are determined to reform whatever deficiencies they find. . . . It seems to me significant that the Japanese people characteristically refuse to see themselves as victims. They know that to accept the status of victim, however justified, can only encourage a posture of passivity . . . and that's no way to succeed. (Tuan, 1989)

They cheerfully meet the challenge of the case, rather than complaining how it is set up.

The second implication is that we must diversify our campaigns. It is better not to stake everything in one place. That may bring trouble, for the family may be mean, the high school gang envious, the company oblivious, and the national judges having their own ax to grind. If you are overconnected to success in one place, in someone else's terms, you lose everything at once.

Worse, the crude terms of loyalty and disloyalty, winning and losing, being accepted and rejected, being somebody and being nobody, do not stay the same. What got you in this week may get you out next week or next month or next year, because the modern world is so interactive from top to bottom that the terms at any one level are subject to sudden reversals.[11]

This is not a new problem in nature, per se, but the tempo, the range, and the intensity are unprecedented. Contests are everywhere; the newspaper is almost entirely a list of the daily results.

But how then are we to last? We may take after the redwood species. Redwood trees diversify, splendidly. Forest fires do not disturb them, for their bark can resist the fire and their crowns are above the reach of most fires. So they are even helped by fires, for their competitors are eliminated. Even if the scale of the fire is monumental, catching their crowns, still they last, for their reproduction is secured in seeds likely to withstand the heat. In other words, they live at many different scales, so that disaster on any one scale is taken in stride (Allen and Starr, 1982).

Thirdly, and finally, we believe it is both right and practical to refrain from mistaking individual beings for the crude parts they play in the modern world. Bosses, professors, and managers may make enormous sacrifices to occupy their insider roles:

On the day he steps down, he passes into oblivion. . . . I do not suggest that, given his sacrifices, the modern business executive is underpaid. I do note, in a somewhat circumspect defense of his liberal compensation, that to give up so much of the only life one is certain (considering the present state of knowledge on the matter) to have is surely worth something. (Galbraith, 1986, p. 41)

Subordinates, students and the altogether unfortunate of this world offer up a surface of going along, often slowly and awkwardly, as if silent, dull, self-derogatory or trite, while being very, very fast in the small and deft movements of cutting loose. They leave their shells behind in the traps, in the judgments and the invasions. Those who want to find where they actually live will have to be tuned at least doubly: to the slow posturing and to the wit of darting away.

Both winners and losers are apt to be what Michael White (1983, 1988) calls "victims of their beliefs," what Selvini Palazzoli et al. (1978) call "victims of the game," or what we could call most broadly "victims of the pattern." There is a charitable attitude in distinguishing a person from his unfortunate pattern. Gandhi struck that attitude about his opponents. Such an attitude need not deny that some of "the victims of the pattern" may be doing terrible things to other people, to derive what look like advantages from where they sit within the pattern.

Since the human being is able to defend his or her group by appearing to be what is called for, that being will be grossly underestimated by a vulgar judgment that reckons his winning or losing at face value. This is why biology and sociology and history and literature and psychiatry—any subject which has to reckon how living creatures work—will sorely miss its subject if it is pegged to seeing its subject on one (vulgar) scale. Hamlet says exactly this to Rosencrantz and Guildenstern, who are trying to convince him to comply with his uncle the king:

Why, look you now, how unworthy a thing you make of me! You would play upon me, you would seem to know my stops, you would pluck the heart out of my mystery, you would sound me from my lowest note to the top of my compass; and there is much music, excellent voice, in this little organ, yet you cannot make it speak. (III, ii, 349–355)

Such a hierarchical creature will not be appreciated by any method which reduces him to one kind of vulgar music.

This is of extreme importance for teaching. Students will (wisely) hide from teachers who want to use them to make a point. They are (perhaps dimly) aware of princes who can seem to be all religion while rubbing out those who get in their way. Students will also (wisely) hide from teachers who are so dull as not to see how their subject triggers far-flung associations to neighboring subjects. Thus, if we call the subject of teaching our challenge at hand, then it will be flat unless the smaller scale, the diversity of the students, is welcomed and the larger scale, the range of the discussion, is enjoyed. This is what Bateson (1979) meant by "the pattern that connects," which is hierarchical in its nature, which is vertical in its complexity, however crude it may be in its tests at any one (vulgar) level. Thus, the minimum challenge of organization in the teaching field is to be able to set up situations in which the individuals can emerge freshly on their own terms, tackle the challenge at hand, and ride it into other domains.[12]

Finally, this distinction between the horizontal and the vertical may help us to be charitable, comforting and more imaginative toward ourselves. In those necessary intervals where we are losing, neglected or unseen on the leveling stage of the modern contest, we can slip downwards like Alice into her play (Carroll, 1862) or upwards like an author who flies to his far-flung friends in his letters. With this vertical freedom we remember what we believe in and delight in and fight for, whether these horizontal worlds agree or not.[13]

PART II

Organizing

2. *Us and Them*

T HE COMMON ANTAGONIST IS a dynamic set of forces that draws people together: that which solidifies Us and clarifies Them. At times the Us takes on a real enemy or set of enemies, at times a more transitory set of circumstances. The solidarity is essential to survival, but if cohesiveness is to endure, conditions must be propitious.

This is poignantly described in "The Open Boat," a short story by Stephen Crane in which four men are cast together in a lifeboat, rowing for many days to an uncertain fate. They become so attached to each other as a group that they cooperate as if one person, totally involved in mutual survival. Snores become comforting signs of each other's continued life; one's weariness is felt by all. But as they get close to land and finally step on shore, mingle with people, and are assisted by them, the group dissolves totally. The story must end. One dies swimming to shore, but isn't noticed much as each is now focused on his own survival, his own helpers.

To survive, cohesiveness is necessary and (especially under constant fire) the more the better. Cohesive organizations move in step with great social accomplishment, from Moses moving a nation, to starting the United Nations, to the Normandy invasion. In securing a social organization, one must be oriented to the importance and power of building alliances and how they can be used to stand against a particular common antagonist. Because building alliances is a controllable force, one must secondarily be prepared for false forms, for a mimicry of loyalty. A sense of Us is no guarantee of moral behavior.

ALLIANCES AND THE COMMON ANTAGONIST

The great social accomplishments of our civilization occur in the inspiring atmosphere of cohesiveness, of a clear sense of Us facing Them. Securing cohesiveness and alliances is essential for intensifying social energies. Otherwise, it is like trying to boil water by pouring it over the stove: The common antagonist is the container. Us is the sense of being on the inside.

We can look at the grander level of Moses' leadership of Israel's exodus from Egypt, Lincoln's inspiring the Union forces for their long and ultimately successful battles, or Martin Luther King's galvanizing a tremendously significant civil rights movement. Each is a reminder on a grand scale of the astounding power intrinsic to a common antagonist. On the more mundane scale, there is the accomplishment of a cohesive sports team, the usefulness of a well-working therapy group, or the accomplishment of a cohesive family successfully facing the modern contest and preparing children to survive and prosper in it.

The importance of a clear sense of Us and Them is not to be underestimated or taken for granted. The container is all important. Unlike the concreteness of a kettle, however, social cohesiveness can be elusive to create and sustain. Without a sense of Us being secured, the group is weakened both within and in facing its outside world. Since all social force is lost without it, the sense of Us must be the first acquisition for participating in the modern contest.

THE SHIFTABLE IMAGE

The common antagonist that galvanizes the sense of Us and Them is a fluid force. Part of what makes it a fascinating focus for securing social organization is that alliance-building can be controlled for various ends. Because cohesiveness depends so much on a shared image of the enemy, we suggest careful attendance to how the image is drawn initially and how it shifts over time.

This is a particularly central issue for a new group insofar as its shared image influences the form and atmosphere of the undertaking. It is important for someone entering a group since the shared image can hold the key to membership access. It can be useful to the intervener to the extent that a common view permits both access to the group and a step towards initiating a change process.

In describing aspects of how humans deal with their tendency towards fear and distrust of members of groups other than their own, Frank (1982) observes how a group bases its actions towards the other on its "image of the enemy." The image is a static slice of time; however, it changes as relationships between the groups evolve. Adjectives describing friends become attached to enemies when they cease to be enemies. It is as if the forces of unity can be mobilized through developing immediate images of a common antagonist against which one must be protected.

Authors as disparate as Aristophanes (*Lysistrata*) and Norman Mailer (*Armies of the Night*) have built stories around images of the enemy drawn to a fever pitch for a specific purpose and then permitted to dissipate into other channels, other fields of time and space. The image is erected with the intention of accomplishing one goal, but must be dissipated for the completion of another. Lysistrata's urging of her female cohorts to unite against their warrior-husbands to demonstrate for peace would have been a much less forceful (and humorous) stance if it were not intended as a prelude to a lusty welcome after the image had served its purpose. "Armies of the night" are intended to function in the dark but do their best work during the light of day back among the indolent enemy in their own midst. So the enemy must be kept within shifting images.

One of the fascinating things about charismatic leadership is its ability to influence the image of the common antagonist so as to create a very personal loyalty, although this is not a position of invulnerability. It is even a hallmark of this kind of leader that personal attachment and devotion be strong and indeed blind. Both authors had the opportunity early in our careers to work under such a leader, when he was brought in to head an inpatient unit at a prestigious mental health training center. Since it was a unit that had floundered, there was considerable excitement about the arrival of the new person. Soon after he arrived he established a program that was very controversial within the larger training setting; nevertheless, he galvanized considerable loyalty within the unit staff. His own conviction about his program, the sense of coherence and excitement he generated with his new ideas, and his own strong, engaging attachment to his staff all combined to make us feel fortunate to be going to work for this man every day.

As the image of the enemy (the larger training setting) was made vivid enough by personal (charismatic) persuasion, we enjoyed being on the inside and much good was accomplished during the robust phase of the alliance. Our hero was suddenly fired. The downturn was sudden and very instructive in retrospect insofar as it made us aware of the need for a broader state of readiness; but while the image was flying, it was flying high.

Animal behavior also reveals instinctive shifts in the common antagonist. Lorenz (1952) has a wonderful example of the stickleback, fish that believe in economy of effort. When encountering an outsider near its home, the stickleback will fight the enemy viciously to protect its territory. The same creature, at a distance from home, will be passed by. The image of the antagonist is partly composed of proximity. In human groups, once inside the tent, within the group boundary, one feels safe and is treated with the rights and privileges of a family member. Once outside, s/he may find the locks quickly changed. A devoted sports fan will immediately make a hero out of the archrival team's best player as soon as he is traded to the home team. And vice versa, the home towners can be quite nasty to the local hero who defects.

SECURING THE ORGANIZATION

How then do we develop solidarity *and* keep it constructive. We call this securing the organization. For instance, let us consider this situation. I did an organizational consultation with a small mental health agency. A triumvirate of the female executive director and two male lieutenants told me that they had been working together for about ten years. The agency was at a point of plotting future plans, but the two men were unwilling to cooperate if they were to be denied executive slots; yet they were quite devoted to the agency's mission and didn't want to leave. In their view the three formed a cohesive unit against the half-dozen other newer staff. But the boss wanted to keep control, so they were deadlocked.

It was quite clear that enemies were around every corner: the other staff, individuals' power aspirations, etc. I asked the three executives to help me get a clearer picture of the planning task ahead of them: not abstractions, but what each conceived had to be done to make them all want to stay. It quickly became clear that there were sharp differences about the mission of the agency revolving around the question of whether they should take on the AIDS problem or continue with the general problems of indigent health. In the course of this discussion, their fights with each other emerged. The executive director refused to concede financial control but had to admit that one of her associates was much better than she at public relations and had a strong community constituency, which was important for funding. It also emerged that the whole job was just not doable by one person.

By the time I introduced the concept of a management team, they were more than willing to buy my image as a way out of the overwhelming work demands they envisioned. The image of the enemy was the future planning task. With Them thus defined, authority was more willingly distributed among the triumvirate (Us).

No sooner was the management team put in place, however, than the new solidarity almost beckoned for a *tangible* antagonist. It wasn't long before the search led to a scapegoat. It was as if the newly formed army needed a battle to test its mettle. One of the employees, a bold, competent, and outspoken woman, was nailed as too controversial to tolerate. The question became: Who of this new triumvirate would take her on? The two men new to the executive wanted very much to do it; the executive director was more cautious and defensive of this controversial employee, but agreed that the reins must be tightened. When I raised the question of whether there was a way to work on this as a management *team*, they were able to come up with a team approach: clearer limits and directives, more accountability to the team. The idea was to give this person clearer room to move. There was a way they could all win. The final paragraph of this chapter of the consultation was written when the three began to implement the plan at the work-place *and* the two lieutenants were given raises commensurate with their new responsibilities.

My task in this consultation was to make it possible for common antago-nists to emerge which were related to the mission of the group at a particular time; this is not unlike the work of group therapists, teachers, business executives, etc. The enemy around which their alliance coalesced was the mountain of work; then the team muscles needed to be flexed. Both interventions were aimed at providing a quick move from problem to solution, staying within the organization's mission, and not taking advantage of an individual. It takes work to secure the cohesiveness.

FROM STRANGER TO US

One has a good chance of establishing entry if one can offer to help the group fight invasion or restore a sense of Us to its members, i.e., help the loser regain his/her footing. Reading the common antagonist can offer a way into the system for an outsider wanting to enter the tent (or build one, for that matter). However, playing and winning the contest of entry at one level can lead to unexpected results at other levels.

The challenge to become part of Us cuts across a range of situations: an outside consultation, intergroup interactions, a new member joining an ongoing group. I am reminded of one of the most elaborate and delightful cinematic games of cat and mouse (a most tentative alliance): Kurosawa's film "The Seven Samurai." The farmers, while inviting the warriors in as protectors, are unable to trust them. Baffled by the mistrust, the warriors meet it with anger and distrust of their own. There are a whole series of tests and challenges, until it is clear that there is a basis for safety in temporarily shifting their (farmers *and* warriors) common antagonist to the outside barbarian pillagers. As soon as the battle is fought and won, however, the remaining warriors and farmers again stand on opposite sides of the line. What was crucial for the occurrence of intergroup cohesiveness was an intensification of the antagonist, a shift in other conditions outside both groups that could permit the situation to be construed differently. The farmers could temporarily value the warriors by putting down their scythes and taking up arms in their own behalf. The warriors could show the farmers a respect for life, in addition to killing. The deeper common threat of mutual invasion never changed.

Therapists and consultants experience this entry challenge all the time. The client group or family invites the intervener to the door and then dares him or her to attempt entry. Selvini Palazzoli and her colleagues propose a class of solutions they call "positive connotation," a solution they apply in both family therapy (1978) and organizational consultation (1986). The class of behavior indicates for the organizational, family, or individual client that the consultant sees the problem with which they are struggling mightily and is ready to ally with them in trying to overcome it. For example, spouses came to a consultation about their relationship after the woman had rented an apartment and, after 20 years of marriage, they were about to split up. They interspersed intense criticism of each other with their asking (almost rhetorically), "So why did we even come here?" I finally said to them that I had an answer to this question: Perhaps they really wanted to try to make the marriage work, but after hating each other so long they had forgotten. This placed me on their side, so that our work could proceed as a team of three exploring their life together.

That positive connotation works at all confirms a point about the image of the enemy which is illustrated in the work of Dyson (1984). In describing images of the Russians, he paraphrased Humpty Dumpty's adage that the image of a group was what the imager wanted it to be, no more, no less. Russian history, for instance, suggested a picture of the Russians as victims who fought ferociously for self-preservation and won. Seen this way, they are a people worried about their weakness, but an international force to be negotiated with, sharing similar problems of global survival. An equally informed view has the Russians as cunning tyrants, bleak and untrust-worthy. One would enter negotiations with quite a different attitude depend-ing on one's image of the "enemy." Positive connotation conveys the inter-vener as on the side of the common struggle.

For example, a very isolated person, with whom I worked in psychother-apy for months, finally took a step in joining a volunteer continuing educa-tion group related to his work. He came in terribly discouraged about the coldness of the leader, which only confirmed his worst convictions about social life. I saw my job as joining him in managing this situation. I said that, while it is true there are a lot of really difficult people in the group, we had reason to hope that he could get something good out of the group for himself. He was impressed that I wasn't discouraged by his terrible experi-ence. He stayed long enough to have a chance to star in the group and experience how his image of the leader and other members changed dramati-cally when they showed some appreciation of him. Following this incident, he had the idea that he might try group therapy to practice being sociable. Partnership against one's (even imagined) enemies is a powerful and encour-aging experience.

Often the common enemy is the threat of change—and one can look at Selvini Palazzoli's elegance as operating to join with the family *against* change. But there is often a loser. So one must also offer hope along with alliance—hope that the loser can be restored. When presented with a fami-ly's identified patient to cure, the therapist may be allowed to help only by starting with this one individual. At later moments, it may be necessary to define the boundary differently and get the whole family involved. If the situation is terribly abusive and enmeshed, we might start with restoring the victim to an equal or winning position, at least balancing the scales some-what before daring to expand focus to the rest of the family. On the other hand, many families will present themselves as a unit and defy starting any place other than the whole group; the family group is declared to be where the problem lies. To stay connected, the intervener's image of the problem to be solved must be shifting.

THE (NOT-SO-) SIMPLE STORY

What is a positive force under certain circumstances can take a surprising if not unpleasant turn as conditions change. As a dynamic and controllable force, the sense of joining can be exploited badly, as seen in therapists' sexual indiscretions with patients, cults mobilized for all forms of evil, and the mundane forms of exploitation in family life, such as child abuse and molestation. What looks like loyalty and alliance is really a mimicry of loyalty for other purposes.

Cohesiveness itself reveals little of the quality of group life; it comes in too many packages. Kai Erikson (1966), though talking about Puritan America and not a small group, emphasized how dangerous it can be for boundaries to shift. While he was focusing specifically on deviance, Erikson offered a frightening exposition of the use of a witchhunt as a common antagonist. At the time of the hunts, the Puritans were no longer revolutionaries. They were moving into unsure times ideologically. What would hold them together and guide their future? Hunting, judging, and killing witches. The sense of identity needed to be shored up dramatically, and internal persecutions were part of that process. It seems an ironic twist that a group originating in protection against religious persecution should later persecute within its own midst. However, this was a group that knew the cohering power of persecutions. At a time of transition and potential disorder, it is no surprise (in retrospect) that this method of rebuilding identity would emerge. Conditions had changed and new distinctions had to be made to protect against social disorder.

In describing the thin veneer of civilization, Freud (1921, 1930) wrote about this devastating dilemma of group life. Our instincts as biological creatures make group formation inevitable for survival, but, whether it is the family group, a large unorganized mass, or a country, once the enemies are kept out we have to face even worse enemies within. The very instincts that are the basis of the group's standing against the common enemy—be it sex, dependency, or aggression—become the basis for uncivilized events within the group. The family has its murderous internal uprisings, the church breeds its mindless obedience, and the army strikes out at risk to its own members. The coherence is never simple.

"A lifetime later" Mitscherlich (1978) retrospectively evaluated Freud's essays, only to find even more reason to believe them. He found more recent terrifying examples of group exploitation of the masses by destructive charismatic leaders. Being slightly more optimistic than Freud, he proposed a solution to collective regression in the "strength of the ego" to stand against the contagion of the mass. The picture he drew was of a decaying society in which the "ego-structuring" forces of tradition, family, and neighborhood were decaying; the lone self-aware and self-discovering individual's ego would survive. The image has some of the desperation of the few surviving condors looking down from their mountain crags as the roads and cities consume their very ecology. An individual ego will be similarly overwhelmed in the face of the unsupportive and deadly environment.

Modern writers make the point, with even more forcefulness and focus on society than Freud, that there is no simple inherent moral value or immanent goodness to solidarity. Solzhenitsyn's *Gulag* is a moving example of solidarity being attained and sustained at tremendous cost to lives and one's sense of decency. In a moving drama, Durrenmatt (1956) describes a poor small community under the spell of an immoral savior who captures the citizens' loyalty by promising them great riches. She systematically leads them to murder one of the central members of their community, who is also a secret enemy of their benefactress. It is a nightmare of persecution built on the cohesiveness of greed.

Lessons from history also reveal that the simple story isn't so simple. On the one hand there is Fisher's (1935) description of the Roman empire facing floods of invaders. They held off one emergency after another, guided by a strong sense of mission. Structures of government, such as administered laws, a money system, and a deployed defensive system, backed a strongly cohesive culture and leadership. This supported stable cohesive conditions for hundreds of years. On the other hand, the feverish ideological unity of Nazi Germany, so graphically described by Lifton (1986), resulted in a culture immersed in death imagery and degradation, the organization of its governmental machinery eventually used for the horrors of "purification."

At times solidarity can be an uplifting force. At other times it can be controlled for perpetrating evil ends while looking like loyalty on the surface. At times it can be left to drift and can then lead to a fortuitously good or bad situation. Group life being ever-changing, even the most planful use of the common antagonist will be difficult because of the complexity of other forces.

SURPRISING SHIFTS

Shifts in the image of the enemy can catch one by surprise. The foundation of cohesiveness is suddenly shaken; the social contract, if you will, suddenly revised. One can never be ready for everything, but without readiness disappointment is even more shocking. A cornerstone of securing social organization is readiness to possibilities of falseness.

From an organizational perspective context is crucial. The simple principle I would propose for handling surprising shifts in the common antagonist is this: Attend to life outside the immediate context.

Seminars provide many examples of groups that have surprising eruptions. In one seminar, a graduate course in group therapy, I found myself laboring with many of the usual seminar frustrations. Starting right off, my initial enthusiasm for the course was dulled when one student dropped because there was too much work. Another said he would stay only if he didn't have to do the term paper. Another student had scheduling problems, which meant she would have to arrive late for several weeks. I felt that, since this was the first time that this course was being offered and the registration was marginal, I should be prepared to take the group as it came; consequently, I was (uncomfortably) compromising on many points. I had accepted conditions with which I felt uncomfortable in other classes — lateness, unreported absences, late papers, marginal participation, etc. — but before these things had not all occurred at the same time.

In this particular seminar, I said during the second meeting that I felt the discrepancy between my enthusiasm and their treating this as just another seminar. They agreed, and for a moment I felt reassured that I was right. From my behavior in other seminars I had led, I was expecting to go about the course following the outline and having a fragmented experience with the group, sharing my frustrations with colleagues and the rear end of my dog.

I felt pushed over the edge in about the eighth week of the term, when I was called at home late on the night before the seminar met. The female student wanted to know how she could get the reading for the next day; apparently it wasn't in the library. Since she had known that this was the reading for several weeks, I was shocked and infuriated by the call, even insulted. My response on the phone was a moderately peeved despair about the eleventh hour nature of the request. I decided to intervene in class. I couldn't stand business as usual.

I told the class what had happened. The student blushed and said that she had been the first one to cross the oedipal line. I asked if she thought I was talking about sex in our relationship, because I wasn't. I was talking about feeling insulted by the request. I described my reaction in some detail. I sensed that they were open to this and asked them for their student experiences of this and other incidents — lateness, absences, etc. How did these events make them feel? How did they think it made me feel?

The initial reaction was that I was trying to "shrink" them. I said that I wanted to break some seminar rules with them, particularly the rule that said that personal experiences in the class group were interferences with the course learning. I presented it as something for us to try. I pursued it whenever data were presented to me. It didn't take long before they were picking up the data themselves. I had to be aware and guard against the class becoming a self-study group, but the quality of their participation made the risk worthwhile. The common antagonist had become our life together. If this shift hadn't taken place, the students and I would have endured our weeks together in a false cohesiveness.

Under some conditions of experimentation and playfulness, solidarity can split open, with emotional surprises for all, including the consultant or teacher. The seminar ends but a specific job gets done and a new kind of process has a chance of emerging and registering in an influential way. As a group leader, one can walk out feeling a bit more heartened by the experience. In the seminar example, I had to push to make the social experiment work. It is also true of some highly cohesive situations that one must be open to surprise when the critical card is turned over by someone else.

In organizations, intragroup developments can offer their own surprises. In one example, the staff, trainees, and patients created the drama. In a community agency to which I consulted, the staff ideology in dealing with a residential chronic psychotic population was egalitarian. In spite of the fact that there was an authority structure, there was an intense belief that all were equally responsible for the emotional tenor of the place, day-to-day operations were shared by all, and they were all honest with each other and the patients. Consultation was initiated because of a director change and a need for an interim plan. As a consultant known to them, I was readily accepted — perhaps too readily. There was a strong wish for an immediate rapport, and I felt under some pressure to learn about their situation very quickly. I had the sense that their cohesiveness was so intense that it would be very difficult for me to get in, as welcome as I was being made to feel. I was also jarred every time I learned that one of the staff members was relatively new or a trainee. They had the aura of a group that had been in kindergarten together. The blurriness made the solidarity confusing. I couldn't tell whether they were committed primarily to their work roles or primarily to each other, or both. I imagined that this would become clearer as we worked on their interim management plan, which was rather easy to construct during the first two meetings.

There was something unsettled in the group, however, because the members wanted me to come back. The conversation got more general over the next couple of meetings, moving to patient care issues, including the trainees' role vis-à-vis patients. As the conversation focused more on individual patients, one in particular stood out, very uncomfortably, because she had recently called her parents and told them unsettling things about wanting to leave the facility. Just prior to the sixth consultation meeting, the father was on the phone to the director. One of the young male trainees, increasingly agitated as the mystery of the phone call was highlighted, told of his sexual relationship with this patient, which was about to be revealed to the staff through her father. The trainee had invited this patient to move in with him; thus, she wanted to leave the facility.

The staff was astounded and enraged. The apparently solid coconut was split open and smelled rotten inside. Much to their surprise, their enemy was within their midst. They had deceptive internal security which left them open to an amoral fifth column. Assuming responsibility based on unqualified mutual acceptance gave one member a chance to defect emotionally. The consultation ended soon after this exposure, as they could now work with each other to handle this crisis and correct staff process. Follow-up revealed the enemy had been their own unmonitored morality, which had not been addressed heretofore by either patients and staff—as some Panglossian acceptance of good intentions. Nobody had seen beyond the surface loyalties. In a subterranean way each person had been left to his/her own moral devices. Clearly, reins had to be tightened.

In conclusion, in securing organization, one must evoke a sense of Us and Them. The dynamic forces of cohesiveness and alliance draw the common antagonist into clarity. Within the sharpness of Us and Them great power and accomplishment can be generated. Since these are changeable social forces, one must be prepared to monitor misuse and falseness.

3. *Vertical and Horizontal Readiness*

B ECAUSE OF THE MANY LEVELS that come to bear upon most struggles in
the modern world, having advance warning—or intelligence, as the military
say—is critical. We must be looking into the next compartments to see what
is coming towards us. We cannot afford to be like the dolphins:

Even dolphins with their theoretical potential to be humans' intellectual equals (some
would say they are potentially superior) devote their considerable brain power to the
control of their immediate environment, the sea, to which they are superbly adapted,
and they seem not to have been beset by the urge to know how their local environment fits into the greater environment of the total Universe—that urge has been the
driving force behind many of the most significant intellectual achievements of the
human race. (Gribbin, 1977, pp. 2–3)

If the dolphins were more like us, they would be studying events on land, to
protect themselves from the activities of man, and they would be studying
events in their own organs, to protect themselves from the activities of
microorganisms.

But such imaginative range can lead to overstepping, so it must be balanced by a ruthless monitoring of the crude requirements at any level of
organization. Think of Wilhelm Reich, who jumped from a view of the
"constant attitude" of his patients downward into the body compartment to
see how the constant attitude appears as a fixed posture, and then upward
into the social compartment to see how the constant attitude appears as a
political gesture. To Reich this was very exciting—so exciting that he made
grave miscalculations about what the psychoanalytic establishment could
tolerate of his setting loose the body with his orgone experiments and what
the Communist establishment could tolerate of his sexual clinics.[1]

RECOGNIZING THE REQUIREMENTS OF BUSINESS

One way to tune in on many levels while staying absolutely clear about
the crude requirements is to think of the great world of human commerce as
a simultaneous radio broadcast from very low to very high frequencies.
Most people are tuned into narrow, highly amplified bands. If you are going
to be more subtle and wide-ranging in your own tuning, you may also want

to recall that reaching your fellow man is likely to depend on saying the right few words on his wavelength.

In general, you will be able to reconnoitre the neighboring compartments if you remember where and when the crude lines of property are drawn and redrawn:

One hundred and twenty acres, according to the County Clerk, is the extent of my worldly domain. But the County Clerk is a sleepy fellow, who never looks at his record books before 9 o'clock. What they would show at daybreak is the question here at issue. Books or no books, it is a fact, patented to my dog and myself, that at daybreak I am the sole owner of all the acres I can walk over. It is not only boundaries that disappear, but also the thought of being bounded. Expanses unknown to deed or map are known to every dawn and solitude, supposed no longer to exist in my country, extends on every hand as far as the dew can reach. (Leopold, 1949, p. 44)

Leopold, like Reich, had imaginative range, but he was also absolutely clear about where the property lines lay at 9 o'clock in the morning.[2] At that hour Calvin Coolidge's truth takes over: viz., "The business of America is business" (Heilbroner, 1989, p. 103).[3] You may derive the advantages of intelligence if you can read at different levels, so long as you can keep in mind the business requirements of the single level or frequency band you are addressing. If you do not recall these business or territorial requirements, you will set in motion a group of angry, single-minded people, determined to put you in your place! Nothing else will be on their minds.[4]

HAVING A LOOSE, UPTIGHT ORGANIZATION

Even the best intelligence is going to anticipate only some of the shocks coming towards us from larger and smaller worlds. We are going to lose unexpectedly in this modern world in which no single compartment can be cut off for long from these outside influences. Hence, it is crucial to be able to lose gracefully, gathering up one's powers for another day. How does one fight hard and yet take losses in stride? This capability depends on being able to keep one's involvement clear, viz., between the battle and the campaign, between the campaign and the war, between the war and the Lord's work. The deeper levels secure the shallows, because a defeat may be taken as but a small part of the larger venture. This allows the organization to be fierce without being too uptight.

As Red Auerbach, longtime coach of the Boston Celtics basketball team, knew so well, a successful organization has to keep a careful watch on tightness:

Basketball ain't no democracy. A coach can talk a lot, even yell. All that matters is what is absorbed by the players. All I liked to say was, "We're uptight." I'd tell them that, then I'd add that's how I liked them. Then, I'd ask them to think about that other team. Think how those guys must feel. They're playing the Celtics. (1986)

Notice how this down-to-earth man gives a message about tightness on three different levels: observed with disapproval, liked anyway, and discounted by comparison with the other team.

All sophisticated organizations, athletic or military, educational or commercial, have to have this capability for intensity which is graceful, unhurried, even effortless. Sophisticated movements and campaigns depend on the players' being at ease enough to make very fine adjustments, while stiff fighting takes a tightening up of the ranks. Either capacity alone is likely to be catastrophic in the long run, looseness becoming disarray in the face of dangerous foes, tightness becoming so wearisome that it cannot be sustained. (Gosling, 1979).[5]

The utilization of many different levels may allow the necessary looseness or tightness for the battle at hand, depending on which is called for, when both capabilities are in service of aims at a higher level. Those who operate in politics with secure family or with moral or religious beliefs in the background are able to be much less driven about the fate of any given tactic or even strategy. They are freer to move as needed, even to take defeats as lessons rather than catastrophes (Horkheimer, 1972). The game is just the game. The game is not the season, the season is not the career, and the career is not the life: This clarity of the hierarchy of aims or purposes is a broad requirement for a relatively secure organization in our times.[6]

For instance, I have a patient who is a medical doctor, but an atypical one like Lydgate in *Middlemarch* (Eliot, 1871) for his scientific dedication and lack of attention to money. When he came to me, he complained bitterly of his colleagues, his friends and his wife. He stiffly battled them all. The colleagues always voted their own pocketbooks. The friends could listen about science for no more than five minutes. The wife could not be held to the budget. He was continually exercised, and defeated all too often. You could say that he refused to see the narrow territorial (business) requirements of everyone around him.

His organization as an individual being was quite ill suited to his locale (his Middlemarch). He only settled down after several years of our conversation twice a week in individual psychotherapy, when he could finally draw the crucial distinction between his great love of science as a private matter and the strategic and tactical problems of daily business. What his colleagues, his friends, and his wife did could be tackled lightly because he could afford to lose in these matters of less importance to him; surprisingly, this looseness made him more deft at winning these contests.[7]

A relatively secure organization (Chapters 2, 3) will read well in the dark in which all organizations (of one person, of few or many persons) have to carry forward, not quite knowing whether the next corner will be like recent corners or quite a different turn (Chapters 4, 5). Such an organization will allow freedom of movement, being difficult to trap at any one level (Chapters 6, 7). When set back such an organization will be ready to make comebacks by constructing counterproposals (Chapters 8, 9, 10, 11). Therefore, it will last and even allow its players to enjoy this potentially terrible world (Chapters 12 and 1). We have constructed our book to show such an organization in just this sequence of action. Now we tackle three case problems of securing organization, in order of increasing difficulty.

THE BRIEF PSYCHOTHERAPY CLINIC: STRICT MEASURES

I wanted a situation in my department of psychiatry in which the ten to twelve senior residents and psychology fellows could get help from one another with their own brief psychotherapy patients. They need a protected space, for the trainee or faculty member who shows a case in the department at large is fair game. Yet they need vigorous discussion of alternatives. After all, there are many possible lenses to use concerning the patient's life, which will open up fields of altogether different grain and extent, from the narrow field of the patient's physiological disturbances to the largest field of huge, imposing social problems (Gustafson, 1986, 1989b). A patient could be stuck on any of these fields, but any single clinician will only see through some of these lenses concerning a given patient. Hence the great benefit of friendly colleagues who use different ones.

I have now conducted the Brief Psychotherapy Clinic for ten years. Several measures have proven reliable. The first has been to tell them my requirements: to be on time, to let one of us know if illness, vacation or emergency will require lateness or absence, and to prepare for all our discussions by reading. I tell them that the centrifugal forces (the diverse purposes) of the department will pull our clinic apart unless we pull together strictly. They can be in—or out if they cannot abide by these requirements. This is what Robin Skynner (personal communication) calls one of the great simplicities of group life: You get a ragged crew if you allow lax behavior but a proud crew if you ask them to live up to their capabilities.

The second measure is never to allow the presentation and discussion of a case without a focus on what help the presenter *wants*. When that need is not stated, a breach is opened for hounds and hares, the presenter trying to fly ahead, the discussants trying to sniff out his or her weak points. I ask the presenter to tell us what he or she is having difficulty with: Why does he or she ask for our help? Once the presenter has shown a point of vulnerability, the hounds are very friendly and extremely vigorous in their attempts to find new paths for the presenter to take with his or her patient. This is what Winnicott called "meeting the challenge of the case" (1965): the aggressiveness is put in the service of helping the petitioner. This second simplicity of organization makes all the difference: whether we have the hunting of the open field or the hospitality of the tent (Klein, 1959).

A third measure is for myself alone. I do not try to solve the case myself. This would only reintroduce the presenter as quarry, myself as the hunter. I pose problems (Freire, 1970). To the presenter: What are you asking the group for help with? What is your own view about why and how you are stuck? To the group: Your views are A, B, C and D? Back to the presenter: Which of these views seems most helpful to you from where you sit? After both presenter and helpers have had their say and been correctly understood, I will make a small addition to their work, which remains acknowledged as *their* work. I (mostly) spare them my intrusions, my corrections and my ignoring of their striking talents. I acknowledge all contributions (that I notice!) which have moved the group, the presenter or myself. Thereby their diversity is protected from the usual fears that subordinates have to have of their bosses. I will take care as best I can not to invade, judge or snare them. It could even be said that they score at will against the problem posed. What I get, nearly every week, is a remarkable array of individual differences, as if the animals that frequent the stream at dusk could appear in broad daylight.[8]

All three of these measures separate the territory of the clinic from the dangerous open spaces of the department: the strictness of commitment, the rules of their proceeding with each other, and the rules of my proceeding with them. As I hold these measures tightly, I find them discovering great freedom to emerge as individual members, to take up being themselves. I am not exercising my authority by position, viz., not insisting: "Because I say so." Instead, I am exercising my authority by proposal, viz., saying: "This is how I propose we proceed. . . . " This tends to bring about a very elaborated code in the seminar (Bernstein, 1973), because my proposals are challenged, revised and improved by the members' putting them in their own hands and then in their own words. In this playful sense, they are dominant over me (while I still run the place).

But there is one more, a fourth measure, which is also indispensable. I hold, for us all, that there is no right way to do psychotherapy, but many different schools, methods, strategies and tactics. There are only trade-offs and different inclinations personal to themselves, so that any given move or recommendation will have certain advantages and certain risks, warranting clarification (Popper, 1957). This means that the presenter has attempted something he or she has felt inclined to do or say, which always has something to say for it, something to be wary of. The same goes for all the helpers — and for me.

This fourth measure frees them up to bring in whatever they are excited about from the larger worlds of the schools of psychotherapy, their reading, and their various experiences of life. There is a resonance between their individual contributions and this larger world. According to Deutsch's theorem (Platt, 1970), when the most powerful component of an organization resonates with some entity larger than the group, then you can expect transformations of the group. So this becomes something other than the usual seminar in the usual department activity. This is not invariable, but it has returned to refresh me time and again, for the last ten years.

The dangers, as I have written, for reliable organization come from smaller or larger compartments. The shock which hit me this year was that our chief source of fine cases stopped flowing. Instead of sending about twenty well selected patients a semester, our Student Health doctors, who run the free general health service for all university students, sent us but two. I believe I had acted no differently this year from any other year. I began the year as usual by showing the Student Health staff a videotape of a fascinating case they had sent. Their discussion was extremely lively, vigorous, thoughtful. The room was packed. So why had this black box, a mile away, stopped turning out the fine referrals we had worked together to elicit for seven years? Being altogether external to the place, a once-a-year visitor, I am very poorly placed to find out.

I was shocked as no cases appeared week after week. This was simply unprecedented — right when I was doing the best work ever, the trainees as well. There was no relation between the remarkable emerging individuals in the clinic, the collective level of work led by myself, and what had happened in the Student Health Service. Not so far as I can tell.

What I think has happened is that psychiatry has undergone a change in relation to medicine: It has discovered "anxiety disorders" and "affective disorders." Probably new clinics by those names appeal more to the medical doctors. If a patient is anxious or depressed (all of our cases for brief therapy have been anxious or depressed), they need only send the patient to one of these two clinics. There the patient will get drugs, behavior therapy, or something.

Whether or not this hypothesis is strictly true or not, I could not help but notice that I had put the continuance of my clinic in the hands of a group of medical doctors a mile away whose own needs would dictate the flow of their referrals — a black box tuned to some narrow band of frequency to which I have a very small access once a year. How foolish. I reconsidered.

Given that my reputation is most secured by the trainees who watch my work day in and day out, I reckoned that the most reliable supply of cases would come from the participants themselves. After all, they are on the firing line of all the primary care of the department: intakes, hospital consultations, emergency services, health maintenance organizations, mental health center, and so forth. Also, I have secured places for them in many private and public practice groups in town. Therefore, I reorganized the Clinic so they secure their own cases from their primary care responsibilities and from their elective placements. I provide the setting for consultation about preliminary interviews, trial therapy, or later therapy problems. My clinic now depends on ten or twelve sources of cases, on the well-being of my entire department, the medical school, and of practices in town—not as before on a single source, over which the extremely shifting health market holds sway.[9]

After World War II in England, when the National Health Service and the Royal College of General Practitioners were put in place, the G.P.s were overrun with patients. Not just the welcomed problems of medical diagnosis and treatment but also troubled lives were brought into the consulting room. Doctors found that they had to deal with the latter as often as the former. There was no getting around the fact that half the patients were not ill per se, but unhappy. They would keep coming, one way or another, in the guise of an illness. Who could help the G.P.s?

The proposal of Michael Balint and a group of socially minded psychoanalysts, mostly from the Tavistock Clinic in London, was to offer General Practitioner Groups or G.P. Groups or Balint Groups as they became known, in which about six G.P.s would meet weekly as a seminar under the leadership of one of the psychoanalysts to discuss the case situations presented from the day-to-day work of the G.P.s. The analysts would not presume to know how G.P.s should manage their caseloads, but rather help the group of G.P.s to help each other in the territory they knew best. These were self-help groups (Balint, 1951) assisted by analysts.

About ten years ago, in our medical school, I proposed to a professor of medicine who ran the general medical outpatient clinic that the residents working there might well be in the predicament of the English G.P.s and might welcome a chance to have their own Balint Group, which I would offer to lead. He was very glad for my offer, especially since the three residents working in his clinic seemed to be extremely angry about their day-to-day interactions with their patients.

The group worked out beautifully, as follows. The three residents were very glad to get an hour off a week from the clinic they mostly hated. They were very glad to present impossible cases to me, about which I could do nothing: I would take upon myself the helplessness that they wanted to be rid of. They were very glad to get some cathartic expression of their own pent-up urges to torture someone for making them feel helpless. They tortured me. Finally, I was able to show them how I handled being made to feel helpless in the hands of torturers: I demonstrated to them, for each specific case presented, how we were enacting the very problem from the consulting room in our own interaction. They did to me what the patients did to them. I felt what they felt on the receiving end. In other words, they were turning passive into active (Weiss and Sampson, 1986). As I caught on to this activity of theirs, they felt deeply understood. We could then discuss the different ways they were trapped by patients, the different ways each of them tended to be caught, the different ways they could propose to each other to get out of helpless positions or to get some constructive use of the anger so amply aroused. In brief, there was a very nice resonance of relieving them from the clinic, victimizing a psychiatrist, and relieving themselves of destructive urges, which could even be turned around to constructive action. We met the challenge of their troubled interactions.

We got more ambitious. After several more exciting years, my colleague, the professor of medicine, proposed requiring Balint Groups for all second-year medical residents. If the pilot project had succeeded, it was time to do the large experiment. He and another professor of medicine and I would each conduct a group. I would also assist my two colleagues in what would be their first attempts to lead Balint Groups, and they would assist me with my group, on a weekly basis.

The chairman of the department of medicine and the medical faculty approved the new required seminar, set aside Monday noons as protected time, free from all but emergency duties, and even supplied lunches for all the participants. This was unqualified support.

This is where the trouble began. The residents showed great resistance. Most were very difficult to reach by telephone to schedule appointments. Most missed one or more appointments, even when arranged. Many signed a letter of protest: "No extending our Monday work day by one hour (the work not finished in the Monday noon hour will only get tacked on at the end of the day)!" No forced psychotherapy for them, thank you! They would take care of their own problems.

Still, we persisted, somehow interviewing all of them, explaining our purposes, asking each of them to give it a fair try. Then, something very interesting happened. My group didn't show for the first meeting at all. The group of the female professor of medicine (medical psychology) half showed. The group of the male professor of medicine (internal medicine) mostly showed. This pattern persisted. I dropped my group. The medical psychologist struggled with hers. The internist very much enjoyed his group, which was consistent and interested.

If I had taken this personally, I would have been very hurt. Here I am, the most experienced leader, never getting a chance at all. But I did not take the rejection personally at all. Actually, I very much enjoyed my preliminary interviews with the residents assigned to my group, where each made it very clear that he or she was not going to join a group led by myself for the purpose of looking into difficult interactions with patients, families, nursing staff and medical colleagues and faculty. I was deeply impressed by the coherence of their peer culture, banding together against being looked into by this outsider, refusing to comply with the orders of their chairman backed by the entire medical faculty.

I was entirely prepared for this disaster by my previous acquaintance with the medical resident peer group culture, so well described by Mizrahi (1984a, 1984b). It is difficult to appreciate just how vulnerable these young doctors are to making serious medical mistakes and thereby losing confidence in themselves altogether. The press of work is great. The holes in their knowledge are great. So much can go wrong.

What they seem to do is to group together into a kind of mutual protection society. The cardinal principle is that only medical residents can judge medical residents. No one else knows what they go through: Not patients. Not families. Not faculty. Certainly not psychiatrists. Their own judgments of one another are forgiving: The rule is to deny, justify or get rid of mistakes. As one resident said to another in one of our groups, "The mistake departs with the paperwork. Forget it."

The great weaknesses of this peer society are apparent. What is protection for the residents is seen as resistance by the faculty and as not caring by patients and families. But the mutual protection society is the decisive level.

What I believe we ended up with was a bow to the medical faculty, the great power over the heads of the residents. They would comply with the Balint Group led by one of the internists, less with a group led by the woman medical psychologist from within their department, not at all with an outsider professor of psychiatry. Very neatly arranged. The peer culture is expert at making such bows, while defending its own peer court as the ultimate authority. I accepted this result gracefully, if I may say so, enjoying the weekly meetings with the internist and the medical psychologist to assist them with their groups.

The follow-up is that both Balint groups lasted the year with the participation of about half of those required to be there. The group led by the internist struggled with some members very hostile to the work of the group, while the group led by the medical psychologist got stronger in its commitment, interest and imagination, largely due to the peer leadership of a mature member of the group. This is what Redl (1946) called the influence of the "good example," versus that of the "bad influence."

In groups that are highly ambivalent about the nature of the work of the group, the swing depends very much upon *which* peer leaders (i-1) resonate with the group (i). It could be said that the chief job of the leader is to help "the good influences" along. In general, this has to be done obliquely, indirectly, subtly, or the assistance will only drive the group towards the "bad influence." I believe it is very important to treat both subgroups as potentially constructive in shaping the work, because each subgroup tends to be the champion of different demands for working conditions: viz., to go fast, to go slow; to be dependent, to be independent. A leader that backs one pole tends to drive the other pole into withdrawal or hostility. See Gustafson et al. (1981) and Gustafson and Cooper (1985) for many illustrations and further argument about managing subgroup struggles. Still, we are often limited by the initial composition of the groups: whether there are peer leaders present to take over and whether they are peer members whom the group cannot stomach. We set up the best organization we can arrange, but this may not suffice to manage the composition. Gleick (1988) refers to this as "sensitive dependence upon initial conditions." Every athletic coach has been humbled by it.

Notice that the first Balint Group never gave us a view of the level of the peer court (Bach, 1954). The outpatient clinic sequestered three residents there full-time. The Balint Group was an actual free hour from that dreaded clinic, which gave the freedom I have described to make the psychiatrist bear their helplessness and rage. This was a resonant special case, an event in a closet, if you will, which was a great exception to the dominance of the peer culture in the hospital at large. Only when we widened our field to take in the entire hospital did we run into the extraordinary struggle between the peer court and the medical faculty, in which I had to be sacrificed. Fortunately, I was ready and willing.[10]

A FAMILY THERAPY TEAM IN THE MILAN TRADITION: FULLY COMPLEX SCALING STRATEGY FOR ORGANIZATIONS

The most highly developed forms of organization have a complex vertical scaling strategy (Allen and Starr, 1982) for bringing to bear other levels to meet the challenge at hand. Such scaling allows a simultaneous reckoning of many different fields of concern. It is equally important to have a kind of horizontal scaling strategy (Allen and Starr, 1982), through which expected disturbances that occur over different intervals of time can be incorporated into the repertoire of the organization. The organization can work as if it *expects* to be disturbed.

The Madison brief family therapy team (Gustafson, 1989a) is such an organization, depending upon both vertical and horizontal scaling strategies for forwarding learning at a very rapid tempo. Let us take a look at the vertical scaling first, which is somewhat familiar to the reader from the case study of the Balint Groups project.

In contrast to the situation in Italy (Selvini Palazzoli et al., 1978), very disturbed patients and families in this country almost always come with doctors who are giving them some psychopharmacological drug. Such a doctor can be the most important member of the extended family, for without *him* or *her* there may be little sleep or peace whatsoever. As the Milan team wrote in their famous essay, "Snares in Family Therapy" (Selvini Palazzoli and Prata, 1982), attempts to do family therapy recommended by the family psychiatrist are fated to fail, because the family is likely to put in an appearance to keep the doctor in tow, but no more. After several such defeats, the Milan team refused to see families who had already secured another kind of treatment such as psychopharmacology.

Because we were anxious to work with the most disturbed and disturbing families, we did not want to come to the same recommendation, so we attempted a number of family therapy cases, *reaching* as it were past the family psychiatrist to get to the family. We confirmed their finding. We never succeeded, for the family psychiatrist was the crucial player to be retained by the family. The families either did very little or began to do some very new moves but then caught themselves, behaved crazily, and reintroduced the family psychiatrist as the prominent personage.

I soon realized that we were getting our levels of organization muddled. If the crucial conservative game is the family plus psychiatrist, then our consultation that dove to a smaller level of the family was not meeting the challenge of the case. It would be better to restrict our consultation to the individual asking for our help, almost always the sinking psychiatrist caught in the family mud. We would watch the other levels very carefully and acknowledge them very judiciously in our final recommendation to the family psychiatrist, but it would be to him or her that the message would be given (Burnham and Harris, 1985; Burnham, 1986).

A common request for consultation comes from a psychiatrist who is being swamped by calls from a borderline patient and his or her family. Let us take a particular case which I refer to as the Case of the Glue Team and the Crowbar Team. To summarize several hours of interviewing, allow me to say that the psychiatrist hoped to be called less by the girl's mother reporting that the girl was suicidal again. Unfortunately, the more the girl's father ferried her over to the foster parents to get her to "grow up," the more the girl alarmed her mother by talk of suicide, prompting the mother to call the psychiatrist. The more the psychiatrist and the social worker backed the Crowbar Team of the father and foster parents, the more the Glue Team of the girl and mother stuck together. Indeed, the mother and daughter sat together on the left couch looking like doubles of each other, while the father sat on the right couch with the foster parents looking like he had found his partners as well.

We didn't say what I just wrote. What we said was that the family psychiatrist was going to be called even more the way things were going, because the harder the separation team worked, the more the closeness team got together, which meant calling him about suicide. Now that the mother was thinking of part-time school, the prospects for him being called looked unlimited to us, because the closeness team would be doubly threatened. The psychiatrist was very relieved to see how he had been playing into his own misery by backing the separation team.

Now such a consultation may be more or less on the mark. If we are able to tackle the chief concern of the psychiatrist in being mixed up with the family, while catching the family game and the exquisite role of the patient, then we are likely to have a grateful doctor. If we even catch the slow but catastrophic change in time that threatens the family, to show how all the other levels are responsive to this once-in-a-lifetime threat, then we may even bring about a major shift in the doctor/family game. In this case, the impending threat was the parents' retiring to another clime, which would break up all the other levels to the game. The patient might get herself together once the game was up. It is as if every level becomes exceedingly clear once we hold firmly to consulting to the family psychiatrist. If we do not, everything is muddled and we are in the mud with the family psychiatrist.

The reader may be interested in the follow-up from the family psychiatrist on his enmeshment with the Glue Team and the Crowbar Team. I wrote him fifteen months after our consultation to express my interest in the outcome and he telephoned back to tell me, essentially, the following: The family had settled down. There was some push towards "psychosurgery" by the mother (and daughter Glue Team) after our consultation, but a member of the Crowbar Team put the kabosh on this. Then the family psychiatrist focused in with the mother on "how her anxiety was driving the system," which "helped a lot to quiet things down." He sees them only occasionally, their "great energies" once leading to a consult about behavior therapy, but mostly they have settled down. He is greatly relieved (and, as I noted, quite clear about how he was driving the system, even stabilizing its uproar).

But we are not so accomplished as always to get the vertical scaling so perfectly. Indeed, our ambition is not to avoid mistakes but to learn from them as fast as possible. We expect to get disturbing feedback, because these extended families are so complicated that it is impossible for us to get every one of them right in a single interview. Such troubles we have arranged to take in stride, even to turn to our advantage, because we learn (profit) more by our failures than by our successes (doing what we already know), which we can then turn to advantage for our next families. We have learned, as the ecologists would say, to incorporate the perturbations (Allen and Starr, 1982), which would otherwise wreck us. These occur at different frequencies, some coming quite suddenly, some slow, some slower. We have arranged a horizontal scaling strategy to meet these disturbing waves on their way to crushing us, to usher them in.

First of all, we expect to get sessions occasionally canceled at the last hour. Last-minute cancellations can be rough on our morale. But we have incorporated this disturbance into our routine, taking the hour to go over our last communications with the doctor/family, both our written summary and selections from the videotape. Since the cancellation nearly always is due to an oversight on our part, we eagerly look forward to reviewing our summary and videotape, knowing that we are about to learn something of great importance. We are about to get better.

Secondly, we have arranged a monthly disturbance for ourselves, which is to have one of our three teams present a case with which it is having trouble. (Our team is actually an ensemble of three teams.) Once I made a dangerous error when I proposed a theoretical discussion for the monthly meeting. What we got was four different discussions, like the famous horse which was pulled apart by cruel masters pulling from all four quarters.

We all pull together if one of the teams asks for help, when it is quite evident from the start that it does need help. For instance, when our team presented the Case of the Glue Team and the Crowbar Team, the team members were feeling quite successful. So we showed the final message to the doctor and family, saying to our colleagues: "Let's go back over the tape now that you have seen the conclusion, so you can help us see what we overlooked!" Indeed, they were remarkable as usual noticing that, while we caught the relation between the consultation, the doctor plus family, the family teams (crowbar and glue), we had almost completely overlooked the patient in our final message and had said too little about the great threat to the game from the retirement. They noted that the patient's response to the message had been: "Why are these people interested in helping me?" Indeed, she became lost in the crowd after we left the interview, which became a kind of party for everyone but her. Clearly the helping teams were getting a little society out of her being the poor patient. That game could not last forever. As one of our colleagues rightly concluded the evening's discussion: "Such patients often make the most remarkable improvements, when the family game comes to its final halt." We could do a better job of helping them all anticipate that fateful day.

A third disturbance we arrange for ourselves is even more infrequent. Several times a year, we provide observation groups so that outsiders can observe our work down the hall on closed circuit television. We have borrowed the procedure from one of the Milan teams (Boscolo and Cecchin, 1982). The gist of the procedure is that the five or six observers work with a member of our team in a room that has a videotape monitor of our interactions with the doctor and family and an audio monitor of our team discussions behind the one-way mirror. They prepare a message to us about *their* view of our relation to the doctor and family. They deliver their message to us after the doctor and family have finished with us for the day. Then we have a half-hour to entertain this message, discussing *their* hypothesis about us in relation to our consultees. This is always very lively and spirited and undefensive, since we have placed ourselves in a position to hear their message as *their* hypothesis about us. Everyone is entertained. When we used to have outside observers with us behind the mirror inserting themselves into our work, we were not so pleased. Outsiders can make important observations if you can arrange not to be thwarted by them.

A fourth, most infrequent disturbance is to give performances about our work on larger stages such as departmental case conferences or national meetings or national publications of family therapists. We have not had a good routine about these most infrequent events until very recently, which meant that we took some hard blows. When a level is not fully defined as a stage of its own frequency and scope, then the tendency is to accommodate it to the next smaller level.

In one presentation to a departmental case conference, I found myself talking about the family as I would at an observation group. I was disqualified by a series of five colleagues, who reminded me by their behavior that those who are foolish enough to show videotapes at departmental conferences have lost their bearings. I was fair game in a brief but unrestricted hunting season.

In a second presentation, I accepted without thinking an offer by a well-known editor of a family therapy publication to write a review of Selvini Palazzoli's two new books in the Milan tradition. He warmly suggested that he would accept whatever I wrote, since he admired my writing. Little did I anticipate that this czar intended to accept what I wrote, only if *he* could rewrite it from A to Z. He felt entitled to do this as the successful judge of the popular taste in family therapy. After all, this is his business (territory). I had had little idea of the scope of his proprietorship! These larger stages have their own crude requirements, which we must be ready to meet. I subsequently found a better place for my review, in a journal with a serious technical interest in the methods of the Milan teams (Gustafson, 1989a).

In summary, our horizontal scaling strategy is *actively to take into our work the disturbances which would otherwise befall us when we were not ready for them*: late cancelations on occasional weeks; differing perspectives of colleagues monthly; outside perspectives of sympathetic and curious outsiders in observation groups several times a year; very outside perspectives of hostile rivals, such as in our department or in national publications or meetings, less frequently.[11]

CONCLUSION

Vertical and horizontal scaling strategies allow us to do what all the other animals must do (Allen and Starr, 1982) to last and flourish in a relatively hostile world which is ready to invade, judge and snare us. We filter out disturbances until we are ready for them. We incorporate the disturbances into our routines, so that we bring them (as much as possible) under our control. We diversify our scaling. We replicate by bringing new colleagues behind these protective barriers.

But the range that we must master, vertically and horizontally, is greater than any other social animal. Sir Thomas Browne (1682) once described man as " . . . that great and true Amphibian whose nature is disposed to live, not only like other creatures in diverse elements, but in divided and distinguished worlds." Little did Sir Thomas imagine that this land creature would fly as well as swim, that she would alter time as well as space. She would need to read not only other compartments of space but also other frequencies of time. Hence, her need for both vertical and horizontal scaling.[12]

PART III

Reading Situations

4. *Gaining and Renewing Clarity*

BETWEEN ORGANIZING AND acting there must be a clear reading of a situation: how it works, its strengths and weaknesses. The patterns that connect us, however, are like clouds, like storm clouds that pass through. Clarity is possible if you keep an eye on the edge of the cloud, where its shape is distinct though ever-changing. As one's eye moves to the interior of the cloud, the shape is lost, except in memory. Here we pose, on the one hand, a strategy for anticipating the pattern that connects, reading and holding onto clarity as the social game unfolds; and, on the other hand, a strategy for moving vantage points to renew clarity when relationships are overtaken by storm clouds, as inevitably happens.

GAINING CLARITY

In pursuing coherence, we are trying to "grasp what in the world is happening" as group life proceeds (Mann, 1975). It is incredibly useful and orienting to have some way of describing the pattern that connects people in a particular situation. Mann talked about this problem in down-to-earth terms and was clear about certain very useful guidelines. He developed an "operative metaphor": winners and losers—the continuous struggle for dominance is common in groups. Once he delineated the pattern, he used it as an operating base for understanding a whole range of interactions. He took the win-lose theme as the edge of the cloud and oriented himself to it in order to weave together the events of his groups as they unfolded. The complexities of group life compelled him to use the metaphor across different levels of the group—from peers to leader to the larger cultural context.

Mann aims for a loose but clear set of ideas as a mooring, what might be thought of as a theory of the current situation. He then adds and corrects his metaphor by going back and forth from the ideas to the experience. The process of building a theory of his immediate environment is a continuous one. When reading Mann one is reminded of Lewin's (1945) prescription that there is nothing so practical as a good theory.[1]

A useful operative metaphor seems to have two important characteristics. First, it makes sense of the situation. From animal training (Hearne, 1986a, b) to organizational consultation, it is good to have a picture of the way social life works that appreciates the depth of our connection with one another. Second, the metaphor develops a responsible, moral, positive basis for action.

One major obstacle to gaining initial clarity is being persuaded by another's understanding of a situation. A belief that is clarifying for one person can be deadening for another. For instance, a scientist I was seeing in psychotherapy came in rather disheartened. This surprised and puzzled me because he had recently pushed for an expansion of his job role and had become head of a research team on a new project. He began to say how when he had met with his new number two man in the operation he had realized how small a piece this project was in the larger picture. This assistant, who should have been inspired by their mission, instead seemed almost depressed by it. I knew that pushing for the assignment was a big step for this scientist. When I asked more about this assistant's attitude, it became clear that he was a stubborn, unqualified man who was disgruntled because he had been passed up for head position. He didn't want to be subordinated and had an aggressively uncooperative attitude. My client found his attitude contagious. This had happened to him on other occasions, but now victory was closer at hand than it had ever been before.

I said that he needed to watch for such disqualification and envy in order to protect his own enthusiasm. He had lost inspiration by subscribing to the assistant's viewpoint. He not only immediately realized what had happened to him, but soon developed a plan of action: He would give this assistant an ultimatum—either work or leave the team. The clarity of his own excitement about his work advancement was, for the time being, secured once again.

Often, to secure a sense of clarity it is important to keep initial excitement relatively unassailable. When another's critical view of reality does get through, one must titrate it emotionally, ask questions about it—questions of oneself and others—to assess its validity. Clarity is fragile and deserves protection and nurturance.

Another common obstacle to clarity in meeting the challenge of the immediate case is an overcommitment to theory. Rather than being too unprotective of one's spirit and beliefs, one treasures them and stops collecting data because it might disconfirm these beliefs. Being closed to the immediacy of the case can occur in at least two different forms: holding onto a theory that is very difficult to apply, or holding onto a theory that can be applied so elegantly that it explains everything and nothing. In both situations intellectual clarity is preferred to connection.

Some theories are just plain difficult to use. This probably means that an intermediate level of operation is missing; however, one might not realize the piece is missing until faced with a group in which one must *do* something. Since theory is by definition abstract, the problem comes in translating theory to practice.

Sometimes a set of ideas is so manageable and compelling that there is an inherent joy in applying it—almost the way children enjoy repeating over and over again a game they have recently mastered. This weighs the odds against specificity; the theory is too easily applied and false positives are likely.

Clarity and connection are interlocking; clarity is most secured when it is connected with the case. What this suggests is the interactive nature of gaining coherence: One has an *idea* or experience about what is going on, one *gets involved* in a situation, exposes one's clarity to the situation, one has *beliefs confirmed* or *disconfirmed*. One works to avoid what Popper (in Magee, 1973) calls the error of "historicism" by not assuming that an explanation connected with past events will serve to predict the future.[2] Active experimentation offers the answer.

Renewing Clarity

In the normal course of events, relationships become unclear. The challenge is both realizing when we are in the fog and having a strategy for recovering clarity. When outside the cloud and able to see its edge, one can get reliable bearings visually. Once in the cloud, surrounded by unclarity, one must rely on instruments. One of the greatest challenges for a new pilot is relying on instruments, knowing that one *must* switch vantage points for reliable orientation.

Action strategies are based on being able to experience the difference between reading the edge of the cloud and being in it. If we know when we have slipped into the cloud, we are able to put aside (temporarily) an unhelpful conviction or operative metaphor about what is happening. I find it useful to have a number of vantage points with which I can experiment in order to see things in a different way. These different vantage points are "musts" for reorienting.

Loose Coupling and Shifting Emphasis

Loose coupling refers to the notion that it is possible to hold more than one idea or belief at a time and to shift from one to the other. When operating with one particular idea, one can be convinced and vigorous. In fact, we can become attached to our ideas with the same force with which we become coupled to other people. Ideas are no less demanding, in part because they are attached also to teachers, mentors, and/or deep beliefs we hold about how the world works. It is probably useful and adaptive that we are able to get so wedded to our ideas, since at the other extreme is lack of conviction and continual wavering.

Being loosely coupled opens up the possibility of a middleground, of shifting to a different point of view. In discussing vertical and horizontal loose coupling, Simon (1977) suggested the value of keeping interrelated ideas separate. It then becomes possible simultaneously to hold ideas referring to more than one level. For instance, in describing advances in understanding and writing about history, Hughes (1964) makes the point that the more recent advances in historical vision have come through both the belief in the exercise of creative thought *and* adherence to directly perceived evidence of the vanished past. These ideas, held at very different levels in this academic discipline, are only apparently incongruous.

Bion had a way of shifting emphasis by having a theory with two central ideas to which he could be loosely coupled. He had a set of group conditions identifying work, and another set identifying irrationality. Both needed to be kept in mind to make proper internal judgments about situations. He believed that a group was either doing its job or acting irrationally. When the group was working well, he just watched it. When group members were being irrational, he experienced disbelief. His sharing of his disbelief was a tactic both to recover his own clarity and to get the group back to work.[3]

A couple in a long-term small business partnership, were committed to a single idea about why their relationship wasn't working when they came to me for consultation. But the idea was different for each. Each was committed to blame, believing the other person to be at fault. The man and woman involved had been fighting viciously recently, so badly that they were considering breaking up their partnership. To confuse matters, they had also been having a romance, complicated by the man's being married. The critical incident precipitating the consultation was the woman's involvement in an independent romance. They were convinced their personal relationship had nothing to do with the partnership hostilities. He blamed her for attacking his work too harshly and frequently; she blamed him for being too helpless. As I listened to their explanations, I could sense that it would be easy to stay out of the fight, but then I was outside—watching and helpless.

I underlined for them how prominent blame was for them both in their interaction. After being pressed to explain why they blamed each other, I said that I didn't know, but I did think they shouldn't stop until we understood why it was so important. I suggested that they needed the blame right now, as well as the distance it produced. This prompted the man to talk about how maudlin the woman had been many years ago (during a more positive time in their relationship) about an incident in her life involving loss. She was overly sentimental, he thought, and very prone to melodrama and tears. It was a time before his marriage when they were struggling about what to do with their relationship. He became more and more humorous and within a couple of minutes they were looking at each other fondly and laughing hilariously at this man's monologue about her being so sentimental. I said that humor, along with blame, might work to regulate distance, but we would have to see.

The atmosphere was cleared by the shift of emphasis.[4] The ideas were both within the same level of their relationship—how they themselves were getting along—but a different part of the interaction was punctuated. Their rediscovery of humor with each other opened up our conversation tremendously; it gave perspective, which finally clarified the origin of the blame: hopes unfulfilled from a tender time which they hadn't yet left behind.

Reversals provide a shift of emphasis, but do so in a dichotomous way: Because of sharpness of an opposite, the drama is often highlighted. The usefulness of thinking in terms of reversals is that the balancing idea or feeling doesn't have to be searched for too hard; it is apparent in the single idea itself.

Gosling (1979) is helpful here. He notes how groups can head in one direction too long. It may be a good direction at one point in time, but it gets into deeper water as it is held onto unrelentingly. In describing the development of his "underconstrained" general practitioner training groups, Gosling noted the groups' movement back and forth between exposure of the doctor-patient relationship to the corresponding exposure of the relationship among the doctors; each could be kept within bounds to maintain acceptable playfulness. When, on the other hand, the group was moved into a wider international context, its members moved unchecked into a position that portrayed them as "downright foolish"; they hadn't automatically accounted for new context. They moved as they had at home, and it was terrible abroad. It is always useful to be able to put into action an opposite or balancing point of view—or at least to have one in mind.

Broadening and Narrowing One's Focus

When explorations in the immediate environment do not lead to renewed clarity, one best explore other aspects of the social terrain. It is useful to take positions that give a view of the larger environment impinging on the group or look at the subparts of the situation, such as the people in the group.[5]

Deutsch encourages communication upward or downward from the center position, depending upon where one is caught. If, for instance, one gets overconnected to an individual in a system, one can become very unclear about the larger issues. If the work with the individual goes swimmingly, the consultant can live with unclarity about the larger picture. However, if the work with the individual is mired down, one way to clear things up is to take a position that reconnects the individual with the larger context.

In an example from my consultation work, a president of a small manufacturing company was seeking advice about her expanding business. She had recently doubled her production staff and hired middle managers for the first time. She was a rather reclusive person, inclined to be distrustful, and saw herself as a poor delegator. She preferred to keep control over all aspects of her factory. In discussing her new administrative assistant, she bent over backwards to expose her own weaknesses as an executive. Only in bits and pieces did she reveal that she had started the business and taken it a very long way through her own efforts. While very competent at managing people, she had become so preoccupied with her own interpersonal limitations that she had difficulty knowing how to think about her assistant's position. She was very unhappy with him because he was always coming in with questions and bothering her when she was working on overall company issues. The subpart levels here were her self-preoccupation and her being riveted on this one person, both of which obscured her knowing what was needed in her larger work group. The situation only made sense to her as a statement of her inadequacy as a person.

As a consultant, I stayed close to the work situation, in a sense moving away from the subpart toward the "bigger picture." I took the position that this assistant was pointing out for her a new level of her company, namely, that she *had* to have structures and rules for gatekeeping for herself (and others). There were so many people now that, lacking some order to their interactions, nobody would get anything done. I suggested to her that in dealing with her assistant she regulate his contact with her, giving him some specific meeting time every day if need be, but no other times. She was immediately relieved, took the suggestion, and solved the problem. This was an all too easy example of lifting people out of one level into another so that they can recover their own ability to act well on their own behalf and stay in a generative frame of mind. As a consultant I found it helpful to be detached enough to seek a level other than the one defined by the client.

Sometimes one's understanding can be thwarted by outside forces. If the members can't stand against the invasion of outside forces, generative interaction is limited; the bodies aren't present or they are too frightened or exhausted by battle to prevail. Freire (1970) offered examples in a framework that suggested narrowing the focus to reduce the effects of the oppression. He was setting up literacy programs for liberated peasantry in post-revolutionary Brazil (as well as other countries). The peasants were trained by their oppressive culture to be unthoughtful as well as illiterate. Their construction of their social situation put them in a helpless position. They expected to be passively taught, and yet being passive was part of the dominating cultural metaphor that kept them illiterate. Freire's method involved posing problems for individuals with drawings — asking the members what names they gave to images and objects important in their daily lives. Generating words in this way turned out to be extremely enlivening. By answering these questions, the peasants, following Freire's lead, challenged the stultifying effects of the larger culture. From images emerged an interest in words and reading. Through an interest in the immediacy of their lives and their group interaction they found a space free of the oppressiveness of their imposed (political, social, etc.) passivity; within this space they could seek current meaning.

Reading Enactments

Another approach to renewal involves attending to nonverbal aspects of social behavior when one is sinking into obscurity at a verbal level. Hearne observed that "objectivity depends on models of the world and of language which require precisely the flat-footed and contaminated sort of straight line that cats are dedicated to undermining for the sake of clarity and richness of discourse" (1986b, p. 81). Such could be said of groups as well. Groups abhor straight lines. Often the straightest line in pursuing meaning is through the rich underbrush of nonverbal discourse in which the words are embedded. Like Hearne's cats, groups often refuse to be understood in *the* terms we as participants or leaders choose, nor will they contain their penchant to demonstrate "revisionary impulses." In some sense, to appreciate enactments one must be only loosely coupled to verbal communication.

To even hope to stay up with the group's immediacy and individuality, it is useful to be able to see the group continuously enacting dramas in which one gets enmeshed as one of the players. The problem is like arriving late for a movie or play and trying to figure out plot from a slice of the action taken out of the middle. The group is constantly acting, there is no libretto that goes with it, and most of the time one is focused on verbal interactions.

Weiss and Sampson (1986) talk about this process in individual psychotherapy. They believe that people most often can't put their central problem into words; instead, they proceed (unconsciously) to enact it in the therapy relationship. While their argument is very much connected with classic psychoanalytic discussions of transference, they add the notion that these unconscious dramas are special tests for the therapist — tests geared to discover whether the therapist will treat the patient any better than a crucial person from the past (such as a parent) has done. Unbeknownst to him/herself, the therapist has a role in this drama — that much can be anticipated. Often the drama unfolds very early in the therapy relationship, before the therapist actually knows much about the person. The challenge is to construct meaning in the current slice of behavior, to find its significance in the drama that is the person's life. The appearance of a larger system dynamic in a smaller part of the organization has been described before (Turquet and Gosling, 1965; Menzies, 1960; Cooper, 1977). What needs to be emphasized here is that it can be *enacted*, not just verbalized.

There is no key to reading enactments, but there are some guidelines. Remember, the map will differ from the territory. The primary guideline to reading an enactment is to take it as it is given in the here and now. Take note of the behaviors. In a consultation I did with a staff group of a mental health day treatment program, the presenting issue was problems with morale and integrating a new staff member, who was seen as a provocateur with colleagues. The conversation occurred within the staff group in a very orderly fashion, except for the fact that the director would periodically dash across the room to the door to smoke. He sat as far away from the door as possible and made dramatic stage crossings. I couldn't connect it with anything being talked about, but it reminded me of someone choking and struggling for air. Since there seemed to be considerable interest in the topics as presented, I decided to stick it out. Communication issues were worked on well in one long session, as we laid out revisions in meeting structure and defined roles more clearly. There was a sense that they were all pulling in the same direction.

There were several other consultation meetings, but no desperate cigarette sprints. Then, in a two-month follow-up meeting, staff began to argue with the director. Some said he wasn't available for private meetings, while others perceived him as doing all negotiations behind closed doors. Again the director was up and dashing across the room to the door to smoke a cigarette, almost, but not quite, leaving the room. As the discussion evolved, senior staff, who enjoyed their private meetings with the director, defended him, while the newer or lower-status staff, who felt excluded, attacked. It seemed reasonable that staff who had worked together for a long time would have a close relationship, but here was the enemy closing in on the director, and he headed for the door.

A secondary guideline, for a fuller appreciation of the enactment, is explicitly seek context. I asked if these dramatic stage crossings were often part of meetings. The director said sheepishly that he didn't want to pollute everybody's air with his smoke; it was his own problem. How did he decide, I wondered aloud, which interactions were safe for the public consumption and which were reserved for his own problem? He said it had to do with people towards whom he felt friendlier; they could confide in each other. Were these confidential topics that pertained to the program or were they strictly personal? Most of "confidential" had to do with work life outside the program. It emerged publicly for the first time that the director was telling confidants more and more clearly that he was considering leaving, making other plans, getting involved in other professional activities that took some of his energy away from the program; moreover, he was listening to the same kind of conversation from other staff members. At a subgroup level, they were like a fifth column, speaking treason behind closed doors. The director was worried about exposure and was (covertly) enacting the tension about wanting to be both inside and outside the door of the program. The verbal interaction wasn't nearly as revealing as his dashing to the door periodically and dramatically.

Was the director's talk about leaving a private or public matter? From his point of view, nonverbally, dramatically, some of both. The enactment was the lever that contributed to lifting the dilemma to the surface. In the first meeting, the drama probably was a combination of both his concern about leaving and the question of whether the troubles in the agency were a private matter or should be made public to a consultant.

CONCLUSION

It is important to have strategies for gaining and renewing clarity. Several postures, covering a broad terrain, have been described to get free of tight

holds of oppressive levels and verbal orientation. Perhaps the most important guide is one's internal sense of when one is clear or unclear about a
situation. "The discovery we all have to make for ourselves is the following
postulate: the environment as we perceive it is our invention" (von Foerster,
1973, p. 288). Our inner maps may be at times our clearest guides. When
they fail, our morale is at risk.

5. *Protecting Morale*

WHEN A FAMILY OR A GROUP at school or a business organization looks for some hope to be fulfilled but nothing comes through at all, then morale is apt to be dashed. Hence the importance of understanding the several ways in which a null result can be anticipated and overcome. When a family therapy team or a therapeutic group or a political organization looks for loyalty to its cause but discovers that the cause has become the housing for larger or smaller purposes which do it injury, then morale is apt to be lost in disillusionment. Hence the importance of understanding the several ways in which a social body can be invaded, judged, and snared from within and without. When looking for what is coming towards any organization, we will see too little if we look only on the field of play where the organization is directly challenged. Such looking ignores larger purposes on larger fields and smaller purposes on smaller fields, which will determine or reverse outcome. Such tunnel vision will be promoted by our antagonists! Hence the importance of reading past surfaces to see what is coming and to make adequate preparations. This is the kind of systemic pessimism (Stierlin, 1988) which will defend us well, so that optimism can prevail.

Individual patients usually have too much anxiety, which needs to be reduced; however, it is equally true that they often have too little anticipation of what will befall them in the social world (what Sullivan [1956] called "selective inattention"), so that they end up defeated by what they have not seen coming. This is demoralizing and even downright depressing. Although much help can be given to individual patients by attending to their inner worlds and to their enactments of difficulties in the consulting room itself (Bennett, 1985; Frank, 1971), this help can overlook the crucial structures of the modern contest, which only come into view in the larger lenses that look at the fields of the family, of group situations (including those of teaching), of the organization in which the patient dwells, and of potentially over-whelming large-scale social problems (Gustafson, 1989b). No amount of self-knowledge will entirely prepare the patient for this surprising set of landscapes. They take on a life of their own, which has little to do with the patient as an individual being.

A therapist well versed in the situations in which just about anybody would become demoralized has a better chance of preparing his or her patient for the world. As Sullivan wrote (1954), there is little that is more important for patients than to recognize and give up what he called "routinely futile operations." But to know what is futile for patients, and thus demoralizing, is to know what is likely to fail in the world. Hence, this entire chapter could be taken as an education for individual therapists about where society is apt to get our patients down.

In other words, we can help our patients with "objective self-possession" (Mann, unpublished) in the world by showing them how it works for or against them: viz., what will panic father and trigger him to unmerciful tirades, or what will put the thoughtless friend firmly in her place. Often, I find this leads right back to the traditional subject matter of deep feeling, anxiety, transference, and so forth, back to what David Mann (unpublished) calls "subjective self-possession."

But we who are not patients are quite as vulnerable to society because of our involvements with families, groups of all kinds, teaching, organizations and large-scale political movements, until we become adept at anticipating for ourselves where morale is very likely to falter. So let us begin our look at three hazards which turn up everywhere.

WHEN NOTHING IS ABOUT TO HAPPEN

Humans are as wily as fish. They feed in certain, select places. In great stretches of the river or of the lake or of the ocean, you will hardly ever see them. They are potentially present everywhere in the water, but they use only a very small bit of their potential space. Fishermen who seek them everywhere will be extremely frustrated, eventually bitter.

But fish are relatively simple about their presence compared to us. They are either there or not there. We have infinite capacity to be partly there, partly in ten other places, partly at one level, partly at ten other levels. The social world is for us an enormous array of shells, nests, fields, habitats, from very small to very large—an enormous potential, most of it unused at any one time.

Therefore, looking for where people are alive takes more skill than fishing, great as that art is in its technical demands. I recommend a kind of double strategy. First, you need to know the array of hiding places, from very small to very large. Second, since most of them will be unused at any one time, you need to know how to put markers out in front of these places, to see if any life is deflected (Havens, 1988).[1]

Yet there are some rules of thumb for locating people. I call these the seven Modern Conservation Laws of Presence.

(1) Without a common threat or opportunity, do not expect presence. Committees, parties, seminars, business as usual, are routinized. Presence is being conserved elsewhere for something more serious, or more playful, where it will gather sharply.

Another way of saying this is that the common purpose of many groups we encounter is so minimal that presence is not necessary to their function: like riding on a bus together. Sartre (Laing and Cooper, 1964) called these serial groups, because the members are merely the series that got in line for the bus (1, 2, 3, 4, 5, etc.). Individual identity is irrelevant. The purposes of the members of the series have no relation to each other, other than that they share the tactic of riding the bus. This is why Sartre said that their relations are practico-inert (practical in the use of the common vehicle, but otherwise inert). So much of the modern world is like this. Whereas the 19th century in America was replete with mutual help organizations (de Tocqueville, 1835), we now depend on bureaucracies for finance, health insurance and even burial, rather than each other. So much of what we do with each other—in school, in business, in meetings—is wait for the obligatory ride to be over.

(2) Do not (usually) expect to find those you fall in league with on one level at other levels. The search party forms and the search party dissolves. The team plays hard together and the team replaces its members all too readily. Emergencies are met. Profits are taken. We disperse again (Crane, 1898). You can expect to mobilize a great deal of presence, to use Winnicott's phrase "to meet the challenge of the case" (1965). You can expect a few overtones, of larger hopes shared, and undertones, humorous and sexual. But the rule is to restrict presence to the level in question, again conserving presence.

(3) The great exception to laws 1 and 2 involves the young, the upcoming, the not yet fixed, who are greatly given to connecting on many levels. Saint Exupery's *Little Prince* (1943) is just such a character. They love to be given the chance to be themselves in many different ways, in meeting the challenge of the case, thus riding into larger worlds they have not yet known. This is a vertical capability, to move up into fields of greater extent, to move down into fields of finer grain, as needed. Like dreaming, this implies a negative capability (Keats, 1817), to be let loose of crude horizontal demands, to find this leeway to sail upwards or downwards.[2]

Nevertheless, presence is still conserved, for these great dreamers see very little of who it is that sets up their dreamscape, take it entirely for granted, drop it in a second. So the adventure subsides, just as it rises, easily and even fervently.

(4) If there is no presence upon a given field, look to larger or smaller fields as the relevant hiding places. Let us take several commonplace examples, starting from the smallest scale, then enlarging.

For instance, psychotherapists in public institutions have often noticed that their patients seem to sleepwalk through their individual psychotherapy sessions. Where have they gone? A chief of psychiatry was astonished one day to notice patients conversing in the waiting room of his department when the residents were away. It turned out that coming to the mother institution was what drew them. Residents came and went. Their weekly conversations in psychotherapy with the residents (supposedly the treatment) were desultory at best. Nothing much seemed to happen on that level. The "transference to the institution" (Reider, 1953) counted for everything.

The marital conversation can disappear in a way which is only more complicated by the range of places that divert the couple from being present for each other. A typical story of the American marital tragedy goes like this: A powerful man and an attractive motherly woman enjoy their sexual relationship, their complementary virtues, their hopes to bring up kids together, the complementary difference in their families of origin, bowling, and working in the factory together. They discuss it all. However, when she gives up her job to stay at home with their young children, their conversation about people at the factory stops. He begins to talk more to his bowling pals, she to her sister. Sex becomes flat, their complementary virtues divisive, the bringing up of their kids a chance to take turns, so each can get away into separate worlds of her family, his bowling and work adventures. Soon he has found a different woman at bowling and work, with whom he discusses his disappointments with his wife! Several years later, she finds a man she can talk with, who understands what she is missing from her husband. Two new conversations have taken over putting the world together, from large to small. Another marital conversation is no longer happening.[3]

Entire halves of groups are commonly missing. When the cancer patients' group gets together on one of our oncology services every week, the prevailing wind favors half of the group. Sometimes those who urge a positive attitude in fighting cancer get the upper hand. The group is about making every day count, the latest discoveries in chemotherapy, and marvelous doctors at the university hospital. Those in tears and rage cannot be found. Some weeks the usual southerly wind has disappeared, replaced by a storm coming upon us from the north. The group is about dying too young, failing families, and outrageous attitudes in doctors. Those who counsel putting your private feelings in your back pocket have no say at all. You wouldn't know they were even there. Often the leaders are captives of the subgroup which is in the saddle, missing the subgroup which is looking at the floor.

Entire groups fail to jell. The sensitivity group of our first-year residents is dispersed into the hospital at large, where each young doctor carries a heavy load late into most evenings. They have a few seminars in the department, but mostly each is on his or her own. Some are married, some have kids as well, while some are single. Some years the group jells, some not. This past year some preferred the consolidation and support of their own families, while some were pulling hard for more mutual support in the sensitivity group. Mutual resentment led to both subgroups staying away, and the sensitivity group didn't jell. After all, there was a modicum of amiability to be conserved for seminars in the department and all too much to do in the hospital. So nothing happened in the sensitivity group this year.[4]

Even organizations come and go with the wind. When the early days of the Reagan administration sounded out here like preparations for nuclear war, when the Secretary of Defense was talking to the press about firing nuclear weapons "across the bow of the Soviets as warning shots," faculty from the entire range of the university got together like the Minute Men at Concord against this terrifying threat. We built an interdisciplinary organization around monthly evening lectures by national and international experts, seminars with the faculty group the following morning, and summer institutes for college faculty in the midwest region. But as the Reagan administration became more conciliatory, the public less terrified, the faculty slid back into their own special academic worlds. The physicists went back to physics, the educators to teaching, and the psychiatrists to psychiatry and some political scientists were willing to keep talking as if the world was theirs anyway. The previous diversity of voices became the insistent voice of political science, which was enough to make anyone resume a smaller subject. The threat had dropped below our common horizon.

This is how the planet itself may disappear. Great opportunities, such as space travel, as well as great hazards, such as nuclear winter, bring it into view. Very few individuals live on this world stage, however. Most who are interested at all are creatures who look at the lesser stage of national security, which is greatly more rewarded. We get frenetic activity in the service of defending us against the Soviet antagonist and third world ferment and monetary collapse. We get too little word about the resources of the planet.

All of the expected presences that seem to fail us can be borne much more cheerfully when we are prepared for their absence. We can put our hopes in more promising places.

(5) When entire fields are vacated, individual beings then may discover something in common. Two of them are apt to feel like stealing away together. I was at a department retirement party one fine summer evening, where everyone was to rub elbows with allies. Fortunately, it was inside and outside the house. The obligatory talk was its usual desultory self, what Winnicott called the "mildly depressing nature of social life." But I found that mention of the pleasures of sneaking away in the summer found takers all around.[5] If shallow, shifty alliances are necessary to us all, if measuring everything is the beginning and end of the lives of professors, then look for them to seek an out for themselves, behind these obligatory appearances. They can be found jogging at noon and watching arrivals at the farm pond all afternoon.

(6) Often, the shared presence of an entire group is within reach, but the two halves of the group cancel each other out. Sometimes, the canceling can be reversed. This is extremely common in the field of group therapy. Take our cancer patients' group, for example. Some of these patients and family members tell so much of their catastrophe that they trigger other patients and family members to stress everything that is going well. This entirely optimistic outlook can drive the desperate to tell even worse tales (Andrew

Kessler, personal communication). These tales drive the optimists to be more insistently optimistic. This keeps going around in what is called a strange loop (because more optimism begets more catastrophe and vice versa) (Cronen, Johnson, and Lannamann, 1982). This is ordinary in group therapy.

A second ordinary and strange loop occurs between the desperate patients and their group therapists. The more lost the patients become in their strange loop, the more they expect the group therapists to take over. The more the group therapists take over, the more passive becomes the group.

But then some of the patients will have to resume their painful tales, because they cannot stand all this passivity for long, which will only drive the optimists into their frantic activity again. When these two strange loops seem endemic to the group therapy, many patients get out of them by quitting the group. This seems their only recourse.

Fortunately, the group therapist who understands these two ordinary and strange loops of group therapy can refrain from making them worse. Often, it is possible to get free of them. The peer loop can be interfered with most simply by taking an interest in both sides, in turns. They become so self-preoccupied that they fail to provide this for each other. They may even fail to interact.

I once did a simulation of group therapy for the last session of a group therapy course. Students so ferociously alternated between wild disclosures that you might hear in a soap opera and window dressing you might see on Fifth Avenue in New York that they seemed to be ignoring the need for listening to one another altogether. That day I waited too long before showing my interest in what they were doing, so the group went dead. They became utterly demoralized. As Robin Skynner has emphasized so lucidly, the leader is the person of last resort. Once he is fully aware that interest and curiosity (Cecchin, 1987) are often in short supply in the strange loop for the peer groups, he may stand ready to come in with them before too long. (This timing is discussed in Chapter 8 as "the lull hypothesis.") Once he is aware that groups can fail to interact at all, guaranteeing failure in group therapy, he may stand ready to invite their interaction or provide his own with them.

But this activity runs the second risk of the strange loop between the fully responsible doctor and the increasingly passive group. Once he is aware of this second ordinary pattern, he will catch it as it occurs, declining the great performance. He will give a little, then make a transition that hands responsibility back to the peers. This creates the possibility of the two great charmed loops of group therapy, which one may be privileged to see someone like Robin Skynner carry out so effortlessly, which make the ordinary, strange loops of group therapy look so needless (Skynner, 1987). The first charmed loop is that admired disclosures lead to more disclosure, which leads to more disclosure. All feel very successful. The second charmed loop is that a little responsibility at the right times and right places by the leader leads to more responsibility by the group, which leads to a little responsibility again by the leader as needed.

(7) Finally, the last Modern Conservation Law of Presence is that most people you will meet will be players of one game or two, who, therefore, will not be present for anything outside their game. They simply will not be listening and watching for anything else. Concerning their game, they will be acute, even watchful for chances to win and chances to disqualify competitors. You can hardly comprehend the extent of the subjects they will tune out, unless you imagine the grocery clerk who has to record the list of charges at the cash register, the builder who has his list of six jobs going at once, and the medical student with his list of diseases in the differential diagnosis of abdominal pain, chest pain, headache, and so forth.

The modern contest has selected out instrumentalists such as these everywhere by discipline, as Foucault (1980) suggests. They win the contests for places. They drop out where they don't win. They qualify those who qualify them, and disqualify those who could disqualify them.

A little sympathy for them is reached once you consider that their lists are twice as long as their days and all important. They simply lack the time to listen for long. Oliver Wendell Holmes called this conceit and recommended it to us all as absolutely necessary:

Little localized powers, and little narrow streaks of specialized knowledge, are things men are very apt to be conceited about. Nature is very wise; but for this encouraging principle how many small talents and little accomplishments would be rejected! Talk about conceit as much as you like, it is to human character what salt is to the ocean; it keeps the sweet, and renders it endurable. Say rather it is like the natural unguent of the sea fowl's plummage, which enables him to shed the rain that falls on him and the wave in which he dips. When one has had *all* his conceit taken out of him, when he has lost *all* his illusions, his feathers will soak through, and he will fly no more. (p. 8)

Little could Holmes imagine in the mid-19th century how such instrumentalists would prosper and multiply in the late 20th century. As *The Little Prince* (St. Exupery, 1943) discovered in his far-reaching travels, it has become unusual to come upon a person who is free to look up from his lists for very long. Conversely, it is usual that if you can improve someone's procedures, he will be satisfied with himself, and indirectly with you.

When the medical students learn interviewing in a group with me by practicing with patients, they are very, very content to learn how to conduct a mental status examination of the patient's cognitive abilities, including orientation, concentration, memory, and so forth. They are not so content with also learning to be interested in the patient's life, unless it can be simplified to a clear story of "What brought you into the hospital?"

When I follow the student who spent a quarter of an hour on the mental status and the student who did a quarter of an hour on "What brought you into the hospital?" with a half-hour of "Maybe there is something you want me to help you with," they all are drawn into the patient's life and deep feelings, just as George Dennison was wholly drawn into *The Lives of Children* (1969). But how fast they put it behind them! Some think it was okay, but a little disappointing because it didn't stay strictly with their subject, "What brought you into the hospital?"; some think it was good; some are deeply moved and even thrilled. I get a C from the first, B from the second, and A from the third.

The best way to stay with them is to be interested in their *doubts* about the interview. This is where each finds his or her particular voice quite readily and even beautifully.

A Darwinian way of stating the prevalence of these instrumentalists is that they have been selected as most apt for the modern contest. They constitute what Tolstoy (1869) called the "swarms" of humanity, as busy as bees (Bayley, 1966).[6]

All seven of these Modern Conservation Laws of Presence keep us well dispersed, not overly connected, which must be of great, even overriding, importance. This is probably best explained as follows:

If species interact weakly, their communities are vulnerable to invasion by another species . . . if they interact strongly, they are vulnerable to almost all the hazards of existence and some will go extinct. (MacArthur, 1972, p. 177)

We seem to gather presence to "meet the challenge of the case," but pull back to maintain diversity, thus protecting ourselves in the two ways that are absolutely necessary: This vulgarity ensures mobilization to any external invasion or opportunity (so we are not picked off singly), while keeping us apart so that we do not fall at once to the same, single hazard. We call this the *thinness*, or thin connectedness, of the social world.

Freud (1921) posed this problem of the *right distance* between us and our fellow men, not in terms of lasting (survival), but in terms of comfort:

Let us keep before our eyes the nature of the emotional relations which hold between men in general. According to Schopenhauer's famous simile of the freezing porcu-pines no one can tolerate a too intimate approach to his neighbor. [footnote contin-ues]: A company of porcupines crowded themselves very close together one cold winter's day so as to profit by one another's warmth and so save themselves from being frozen to death. But soon they felt one another's quills, which induced them to separate again. And now, when the need for warmth brought them nearer again, the second evil arose once more. So that they were driven backwards and forwards from one trouble to the other until they discovered a *mean distance* at which they could most tolerably exist. Parerga and Paralipomena, Part II, 31, "Gleichnisse und Para-beln." (my italics) (Freud, 1921)

Freud then shows how the sediment of feelings of aversion and hostility works to distance us from those most like us.

The evidence of psychoanalysis shows that almost every intimate emotional relation between two people which lasts for some time — marriage, friendship, the relations between parents and children — leaves a sediment of feelings of aversion and hostility, which only escapes perception as a result of repression. This is less disguised in the common wrangles between business partners or in the grumbles of a subordinate at his superior. The same thing happens when men come together in larger units. Every time two families become connected by a marriage, each of them thinks itself superior to or of better birth than the other. Of two neighboring towns each is the other's most jealous rival; every little canton looks down upon the others with contempt. Closely related races keep one another at arm's length; the South German cannot endure the North German, the Englishman casts every kind of aspersion upon the Scot, the Spaniard despises the Portuguese. (Freud, 1921)

Who is not familiar with this distancing operation in his or her extended family, neighborhood or department?

Finally, Frost (1936) put the problem of right distance, not in terms of literal survival or of comfort, that is, objective self-possession (Mann, unpublished), but in terms of keeping one's spirit, or subjective self-possession (Mann, unpublished):

> Probably, you're far too fast and strong
> For my mind to keep working in your presence.
> I can tell better after I get home,
> Better a month from now when cutting posts
> Or mending fence it all comes back to me
> What I was thinking when you interrupted
> My life-train logic. I agree with you
> We're too unseparate. And going home
> From company means coming to our senses (p. 325)

Thus, the thinness of the social world serves many of our purposes, however we may complain of it.[7]

HOUSING LARGER AND SMALLER PURPOSES

If presence is so carefully conserved in the modern world, then generous interest becomes very difficult to resist. But resist we must, very often, because being taken into a business deal, a bureaucratic procedure, or the daily working of a discipline often subjects us to being invaded, judged and snared.

The difficulty comes with sorting out what is help and what is taking advantage, often greatly confounded. The chief device is ancient, but has acquired innumerable new clothes (Bourdieu, 1977): When a party is generous in some way, by bestowing gifts, privileges, honors, or help, it creates a debt for those "helped" and credit for those who give "help," which Bourdieu (1977) calls "symbolic capital." Often, this takes the form of prestige. Such symbolic capital is often better than literal material capital, because it can be converted into material capital repayment when convenient. Little labor is necessary in the interim, while huge labor can be called to one's own service at short notice, as when the magnanimous Algerian family gets the entire village to do its harvesting at a difficult time when all could be lost (while their helpers postpone and risk their own harvests). In modern contests, figuring out the trade-off between the advantages and the disadvantages of the deal is made more difficult because the force of the disadvantage is delayed in its appearance, while the advantage is up front. This is why we think the reader who is fully acquainted with these three delayed disadvantages will bargain more successfully.

Invaded

Be glad you have not been operating a typewriter store since the technological invasion of the personal computer, or making phonographs since the compact disc has come into play. In certain counties, you might not want to be teaching social studies since the born-again people have started breathing down teachers' necks. In other counties, you are apt to dread the administration which is sending you to the state university so that you will teach like all other teachers. We never quite know what *new simplification* will come bearing down on us, but we can be *quite* sure that something is coming soon. Many of us will be put out of commission, while many others will find a ticket to ride.

Some of us are positioned better than others for the sudden tilting of the board which is always about to happen. Think of our extraordinary money system, as managed by the Federal Reserve Board (Greider, 1987). As the Feds increase the supply of money through reducing the prime rate of interest and through selling more government securities, the relative value of money goes down and prices go up. Such inflation actually benefits the middle class because borrowing at present prices to buy things will cost much less to pay back in an inflated future. But it takes value away from those with fixed holdings. Inflation is an enormous wave for redistributing wealth. Now we have just seen the Federal Reserve Board reduce the supply of money, depleting huge sectors of the economy, especially farmers who can't pay back huge investments with deflated money.

Some people benefit whichever way the board is tilted, because it is their full-time job to get the most out of money; to borrow as the dollar inflates and to scoop up the holdings of the losers as the dollar deflates. Some people think ill of these people who devote themselves to this kind of positioning. Galbraith puts this in perspective,

Money also keeps these people out of more damaging pursuits. I repeat myself here: No one who has stood at the top of Wall Street of an evening can doubt for a moment how much better it is that the throng making its way home is in pursuit of money rather than involved with war, religion, or highly motivated political persuasion. On this matter, Dr. Johnson still rules. (1986)

Also, opportunism is a necessary virtue in a highly fluid world of wave upon wave. No organization lasts which is not seeking out new fields of operating, for the old ones are not likely to persist. Keen and Deutsch (1986) call this "learning . . . at the level of large systems":

During the last fifty years, many of the world's governments and political systems have learned to perform many new operations that they did not and could not perform before, and they have *recommitted* some of their old structures and resources, and acquired new ones, so as to create some readily available new structural capacities that earlier they had lacked. (p. 89)

They point to the vast reorganization of water resources, social security, medical care, collective bargaining, military power, nuclear power, space technology, transport, mass communications, computer technology, race and sex equality, and university education.

Readiness to anticipate and ride new opportunities has to be an element of any lasting organization in our time. If opportunism is merely in service of itself, the result is something like Florida real estate or drug dealing. If opportunism is in the service of slower, enduring tradition, the result is more like physics or literature. Think of the only institution in the West which has lasted twenty centuries, the Roman Catholic Church. Here, surely, is an example of traditional beliefs served by opportunism.

Therefore, accepting or being included in a business deal, bureaucratic procedure, or daily working of a discipline had better be with open eyes for the overwhelming likelihood of some new simplification/reorganization coming along soon to alter the landscape drastically.

Judged

If we are to be invaded by waves of new simplification, we are also going to be judged by them as well. And not in our own terms. Large organizations and organizers marshall their divisions, their components, in the simplest possible way. They review them in sequence (Steinbruner, 1974), according to some dichotomy like profit and loss, popularity and unpopularity, publications and the lack thereof. This is how we will be elevated or dropped. Freire (1970) called this the Director Culture, into which subordinates must fit — or disappear. Subordinates have no existence unto themselves which can be seen. Anyone who has ever presented a paper at a large scientific meeting or written for a large and burgeoning field knows that it is very unusual to be heard in one's own terms. In the mass cacophony (Galbraith, 1983) of such rehearsals, little stands out except the simple terms of who got the largest audience.

Understanding the crudity of such judgment, we may also put it to our own use. All we need to do is meet the minimum terms. In other respects, we are free to do as we please. Not so long ago, it was necessary to woo all the senior faculty to find a place in a department. Now, it is only necessary to write twenty articles in journals refereed by the national judges of the field. The deans only count. This is terrible, yes, a loophole for those without conscience, but it is also freedom to work in one's own terms.

Unfortunately, the judging, terrible world often steals in unannounced and speaks from the throat of bosses, teachers, mentors, colleagues, students, friends and even family (Michael Moran, personal communication). We are apt to listen all too well, and too openly, to such judgments of us, as if we were secure and protected by the bonds of loyalty. Only from painful experiences do we learn that children and spouses give voice to causes larger than the family which may denounce us, even cheerfully. Students or colleagues do the same, and so forth. We learn to sketch in the comic mask that the speaker ought to be wearing to pronounce his telling judgment, the mask of a peer group, of a school of thought, of an interest group, of a ruling discipline. Only when we "consider the source" can we set some distance between this judgment and our poor selves. They do what they do. They judge as they judge. It has little to do with me. We place outside ourselves the otherness of others (Gustafson, 1986, Chapter 17). When charity shows itself, how refreshing for us!

Snared

So we must position ourselves to be invaded and judged in the simplest terms. We must also be ready for being snared in bad deals. People at the top of organizations can be expected to spend most of their time with schemes to benefit themselves which are more or less useful to people at lower levels. They will always claim that what is good for them is good for the organization and what is good for the organization is good for the people and what is good for the people is good for the environment, etc. So long as there is some flow of profit downwards, such argument is extremely difficult to oppose. As Machiavelli wrote,

Whenever one does not attack the property or honour of men, they will live contented. (p. 66)

Or more savagely,

Above all he must abstain from taking the goods of others, for men forget more easily the death of their father than the loss of their patrimony. (p. 62)

And,

For it may be said of men in general that they are ungrateful, voluble, dissemblers, anxious to avoid danger, and covetous of gain; as long as you benefit them, they are entirely yours. (p. 61)

However, as soon as profits stop flowing downwards, the argument that all levels fit nicely together breaks down. This is what Habermas called a "legitimation crisis" (1973), where the gears that have enabled the different levels of the social machine to fit together lack the lubrication of profit. Policies which were glossed over in the smoothly flowing regime now can be put in a very bad light and seen to be terrible. The reverse is also true. Policies which have been protective now can be dragged out and sacrificed.

But until such a "steering crisis" (Habermas, 1973), glossing over is the rule, whatever the harm to those on the receiving end. Even when the hidden hand of profit is seen to be bad, strictly illegal or downright evil, there may be hardly a pause before the social machinery is back to full throttle. A memorable example, told to Studs Terkel (1972, p. 213) by Doc Graham, went as follows:

There was a long period during the Depression where the police were taking scrip. Cash had a language all its own. One night in particular, I didn't have my pistol with me, and the lady of the evening pointed out a large score to me. (Laughs) A squad car came by, which I was familiar with. A Cadillac, with a bell on it. I knew all the officers. I borrowed one of their pistols and took the score. Then I had to strip and be searched by the policemen, keeping honest in the end, as we divided the score. . . . I can't say nothin' for 'em, nothin' against 'em. I would say they were opportunists.

Such economic leadership as that of Doc Graham should never be underestimated: It is bold, wide-ranging, rough in the doing, smooth in the telling, and always ready to improvise. Trickle down economics in the field.

Such individuals are met from the very top to the very bottom of social organization. Their cover or gloss, I repeat, is that what is good for them is good for those above them and those below them. Sometimes they are more skillful when they believe or half-believe their own line, as sincerity can be impressive to some listeners. The class of snares generated by their argument is only limited by the ingenuity of man.

In general, the snare has the following structure: What is good at one level is damaging at another level, the second level being out of sight, glossed or covered. Some commonplace examples may illustrate the endless possibilities.

First of all, it is the chief device for fooling ourselves. If I am taken with the notion that I am a good listener, I may tune in to a conversation that makes me sick by not tuning into my bodily reaction. If I am too eager to help a family, I may overlook that they are only coming to please their general practitioner, so they just show up and do nothing, conserving their relationship with him. So soon as I get them going, they quit, also conserving their relationship with him.

Falling in love almost always follows this form. The pair discover each other at some level and overlook to a greater or lesser extent what is trouble at other levels. For instance, they may find their conversation charming, but not quite see that their bodies, their daily interests, and their families of origin have a different coupling. Of the latter level, Carl Whitaker (personal communication) once said, "Marriage is when families exchange hostages." But these other unfortunate levels are not ordinarily seen until it is too late. In this way, reproduction is guaranteed, despite the misfortunes of coupling at other levels.

SURFACES AND GLOSS

We fail to see disadvantages that will invade, judge and snare us later, because surfaces get in the way of our reading other levels to the deal. We are like animals who only perceive in their own compartment (niche), when we often need to be like ecologists (Allen and Starr, 1982) who look beyond the limiting surfaces of a given compartment for what is going to be relevant to that compartment in the long run.

Mostly we see without being aware that what we are seeing is limited by the *extent* of the field overlooked and by the *grain* of our looking. Just as with a telescope or a microscope or a zoom lens that can widen or narrow the field, increase or refine the grain, we become aware of how objects or events come and go as we alter the scope of our looking. Once we have many possible different observation sets, as from the view within a single cell, to a view of an organ, to a view of an organism, we become interested in how events at the level of the cell interact with events at the level of the organ which interact with events at the level of the organism. When there is a phenomenon which can be seen at all of these levels, such as cancer, then we have a chance to see the several levels simultaneously (Allen, O'Neill, and Hoekstra, 1984): the peculiar individual cancer cell, the sheet which takes over the organ, the organ which stops and throws the organism into mayhem. Such superimposing of catastrophic perspectives has generated many useful hypotheses abut how cells are put together into organs, how organs contribute vital functions to the organism.

Surfaces are also created by the grain of looking. When we look at a particular field of a certain extent with a certain grain, say within a single cell, we can notice the components with the cell, the so-called organelles, but we cannot see within the organelles without a finer grain, and we cannot see outside the cell to the organ sheet without a wider extent. Therefore, every field of a particular extent and grain is bounded by surfaces which make for opacity of events which are not of the *right* (middle) *size*. We do not see below the surface to the smaller events. We do not see above the surface to the larger events. Mostly, however, we do not notice that we are not noticing. We just see what we expect to see at the scale we are looking (Allen, O'Neill, and Hoekstra, 1984; Allen and Starr, 1982).

The ordinary surfaces created by the extent and grain of any observation set may be glossed by our clever antagonists, who seek to derive the full advantage over us by this marvelous device.

Gloss, or Pangloss, to use the name of Voltaire's great character, is important to getting individuals to hold still for their usefulness. Here is the start of the episode in which Candide is captured by the Bulgarian press gang:

Two men dressed in blue noticed him. "Comrade," said one, "there's a well-built young man of the right height." They went up to Candide and very civilly invited him to dinner. "Gentlemen," said Candide with charming modesty, "you do me a great honor, but I have no money to pay my share." "Ah, sir," said one of the men in blue, "persons of your figure and merit never pay anything: are you not five feet five tall?" "Yes, gentlemen," said he, bowing, "that is my height." "Ah, sir, come to table; we will not only pay your expenses, we will never allow a man like you to be short of money; men were only made to help each other." "You are in the right," said Candide, "that is what Dr. Pangloss was always telling me, and I see that everything is for the best." . . . (1759, p. 232)

One of the great problems of any organization is to keep bringing in young people to take up the unwanted jobs at the foot of its hierarchy, in return for the possibility of a gradual climb to the more favorable positions. Yet, few of them would come on board if they knew the actual drudge that would become their burden at the bottom. This is carefully hidden as follows. I call it "The Light in the Door of the Black Box" principle. The gloss works in this way: The seekers are interviewed by a very small number of friendly representatives, as it were, in the door of the organization where the light seems very bright. They fail to see what a tiny fraction of the great volume of the black box of the organization they are getting. They sign up. Breaking their necks, a year later, in the hold of the great ship, they will be amazed at how they were gotten to sign up.

Harvard institutions are especially skillful at this kind of glossing, to get young people to give up their lives for the privilege of giving enormous labor for years on end. One of my students, interviewing at one of the Harvard hospitals, was snared by two amazing comments. One was by a nice man on the faculty, who actually took the time to find out what my student was interested in and who then said, "You will be inspired by working here. The clinicians are so great." My student was so mesmerized that he never even found out the names of these great clinicians. The conclusive gloss, from the training director, who was not impressive himself, was: "After you work here, you'll be able to do anything." My student heard this as a Harvard inside ticket to the world. This was true in its own way, but I also heard it differently: After you knock your brains out for 70 or 80 hours a week doing the endless paperwork, you'll be able to put up with anything! The Harvard light in the door can be perfect(ly misleading).

I try to warn students how to read these lighted doorways, these thresholds before the great darkness, but I am not often successful. Like Candide, they want to believe in the best of all possible worlds. I keep copies of Brodsky's "Commencement Address" on my desk for those who are willing to be warned. He wrote:

Such is the structure of life that what we regard as Evil is capable of a fairly ubiquitous presence if only because it tends to appear in the guise of good. You never see it crossing your threshold announcing itself: "Hi, I'm Evil."

. . .

A prudent thing to do, therefore, would be to subject your notions of good to the closest possible scrutiny, to go, so to speak, through your entire wardrobe checking which of your clothes may fit a stranger. That, of course, may turn into a full-time occupation, and well it should. You'll be surprised how many things you considered your own and good can easily fit, without much adjustment, your enemy. (1986, pp. 384–385)

Perhaps it is only by middle age that one is willing to scrutinize one's closet like this, that one is even interested in the study. Yet I wish I had gotten started sooner, which I could have, with help of the kind that Brodsky supplies. Who describes the surprising landscape of group life? Too few.

Finally, we reach the greatest scale of all, the parade of humanity, in such places as Fifth Avenue in New York, or its Russian equivalent, the Nevsky Prospect of St. Petersburg/Leningrad. Here is where surface gets its finest polish, where what is worn bears so little relation to the character within. Yet everyone likes to be taken by the show. I like to juxtapose the Russian and the American versions, worlds apart, yet the same. Here is Gogol inviting his reader to "Nevsky Prospect," where all of Russia walks:

There is nothing finer than Nevsky Prospect, not in Petersburg anyway: it is the making of the city. What splendour does it lack, that fairest of our thoroughfares? I know that not one of the poor clerks that live there would trade Nevsky Prospect for all the blessings of the world. . . . This is the one place where people put in an appearance without being forced to, without being driven there by the needs and commercial interests that swallow up all Petersburg. A man met on Nevsky Prospect seems less of an egoist than in the other streets where greed, selfishness, and covetousness are apparent in all who walk or drive along them. (1835, pp. 207–208)

It is as if all of Russia leaves a clean record here:

All powerful Nevsky Prospect. Sole place of entertainment for the poor man in Petersburg. How wonderfully clean are its surfaces, and, my God, how many feet leave their traces on it! The clumsy, dirty boots of the ex-soldier, under whose weight the very granite seems to crack, and the miniature, ethereal little shoes of the young lady who turns her head toward the glittering shop windows as the sunflower turns to the sun, and the rattling saber of the ambitious lieutenant which marks a sharp scratch along it — all print the scars of strength or weakness on it. What changes pass over it in a single day! What transformations it goes through between one dawn and the next. (p. 208)

If only the clean record could be taken literally! No more there than here. The story Gogol proceeds to tell is a contrast between the shallow Lieutenant Pirogov and the child-like artist Piskarev, both of whom follow women they spy on Nevsky Prospect back to their dwellings. Both are deceived badly by what they thought they saw. But Pirogov lasts, because he is too shallow to have cared very much, while Piskarev cares all too much and is destroyed by how the woman turns out. There is too great a contrast, a heartbreaking distance, between his imagined Bianca of Perugino and the whore he finds.

Oh, do not trust that Nevsky Prospect! I always wrap myself more closely in my cloak when I pass along it and try not to look at the objects which meet me. Everything is a cheat, everything is a dream, everything is other than it seems. You think that the gentleman who walks along in a splendidly cut coat is very wealthy? — not at all. All his wealth lies on his coat. . . . It deceives at all hours, the Nevsky Prospect does, but most of all when night falls in masses of shadow upon it, throwing into relief the white and dun-colored walls of the houses, when all the town is transformed into noise and brilliance, when myriads of carriages roll off bridges, postilions shout and jump up on their horses, and when the devil himself lights the street lamps to show everything in false colors. (p. 238)

And so the morsels are compelled to stand still, watching, waiting to be neatly swallowed.

CONCLUSION

Optimism is crucial to success in the modern world, because it is crucial to business of all kinds. But it must be well defended in a polite Darwinian world of contests. Therefore, we can go about our business more cheerfully when we are alert to the occasions in which presence is going to be withheld, to the deals with delayed disadvantages, to the glossed surfaces that hide both kinds of disappointments from our eyes. We forget too readily that we are just animals, of infinite cleverness, who take over structures, continually, for new uses, for new advantages over our neighbors. We just invent faster than animals who came before us

. . . many, if not most, historical structures are co-opted from previous uses, not designed for current operations. Legs were fins, ear bones were jaw bones and jaw bones were gill-arch bones. . . . (Gould, 1986, p. 54)

Therefore, we invite the wary reader to look upwards and downwards, as well as sideways, when he or she wanders onto Nevsky Prospect and into the smaller enclosures, making up his or her own mind about what is at hand.

Tolstoy put this kind of intelligence about morale in war into the Russian general, Kutuzov:

It is an irony of swarm life, which Tolstoy fully appreciates, that the merely accomplished at once takes on an appearance of the inevitable: when the bees have swarmed and settled it at once becomes clear that it could have happened at no other time and in no other place. . . . As Kutuzov says, "Tout vient a celui qui sait attendre" [Everything comes to him who knows to wait]. To justify oneself in war one must obey the larger law of life, and surrender one's individual will to fate. To be successful is to discern the momentum of the inevitable and to move with it. (Bayley, 1988, pp. 141, 169) (my translation)

We say much the same about intelligence concerning morale in the modern contest. Those who can bear with the thinness of the social world, read its housing of larger and smaller purposes, and not be taken by its gloss, can devote themselves to the love of their own causes with humorous self assurance.[8] Tolstoy called this virtue the most crucial one of all, "samodovolnost":

There are many aspects of bravery, but most depend on the ability to create, as Petya does before his death, a complete world of our own in the midst of alien circumstances. (Bayley, 1966, p. 163)

We return to the subject of depth in a complete world of our own in "Gathering Strength" (Chapter 11). For now, we hope the thin and glossy deceiving modern world is well pictured in your minds, perhaps even as an acceptable world, for as Bertrand Russell once remarked, "Once we accept that the world is a terrible place, we may begin to enjoy it" (Robin Skynner, personal communication). Such morale is likely to be well sustained.

PART IV

Moving Freely

6. *Seizing Moments for Transition*

How is one to move when caught between opposing currents? How can one act in the middle of clashing subgroups? What is to be done in the face of impossible demands? How can one move in the midst of collusion (and other debilitating group games)? Having secured an organization, gotten a reliable reading of the situation, and an initial hold on one's morale, one is faced with emerging ways of moving forward (solving problems, trying to change, future planning, etc.). Action is called for; waiting is no longer useful.

The kind of action described here is not the future-focused move of the opening game, made to establish and secure the organization of the group. Nor is it the more reflective stance of discovering meaning. It is taking a step in the current moment when a step must be made. Emotions are running too high or too low. The group is lost or one is lost in it. One must act or risk losing all. At times the forces are opposing currents, giving no choices but inviting false alignments: at other times, one emotion or one person is so strong as to overwhelm the situation. Transition keeps the situation alive but also feels like it risks identity and orientation (Keen and Deutsch, 1986). Making a move is both crucial and daring.

Sullivan, from the point of view of the individual therapist, talked incisively of the "peculiar significance" of transitions in the typical situation:

Although the making of transitions is strikingly important in the detailed inquiry, it is a necessary part of the technique of interviewing at every stage. . . . When I talk about how to make transitions, I simply mean how to move about in the interview. It is imperative if you want to know who you are with another person, that you proceed along a path that he can at least dimly follow, so that he doesn't get lost completely as to what you are driving at. When he gets lost, very often you do too. . . . (1954, pp. 43–44)

Sullivan describes three kinds of transitions. *Smooth* transitions make relatively small shifts in a topic, so smooth the patient doesn't object and may not even notice. In *accented* transitions, the interviewer announces a shift from the previous subject to a new subject. The interview is being managed, and the interviewer makes it clear that he or she is doing the managing. In an *abrupt* transition the interviewer throws the discussion onto another plane without announcing why, what, or how. The hope is that the patient will forget about what he had been discussing and shift into a new focus altogether. An abrupt transition manages anxiety in the interview, either stemming the tide or opening the dam. The move is an abrupt (maybe even startling) way of either closing off anxiety which is out of control and needs to be stopped or provoking material that points to the pain.

Both Havens (1986) and Sullivan emphasize the importance of orchestrating the interview so one can move freely in the social field. Havens' attitude is also important for us as group participants. It is a given that we will be taken over by distortions, projections, and all the other kinds of thoughts, beliefs, and feelings that people are all too ready to just give away. As group participants we have a whole range of ways to widen perspective and provide balance when things get too off center. When the group sees only one way or only one person with a particular characteristic, it must become possible to "move opposing forces toward an integrated viewpoint" (Havens, 1976, p. 108).

The challenge is to shift oneself and others to face the situation with a wider perspective. The round is lost; what can we do before the game is lost altogether? One can't delay; action must be taken. In looking at another level, one steps back from the immediacy of the paralyzing moment to see the influential forces outside the boundaries of the group or within the corners of the group (subgroups, individual experiences). The transition moves among different levels and loops back to the central task, not off in an idiosyncratic direction.

LOOKING IN ONESELF

One solid guide to recognizing when a situation is sinking is in oneself. One has an internal sense that something is wrong. As a leader, consultant, or member, one has a sense of how the group should proceed in order to accomplish important goals or the assigned task. At some point one is aware that nothing is happening or that what is happening is terribly distorted. The signal is inside the perceiver. I, as group leader/participant, find myself questioning the proceedings and feeling captured by a particular pattern that only makes things worse. It makes me feel that I lack options — none of the choices facing me will improve the situation.

Bion was a master at experiencing the divergencies in groups from an introspective position. His understanding of himself vis-à-vis the group was unparalleled: "The more sophisticated a group becomes and the more it manages to maintain a sophisticated level of behavior, the more it does so by the suppression of one pattern of linked emotions by another" (1959, p. 98). His theory of basic assumptions was a particular view of opposing currents in a sophisticated ("work") group. He saw the dual force operating.

Bion asserted that "in group treatment many interpretations . . . have to be made on the strength of the analyst's own emotional reactions" (1959, p.

149). He was dogged about keeping in mind the group's stated expectations; therefore, he was especially aware of the discrepancy between what the group proposed to be doing with his consultation and what he was actually being expected to do by the members in the group. His own experience told him that if he followed the group's *manifest* directions he would be lost. The expectations were too divergent; "sophisticated" work had been suppressed for other interests. He found inside himself the divergence between what he was there for (his "duty") and what the group seemed to expect of him.

It was the inability to stay afloat in the eddy, the awareness inside himself of crosscurrents in expectations that forced Bion to move. He looked at the unconscious group process — what he called basic assumptions — for behavioral motives that would allow him to become uncoupled from impossible expectations. Two kinds of buoys mark these places over and over again in *Experiences in Groups* (1959).

First, the need for a transition was signaled by an internal experience of the group leader. Bion was so hyperaware of his sense of duty that his mission in the group was almost apostolic in strength. For most of us mortals, such devotion is not likely, but awareness of task gives us a starting point. Only when we are aware, Bion suggested, can we assess our judgments — internal and external — about what the group is expecting from us. In our terms, without clarity about the common antagonist, without securing the organization, we are in an internal muddle about how and where to move when given choices — and we are always given choices in groups.

Second, in preparation for action, Bion posed covert group motivations: "as if the group gathered to sit at the foot of the leader," "as if the group had to fight or flee an enemy," "as if the group had to wait for two of its members to conceive a savior."[1] Defining these covert patterns allowed Bion a sharper sense of *how* he was being drawn away from his duty.

Others have also made important discoveries looking inside themselves.[2] In his marvelous descriptions of family work, Skynner (1981) builds his technical discoveries from missing emotional pieces of the family that he finds inside himself. In working with families, he sees the "real . . . problem . . . always contained in what is not communicated, what is missing from the content of the session" (1981, p. 60). The complexity of his method lies in discovering the missing piece in the therapist's inner experience. His internal experience, his countertransference response, must be returned to the family. In being open to the family members, so that they can really put their issues on the table, the therapist is ready to temporarily become or enact the role of family scapegoat. Skynner really puts himself on the line and stays at the level of his own experience until he can defuse the family bomb and put it back into the family. Without his hyper-selfconsciousness, one is apt either to not connect with the family or to be drawn into the family game. While working from his internal experience, Skynner adds important ideas about making transitions.

The internal signal is a strong identification with a family member's position — his or her pain, rage, neediness; forbidden emotions in the family. Skynner gets lost (temporarily) in the emotional depth of the family group. He doesn't ask Bion's question — what is he hired to do compared with what is the family group expecting? Rather, he asks, what is it like to be a member of this family? He does not just ferret out what is hidden, but experiences, along with the whole family group, what it is like to live (for a while) in this system, until the subterranean forces begin to affect him also; the effect on his internal life is his data. It is the pain, rage, hurt, or other emotion he finds inside himself that he must then reattach to where it belongs: in the family. His first moves are internal, opening himself to the family and entering their (sometimes gothic) emotional labyrinth.

Skynner also proposes a wider range (than Bion) of effective devices for making transitions than only verbal interpretations: "behavioral, educative . . . , advice, task-setting, restructuring . . . modeling" (1981, p. 61). Re-emerging from the emotional eddy is not so easy. With humor and respect for the system, Skynner gives abrupt transitions the feel of a "friendly fight." With this kind of attitude he can get away with all kinds of advice-giving and restructuring.[3]

An example from my consultation practice illustrates moves made from internal signals. I was invited by the head of an inner-city health center to consult with his central staff group of administrators, a group he had managed for about eight years. For many years the group had functioned like a community-based organization — loosely structured, action-oriented to get a job done, primarily responding to external demands, crises, etc. Within the past few months, the director had been wanting to reorganize in order to free up time to do external planning and fund-raising. He had worked out a structure with the staff and put it in place, but very few people used it. He himself still felt vulnerable to demands to perform tasks that he had delegated and requests for information best found elsewhere in the hierarchy.

During the first session of the consultation the problem was amply demonstrated, as much of the time was spent with their going over a real problem with a client. One particular staff person was very frustrated in her efforts to advocate for the client and had gotten everyone involved, taking huge amounts of staff time. When he saw how far behind he had gotten in his other work, he felt exhausted. Staff members were divided, some not being able to get problems solved in the structure, others feeling very frustrated out of the "collective" approach. I held on for the ride, mainly observing and asking questions.

We had agreed to three meetings, a month apart from each other, and I agreed to write them a letter with my summary and recommendations after the first meeting. I said in the letter that "I appreciated the frankness and openness of the discussion under these unfamiliar and stressful conditions."

I went on to describe two subgroups as I saw them, calling them "community-based" and "pro-structure" subgroups. I suggested that for the next meeting we consider their individual pictures of an ideal consultation outcome. I invited them to write me if they wanted to communicate their views before the next meeting. I got a letter signed by six staff members, crossing racial, gender, and departmental lines. They were puzzled and angry and didn't know what I meant by these two subgroups. They were particularly surprised to find that I thought they were open; they did not think they had been, because openness could be "embarrassing and damaging."

When I went to the second meeting, I was aware of feeling worried. I had the sense that the whole thing could be torpedoed. In wondering about the dangers of openness, I was puzzled; I couldn't see the dangers in any person in the group or in their interaction and was ready to look towards the context. After being told that the letter had been distributed to the other staff, I opened the meeting by asking if there was more to say about it. I said I was particularly surprised about the dangers of openness. There was empathic hammering of what was said in the letter: that one could be "penalized by authority in the group for being critical." Openness was threatening, inappropriate, and — by implication — why didn't I know better? I was beginning to feel uneasy. As this barrage of only about four exchanges ended, the first signer of the letter said he wanted to get to the subgroups. I was grilled on what I meant *exactly*. Why did I judge one better than the other? No matter what I said, he just flat out disagreed. His colleagues and co-signer, sitting right next to me, picked up the oar and continued to hit me with it: What did I mean!? I tried to explain myself, moving to managing the manifest request for information. It didn't work because I kept getting the same questions asked in an increasingly angry and petulant manner.

In a move designed to see just how bad the odds were (I'm sure that I was hoping for some support), I asked if the opinions being expressed by the vocal people spoke for the quiet ones as well. Several, including the leader, spoke up, saying that they agreed completely with what I had said. I soon realized that this was the wrong way to go. Not only did it lead to silence, but protesters were not going to be able to fight effectively with their own big gun, who was now on my side. It occurred to me that they were enacting the exact unsafe situation they had described in their letter and that it was best that the silent people be silent. The others were actively attacking me. I began to actively support their action of writing the letter, told them how hopeful it was for our work.

Not long after I began to compliment their letter writing, the attack was transformed. First, there were visible signs of calming down. Then, even more importantly, when I asked for their ideas about what needed to be changed in light of their disagreement with my view, the conversation shifted to how little protection their work role offered their private life. For example, people called staff at home on vacation days to ask routine office questions, and the parents of clients pressed demands when they met an administrator in the supermarket! Practical methods of working on necessary self-protection were pursued by individuals. The danger of confronting each other was the same, namely penetration of the work role to the person being criticized. The original issue, use of the formal structure, was being worked on at the same time privacy was being discussed.

The critical moment for me came with a surprising sense of being treated to disqualifying emotions — accusations, contempt, even denigration. Rather than suggesting to people that they were overly critical, I admired their contributions. This brought about the desired end, namely, that they felt their contributions to be valued and themselves to be reasonable and cooperative staff members. It is often not so simple, in that the consultee may not believe or be able to use the admiration. That opens up a whole new view on things. It shouldn't negate the device itself.

Looking to the Group in the Room

Sometimes the events *in the group* open up before one's eyes in a very dramatic way. They capture one's attention, as in the theater. Then one dips into the experience emotionally.

Classic patterns emerge within groups, patterns that signal a need for transition. In the notion of "peer court" Bach presented an image of group members in psychotherapy as subjecting each other to very careful, and not always generous, scrutiny. In the image he sketched, problems and emotions presented were judged by the peer group, who gave advice, struck the gavel, and moved on to the next case. Bach granted that something positive and therapeutic was going on during this process. "First, the advice contains information previously unattended to. . . . Secondly, the advice [served] as a projection of his own [the advising person's] intrapsychic motivational structure" (1954, pp. 104–5), and thereby gave new information.[4] The picture of the peer court showed the opposing currents of dominance and submission (scapegoating, at the most extreme).

Another form of peer court situation is seen in Laing's discussion of collusion. It happens quite frequently that relationships get counterfeited so that "Peter needs Paul to be a certain person in order for Peter to be the person he wishes to be" (1961, p. 109). Exchanges in the peer court covertly freeze people in complementary relationships to each other. Laing refers to Genet's *Balcony*; Genet had his characters speak what was usually the *un*conscious dialogue:

My being a judge is an emanation of your being a thief. You need only refuse — but you'd better not! . . . for me to cease to be . . . to vanish, evaporated. Burst. Volatized, Denied . . . But you won't refuse, will you? That would be wicked. . . . You'd deprive me of being! (1958, pp. 14–15)

Intimates can't refuse each other. Forward movement is as difficult as motoring an anchored boat.

Peer patterns have been described from many points of view. Goffman (1961), Rosenhan (1973), and others showed how impossible they can be to resist. Expectations in a social environment can be crushing; there is no room to move, only to give in. Observations at the level of social ecology are supported by the experimental social psychology of Asch (1955) and a whole tradition of conformity research. The difficulty we all have standing up to social pressure is no news.

Whether or not intentions are good at a manifest level in organizations, overt or covert politics (Sennett, 1979, Buroway 1979, Jones, 1986) can drastically limit one's choices.[5] Groupthink (Janis, 1967) is a good example of this phenomenon at a policy-making level. Good judgment is stifled in leader and group members alike in the face of paralyzing covert intimidation and a strongly felt need for mutual support. A group organized with a singular value for cohesiveness, which then reads its cohesiveness as once and always positive, can go through a period of stifling conformity.[6]

Another prominent metaphor emerging in groups is Mann's (1975) winners and losers. In order for there to be a winner there must be a loser. There was an almost irresistible tendency in the groups Mann described for the members to spend considerable time establishing a hierarchy of haves and have-nots. He found himself addressing this dynamic vigorously, since the imbalance could drift into a demoralizing scapegoating, balanced on the winning side by an unrealistic sense of power. Again, the peer court was in session, deciding who the saints and sinners were along a whole range of dimensions. While not caught up in the dynamics directly, Mann saw the group's interaction become so patterned and even destructive that action had to be taken.

Sometimes peer tension is best seen as two groups clash over limited resources or incompatible plans. We (Gustafson, Cooper, Lathrop, Ringer, Seldin, and Wright, 1981) have called this a "steering contradiction"; it is the situation in the group when the leader is forced to take a step that potentially chooses the interests of one subgroup at the expense of others.[7] The moment is one of forced choice; even nonaction can be prejudicial. How to get out of the stalemate is the problem in question. An example helps.

Well into a psychotherapy group for perpetrators of domestic violence, the therapist reported a session attended by four members, two oldtimers and two new members. The two seasoned members had a long history of conflict with each other; in fact, about a year before this session they had had a conflict — yet to be resolved — in which one had failed to appear for a social engagement. This had never been mentioned in the group before. In this particular session, one of the experienced members came in ready for a fight. He had been realizing in his individual therapy how much he contained his anger and let others walk all over him. Specifically, he had done that with the incident last year and, damn it, he wanted to get it out and settled once and for all! The antagonist in this pair said he was through with the incident and had no interest in going over it again. He wanted to let it be; he felt that there was too much emotionality in his life and preferred to practice keeping his anger under control. The two new members were quite agitated about this exchange.

The therapist realized that he was in the midst of a rather surprising peer storm, for which members were unprepared, and that the experienced pair wanted support for practicing what the group had been teaching them about emotions.

The therapist's approach can best be described as putting them all in the same (group) tent by reflexive questioning (Tomm, 1987). He intended to actively inspect their life together, looking at the conflict as part of the group process. He primarily asked questions: "What is it like to bring up such angry emotions?" "What is it like to confront each other?" "What would it be like to face each other next week after having this dispute?" By staying with questions that cast individuals into a self-reflective mode about themselves in the group, he kept the conflict under some control. The new members were able to talk about what it felt to anticipate anger, to feel unprotected, to be new in the group with more experienced people. The discussion contributed to a breakdown of the new-old boundary, since they were all participating in looking at their peer life together, rather than at (divisive) parochial interests. In this group example, the accented shift was to another level of experience, which provided the transition.

Peer subgroup clashes are a dramatic indication for a transition. It is deadly to side with either subgroup because of what it does to the other, and ultimately to the whole group. If conflict had been explicitly supported in the above situation (this is not necessarily true of conflict in general), it is likely that the new members' need for support and fear of explosion would have gone unnoticed. They might have defected altogether; even if they had stayed, protecting oneself from both external attack and attacking emotions inside oneself would have become a major concern. While this therapist did not take the only technical alternative, his staying neutral (steering between the opposing factions) was a major move for this kind of peer transition.

Looking in the group, the solution lays in both containing the rout (Turenne's principle described in Havens, 1965) and reflexive questioning. These devices can be very useful. It can be tempting to feel that one must be moving forward boldly and bravely at all times. In the above situation there was no way to move forward and keep the whole undertaking in hand. Rather than cut off part of the group, the therapist chose what amounted to tactical retreat to keep winners and losers in balance, a regrouping which eventually permitted another advance. Rather than encourage either fight or protection, he effectively stated, "we are, after all, in this group together." The very words and spirit of the reflexive questions implied an attitude of steering a common course. The questions asserted that the group was larger than any subgroup and reestablished the common antagonist, that is, their interest in common. It reminded members that they had a common enemy from which their infighting distracted them.

The reflexive questioning establishes on which front the group can once again proceed forward. Perhaps members share concerns about anger and how to be angry and protected from violence at the same time. Perhaps another avenue of exploration will be fruitful. In addition, the questioning inherently corrects for any doubts a member might have about the therapist's working for the greater good of all. Partisanship can be disastrous when there is a danger of a big winner and a big loser. Neutral steering shows the leader as not participating in group games costly to some factions. (This latter concern, incidentally, seems of particular importance in domestic violence situations because there are such traumatic stakes for losers.) There is considerable evidence from phenomena such as scapegoating that this kind of split of subgroups can happen rather readily. Mann described this situation as an observer of a group primarily established for self-study among college students.

This section focused primarily on critical moves coming to the surface in the peer drama. Of course, this does not exclude the leader's experience, since the two often dovetail. We now turn to yet another stage on which the drama unfolds, namely, at the window between the group and its outside context — where the boundary is relatively permeable and mutual influences can be experienced.

LOOKING AT THE SURROUNDING GROUP

Borges has a series of short poems which describe much better than I can what it is to live in larger historical currents, as in "The Exile" (1979, p. 175):

> Someone makes tracks along the paths of Ithaca
> and has forgotten his king, who was at Troy
> so many years ago;
> someone is thinking of his new-won lands
> his new plough and his son,
> and is happy, in the main . . .
> Someone today walks the streets — Chile, Bolivar —
> perhaps happy, perhaps not.
>
> I wish I could be he.

History can be frightful, "destinies which change makes inaccessible" (In Memory of Angelica," p. 177), but nonetheless "the voices of the dead will speak to me forever" ("My Books," p. 179). At times memory and history become the opposing current against which the group flails with continuous lack of success. The group struggles forward with an undertow holding its feet.

Especially in our culture, one hates to think of being influenced by forces outside of one's control. One of the most prototypic situations blocking group movement occurs where members hold the illusion that all the important forces are at a manageable level. One pursues information located somewhere within the confines of the group; yet, information is missing, events are occurring for which members and leader alike are unprepared. Both leader and members might question whether the group is worthwhile. The leader might feel increasingly burdened, having to do the work of seemingly uninvolved members. The source of growing dissatisfaction cannot be pinpointed.

One place to look for the forces that dampen current conditions is in the group's surrounding environment, history, or cultural context. Selvini Palazzoli, Boscolo, Cecchin, and Prata, (1977) described this exact problem in working with families. Until the team looked at the larger (family) context surrounding the immediate family presenting itself with an ill child, their efforts were frustrated. Many other schools of family work, such as those based on the work of Bowen (1978) and Boszormenyi-Nagy and Spark (1984), take this contextual view as central to helping individuals emerge from their own immediate debilitating and collusive group roles.

If one takes the group that presents itself for intervention—the family members or organizational subpart—the simple truth is that one must begin with their immediate experience. It is not uncommon, however, to discover a need for widening the focus to include critical people well beyond the here-and-now group.[8] Without incorporating "the minimum network" (Skynner, 1987), the intervener may ultimately fail to move these particular kinds of situations. It isn't possible to get on top of all the influencing forces, but neither can they be ignored.

I was invited to do my first consultation with the staff of a Catholic boys school. The offer was flattering, the supervision minimal, and my naivete at its high point, as the invitation was received just after I finished graduate school. I met with the teachers weekly and we talked about problem students. These were the most out-of-control children, where slim resources would do the least. I thought I was being helpful, but what continued to emerge was how little good my advice was to them. My supervisor encouraged me to ask why. I had been reluctant to; I expected the worst. Little by little the tyranny of the priest who ran the school unfolded: Irrational restrictions and punitive treatment in general led the teachers to be overprotective of the students, so they didn't report kids until they were really unbearable.

My advice was always too little too late. Finally, I was asked to take on this schoolmaster. I remember feeling terrified at the idea of leaving the consultation room to go to another part of the building to meet him. He wouldn't even talk with me at first, since, after all, I had been hired to talk only with his staff. When I insisted, he listened to some of the issues I cautiously raised on behalf of the group, and fired me, politely and through channels. I had been naive enough not to take into account the strength of the world outside the group of staff and naive enough to think that I could manage it.

I believe I was right, however, in sensing that it was time to make a transition. I had gotten sufficient information from the group of teachers and had felt the desolation of repeatedly fruitless sessions which I thought had been filled with good discussion, useful suggestions, and insights. I had grossly underused my internal sense of danger and their report of the kind of predatory environment that existed in the larger world outside the consultation room. My transition was much too abrupt for the institution. I learned some healthy respect for organizational cultures.

The following incident occurred more recently. I can be happier, in the main, thinking of new-won territory. I was hired by a hospital director to consult with one department. Morale had crashed following the sudden terminal illness and death of its chief three months before. I was asked to work with the staff to develop an interim leadership plan, since the search for a permanent chief promised to be a long one. I was being handed the staff, with the director's blessings.

Realizing early on in my negotiations with the hospital director that he would be interacting with the interim person(s), I decided I couldn't let myself get isolated within the department. The final plan must be workable and acceptable to the director. The consultation was organized *from the outset* to include the director. He was called in at regular intervals to be caught up with the staff's efforts, react, and be part of the next planning step. It was unwise to let stand-offs develop in a group whose morale was so bad; that could only make their life more uncertain. Because an interim promotion (an "acting" position) can be so hard on people who are returning to line staff jobs, staff must have a door open to move back to their regular (permanent) positions at some point. No more losing track of the outside world. A very workable interim plan emerged.

It was important for success in this example to account for the environment surrounding the working team. Peer issues were present as well as internal reactions on my part to various events in the group. Accomplishment of the goal depended on integration with the bigger picture.

CONCLUSION

The single idea of this chapter is the importance of knowing when a transition is needed. Three locations to recognize signals were described, along with ways of managing each. When quick action is required, having a guide can make the difference between using the moment to push ahead or losing the battle—if not the war.

7. *Free Passage*

I DIVIDE THE STREET KNOWLEDGE of social passage into two broad situations: How (being outside) do we know what we can freely bring into a group or social situation? How (being inside) do we know when and how to spring the group free from its apparent groove to some fresh variation? This pair of problems is difficult for all of us, but the passages to be negotiated are similar, from junior high dance class to world congresses of social science.

A witty observer of psychotherapy has said that most people who come for help have one of two problems concerning close relationships: how to get into cages or how to get out of them (Havens, unpublished manuscript). If we step back, farther and farther, we may see social fields of larger and larger extent, in which getting in and out of enclosures is of great concern: getting in and out of not only the marital conversation, but also the seminar conversation, the departmental conversation, the national political conversation, the global nuclear conversation, and so forth. I call this our interest in *free passage*.

Some think that there are rules for what you can bring into a group. If you think in this way, you will miss many of your opportunities. A more freeing notion is that groups recognize what is *not* to be allowed. So long as you do not run over certain lines, you may do as you please. Take the problematic urge to be violent towards good people. You may think this is only allowed towards common objects of scorn or hatred. Not so. For at least twenty centuries, you have been able to get away with mocking good people if you do not break the rules of farce. Everyone at the table is a free target, indirectly, in the telling of a farcical anecdote. There is a grammar of cages, which, if obeyed, allows nearly any content to be slipped in.

Most people know very little about getting out of stultifying or even dreadful social events. They just weather them. Maybe this is a test for our social heroes, that they are undaunted when groups seem to be stuck. They do not go down with the group but freely range up and down, back and forward, to find a fresh turn.

I am reminded of a story told to me in a locker room by a man who had been a lieutenant in the Marines in Korea. When they forged all the way to the Manchurian border, the Chinese suddenly entered the war. Some American troops, including our lieutenant, were completely surrounded, and completely dismayed by the turn in their fortunes. He recalled a meeting of all the officers to discuss their situation, led by their commander, who broke them out of their demoralized state, saying: "You understand we are surrounded on all sides. . . . That means we may attack them in any direction we please."

One may even invent a test for this capacity to spring free of the prevailing convention, as did St. Exupery in the opening of his story of *The Little Prince* (1943). The boy-aviator explains:

In the course of this life I have had a great many encounters with a great many people who have been concerned with matters of consequence. I have lived a great deal among grown-ups. I have seen them intimately, close at hand. And that hasn't much improved my opinion of them. Whenever I met one of them who seemed to me at all clear-sighted, I tried the experiment of showing him my Drawing Number One, which I have always kept. I would try to find out, so, if this was a person of true understanding. But, whoever it was, he, or she, would always say:
"That is a hat."

Drawing Number One looks like a brown hat. Drawing Number Two has the same shape, but it is not colored in brown. Within the shape is an elephant swallowed by a boa constrictor—an imaginative possibility within the lines given.

But it is ever so important to know that most grown-ups do not give themselves this latitude (and longitude);

. . . he, or she, would always say: "That is a hat."
Then I would never talk to that person about boa constrictors, or primeval forests, or stars. I would bring myself down to his level. I would talk to him about bridge, and golf, and politics, and neckties. And the grown-up would be greatly pleased to have met such a sensible man.

Some readers will have already noticed that being astute about the form or shape of cages may help one to get either *in* or *out* of conversations of all sizes. The grammar of cages can secure free passage to bring in what you want, to get out to a fresh variation.

Some skeptical readers will not be persuaded of the grammar of cages by a war story or by such an unworldly story as *The Little Prince*; they would much prefer to believe something like Machiavelli's *The Prince*. Fine. We may soon see that most worldly craft depends upon a similar logic.

Consider the strategy of many current historians, borrowed from Marc Bloch's guide to method, *The Historian's Craft* (1953). As Bloch suggested, historians have only the "tracks" left by men of the past. Many interpretations are freely allowed, but they must not fly in the face of this available testimony. You may be admitted to the conversation of historians if you abide by this grammar. You may also be free to contribute fresh variations of your own, so you need not be confined by their current conversation. Free passage in and out.

As Bloch suggested, the craft of the law and the craft of psychology are no less concerned with admissible testimony and interpretations consistent with that testimony:

Obliged always to be guided by the reports of others, legal action is no less interested than pure research in weighing their accuracy. The tools at its disposal are not different from those of scholarship. They are in fact those that scholarship originally forged. In the useful employment of doubt, judicial practice has only followed, rather laggingly, in the footsteps of the Bollandists and the Benedictines. And the psychologists themselves did not think to seek a scientific object in human testimony, as directly confirmed and elicited, until long after the confused memory of the past had begun to be subjected to rational proof. (p. 136)

And thus we find conversations in every sector of the world, of every size, limited by the forms and shapes in which evidence can be brought into the group, but free in variations that play upon the admitted theme.

Usually, the penalties for transgressing the acceptable shape are harsh. You fall flat trying to come in with a point that will not fit in the shape of admissible evidence, and feel like a fool who has been rightly disqualified. You get swamped with tension, in your head or gut, when you do not find a fresh variation from a tiresome diagram. So we all love the possibilities of free passage.

But we must be alert to the limits of such skill. There are conversations you can be admitted to only by birth, money, gender, race, connections and social rank (Ruth Gustafson, personal communication). The most ingenious shaping of your slant will not get you past the door. You can join certain clubs only by having been born in certain families. You can be a "player" in some stock markets only with so much cash. In many places you are less than a person and more like property as a woman or as a black person. You can be a faculty member only with certain connections to professors. You will probably never be a manager if you have been a secretary (Collins, 1979). The class barriers in America have some looseness, but not very much. The talent for conversational passage must not be overestimated. Systemic optimism is attractive, but it must not be asked to do the impossible (Stierlin, 1988).

BRINGING IN NEW TESTIMONY: ON PLAYING
ACCOMPANIMENT TO THE MUSIC WHICH PREVAILS

Is there a general grammar of cages? Probably not. Every conversation, from the soliloquy to global nuclear talk, has its own peculiar forms, which must be mastered, to allow one to join in, to contribute fresh directions. But there are some recurrent preoccupations, which have been with us in western society for most of recorded time, in the most diverse sectors.

These concerns, ordinarily, must not be transgressed, if one hopes to be persuasive in bringing in new testimony. Invention must shape itself to take care of these crucial lines, including them in a particular drawing put before a group or assembly as a proposal. There may be an infinite number of drawings that include these seven lines, but those that leave any of the seven out are unlikely to carry the day.

The first line is the line of *admiration*. If you do not give it, do not expect to get it, and do not expect to be let in. For several years, I pondered why my students said nothing to me at the end of some seminars that I felt sure were invaluable to them. If they shared my feeling, I was not let in on it. This year, I was struck with the thoughtfulness, wit and humor, as well as the candid facing of difficult problems and cooperation of seminar members, and I wrote them so. Immediately, six of them came by to tell me how much they appreciated that I had noticed! Havens (1986, p. 159) summarizes the range and depth of this line of admiration, quoting Nietzsche:

How poor the human mind would be without vanity! It resembles a well stocked and ever renewed ware-emporium that attracts buyers of every kind; they can find almost everything, provided they bring with them the right kind of money — admiration.

It gets you almost everywhere you want to go (provided you take care of a few other lines, as follows).[1]

The second line to remember is what I call the *loose end* (Gustafson, 1986), following a single reference in passing by Selvini Palazzoli (1985). Groups may be extremely complicated, with so many different lines, like a ball of yarn that has fallen into the paws of the cat. The only reliable way to unravel the yarn is to find the loose end. In the conversation of a group, the loose end lies with the concern in the business being discussed. Any speaker who hopes to have an audience at all must address what "we are all concerned about." Winnicott called this "meeting the challenge of the case" (1965). Even to take up, literally, the words of the previous speakers, is to take hold of the loose end of the conversation. Thus, we may well imagine that the Marine commander not only met the concern of his officers about being surrounded on all sides as a challenge thrown to himself, but also took up the very phrases of his officers as his own introduction, to have their complete attention for the turnabout he invented. Thus, a lecturer to psychoanalysts had better take his starting point somewhere near "resistance" and "transference," or he will not be followed very far down the road. I once started with baseball (as a metaphor) and was off and running before they had the faintest notion of how it pertained to them and their daily business. Best to start right alongside their couches with their favorite words.[2]

A third line which seems essential is what I call the *floor*. If a group goes through the floor, it may not come up again. What I mean is that the bad may overwhelm the good, swamping the boat, sending its members overboard to save themselves elsewhere. The morale of any group is vulnerable to this kind of collapse, which occurs when the benefit of the group looks overwhelmed by its running into what seems to be impossible weather. What is bad for a particular group depends upon the good it proposes to arrange for its members. For military troops, the good is the glory of victory. For medical students, the good is learning about illness while helping patients and surviving call schedules.

The floor of a group may be lost very suddenly, because something overwhelmingly bad can come on very fast. A skillful leader will be ready for these sudden changes in the weather.[3] Inadvertently, I learned something about such preparations from a medical student group I led which benefited the students by teaching them about interviewing disturbed psychiatric patients.

After over ten years of experience with this venture, I arrived at the reliable procedure of having two students interview the patient, each for fifteen minutes. The first did a formal mental status examination, which, being a fully specified procedure, was nearly always successful. Medical students are a class of young beings from a long line of natural selection, which selects those who can follow instructions. So doing mental status exams is like fulfilling their destiny. Their morale is high as they put the patients successfully through their paces. The second student runs a greater risk, which is to do a more open-ended interview to understand the patient's felt situation. Disturbing, terrifying, murderous, despairing possibilities of existence suddenly may be felt acutely by all the students who are watching their colleague understand his or her patient.

Happily, I have arranged always to follow the second student, to enter the abyss where we may find ourselves, by talking with the patient about where the second student understood him best. This takes us back into the frightening material but almost always in a way so that the student is being accepted for getting as far as he did and the patient gets something from me about being able to bear such trouble.

Because of the pressure of time, I made an interesting error this past fall, which shows just how important it is for a leader to take care of the floor of the group. Since all the students would not get to interview twice by the final meeting, I proposed that two of them do the mental status while two of them do the open-ended interview (leaving myself out). A schizophrenic young man began to get across his bitter emptiness when the time was up. Their morale completely broke down. I too late realized my error in taking myself out of the position of being the leader of last resort. The badness of his bitter life broke over them. I was not there to contain it within a good interview, which could have appreciated the patient's courage to persist against such overwhelming odds: "Here he was, still going, despite everything that happened! How did he do it?" The patient would have gotten something from the interview, instead of another bitter experience of being used for the purposes of these more fortunate medical students. The morale of the students depends upon feeling like good doctors, who take from the

patient an opportunity to learn while giving back to the patient some benefits for his trouble. Their leader has to take care that the good mitigates the
bad, for the students cannot take care of this crucial line themselves.

A fourth essential line is what I call the *ceiling*. If a group's expectations
carry too high, they are sure to crash. The same is true for the leader's
expectations. A simple but telling version happened to me when I was
having the advanced residents and fellows in my brief psychotherapy clinic
read the recent book of one of my mentors in preparation for his visit.
Naturally, they found some of his writing helpful, while some of it made
little sense to them. For the very first time of the year, I found myself getting
angry and impatient with them for their lack of comprehension. I was
setting three of them back upon their heels from the heat of my pointing out
what they were missing. I could only apologize, at the end of that day, for
my vehemence. Well, everyone was greatly relieved when I began the reading
for the following week by saying: "It is a dangerous thing to have one's
mentor out for a visit. I believe that every paragraph he ever wrote is extremely helpful. However, I do recognize that you may find some of it
helpful, some of it obscure." They burst out laughing, in great relief. I was
not setting impossible expectations. I went on to say, "Let's discuss today
what is useful for you in this reading, and what is not useful, obscure, or
even misleading for you." That we could do.

A fifth essential line is the (city) *wall* which divides insiders from outsiders: As Melanie Klein wrote (1959), the very same stranger who would be
killed if he were met in the forest would be given great hospitality if he got
invited into the tent. This is why Odysseus always bore greetings from those
who might recommend him and gifts from his own best stores. This got him
into the tent of hospitality, rather than murdered in the harbor. But when he
had lost everything at sea and could not come in strength, he had to get
swiftly to the center if he were to have the chance to tell his story, to make his
case:

> but down the hall Odysseus went unseen,
> still in the cloud Athens cloaked him in,
> until he reached Arete, and the king.
> He threw his great hands round Arete's knees,
> whereupon the sacred mist curled back;
> they saw him; and the diners hushed amazed
> to see an unknown man inside the palace.
> Under their eyes Odysseus made his plea.

A much lesser hero once found himself in a similar situation because the
administrator of his practice group barred him from seeing patients in a
certain sector of the practice. He objected. The entire dispute was put before
the practice group.

The administrator argued, vehemently, that this doctor was giving much too much time to patients, more than any other doctor, as if he were special. He ought to be ousted from the practice.

The doctor had weighed his reply carefully. If he emphasized that his work was so carefully executed that it deserved more time, he would place himself as an outsider to the practice. The group would back the administrator against him. Also, he needed to be very careful about the tone and posture of his answer. Angry defensiveness would also place him as an outsider.

Therefore, he calmly took himself to the center of the practice. In contrast to the hot charges of the administrator, he quietly said that he wanted nothing for himself but the right to practice like everyone else according to his own medical judgment about what patients needed. In this, he was warmly received. The administrator was ignored.

A sixth essential line to any proposal to a group concerns what I call the *tilt of the board*. On any given day, at any given hour, some group members are prospering while others are languishing. Commonly, in a seminar, some students love to go fast while some must go slowly to be sure of getting down the fundamentals they fear they are missing. If the teacher delights in the quick, this usually tilts the board in their favor as the designated winners, while the slow feel lost. They drop out. If the teacher only slogs through the basics, the slow are the winners and the fast are dismayed and go to sleep. Any day, any hour threatens a tilt of the board that makes the teacher excluded by half of the group: either by the slow or by the fast (Gustafson et al., 1981). No matter how interesting his presentation, half of the group will give him no attention and it will fall flat – unless he realizes the direction of the tilt of the board: If he sees that the fast have the day, then doubling back to the slow, to say we must have passed over their concerns, will draw them from their sleep, like an awakening of the dead. The desire of the current losers to recoup is a great force, never to be underestimated, always to be ridden whenever possible, for reasons cited by Selvini Palazzoli:

Such unexpected findings are very valuable, for they force us to think again. In this case, the answer might have come from Montaigne, who already in the sixteenth century said that we move forward more quickly when attracted by desire than when pushed by guilt. In other words, Nina and her father, spurred on by the wish to live, would have moved more briskly than Aldo and his mother, fueled by regrets alone. (1985, p. 31)

There is yet another powerful argument, complementary to that of Selvini Palazzoli, for watching this line I call the tilt of the board and including it in any drawing proposed to a group. This argument recognizes the danger of humiliation to the losers, which can set them against you forever. Sullivan puts the warning thus:

The interviewer can be quite unpleasant, if he is sure that he isn't unpleasant at a point, or in a way, that leaves an open wound. Anything which makes a person feel "small," if you please – a really excellent figure of speech – is apt to leave a long-enduring wound, and to be anything but a help in the further development of the interview. (1954, p. 234)

Always, I believe, in every hour of a consultation to a family, someone in the family is threatened with looking bad, with being made to feel "small" (Haley, 1966). You are not likely to see them again if you do not take care of this threatened wounding. Also, you are likely to see a great thrust of desire from this individual if you manage to back him or her.

A seventh and last essential line to include in your drawing is the *under-line,* or *underlining,* of words or phrases or figures of speech that are partic-ular to each of the crucial players or factions. This takes you into all the different, relevant worlds that need to be understood for you to be accepted by all parties to a dispute. Kuhn explains the world-opening capacity of a figure of speech (locution) as follows, concerning the locutions of Sir Karl Popper, which must have opened up the minds of Popper's students to Kuhn himself!

Sir Karl and I do appeal to the same data; to an uncommon extent we are seeing the same lines on the same paper. . . . Though the lines are the same, the figures which emerge from them are not. That is why I call what separates us a gestalt switch rather than a disagreement and also why I am at once perplexed and intrigued how best to explore the separation. How am I to persuade Sir Karl, who knows everything I know about scientific development and who has somewhere or other said it, that what he calls a duck can be seen as a rabbit. . . . In this situation a change in strategy is called for, and the following suggests itself. Reading over once more a number of Sir Karl's principal books and essays, I encounter again a series of *recurrent phrases* which, though I understand them and do not quite disagree, are *locutions* that I could never have used in the same places. . . . They may, that is, be symptomatic of contextual differences that a careful literal expression hides. If that is so, then these locutions may function not as lines-on-paper but as the rabbit-ear, the shawl, or the ribbon-at-the-throat which one isolates when teaching a friend to transform his way of seeing a gestalt diagram. (Kuhn, 1970, p. 3) (my italics)

And so may such characteristic phrases open access to seven different ges-talts of seven different parties to the family dispute. The seven different pictures may all fit together somehow into a single drawing, but one can hardly get all seven parties to look at one's drawing, unless each party sees its own world included. Each will delight to see his or her own language, gestures and postures in the message. If he cannot see himself there, why listen at all?

In summary, the grammar of cages ordinarily obliges the outsider to take care of seven different lines in order to get his drawing through. An infinite number of drawings may do as well, so long as they include the seven obligatory lines, viz., the line of appreciation, the loose end, the floor, the ceiling, the wall, the tilt of the board, and the underlining of locutions.

One final warning to the reader about skill with the lines. Sometimes, you will get all of the lines right and lose because of a single *point* which lies outside the lines. A single, well-placed point can often disqualify an entirely beautiful argument. Often, this point will turn on a single phrase, as follows:

The great Railway strike in England turned upon the phrase "definitive terms." One side took it to mean "unchangeable"; the other explained too late that they only meant "full and detailed." (Richards, 1922, p. vi)

This is why the astute person interested in free passage will take such great care, on occasion, with every single word, not to provide a point of counter-attack:

An acquaintance is one whose name and face you know, without more than a rough idea of his being and business. A familiar is one you know as much as possible. Words are astonishingly like people. They have characters, they almost have person-alities — are honest, useful, obliging, or treacherous, vain, stubborn. They shift, as people do, their conduct with their company. They are an endless study in which we are studying nature and ourselves at that meeting point where our minds are trying to give form to take it from the world. (Richards, 1922, p. vii)

A single phrase or word can get stuck to a person or to a cause, bringing in its train a whole host of unwelcome or even disreputable associations. This is the single, simplest way to put something or someone out of business. Often, this intent is disguised as a mere question of fact: "Is he a Freudian?" (rather than a person with any common sense), or more openly, "Isn't he a family therapist, not an individual therapist?" Words tend to be dichotomiz-ing: Either you *are* a family therapist or you *are* an individual therapist. To suggest you are neither, but actually a "systemic clinician," is likely to sound like evasion. Therefore, the point of fact must often be granted, to clear oneself of the insinuation: "Yes, I am a family therapist. Now I suppose that means that I am not deeply interested in individuals." Sometimes, one has to accept guilt, not insist upon innocence, to discover the extent of the guilt implied by a word or phrase. I find that most of the strangest and hugest misunderstandings with organizations, classes, families and individuals turn in just this way: Indeed, I must have said *something* wrong. If I can find that point, I have a chance of tracing the large construction that was built upon that point and foisted upon myself.

The single point is extremely important with persons who are desperate. Often, their response to something you do is to stick doggedly to a single fact, question or statement, as if they were saying: "*I* have a point after all. I am not pointless":

An argument occurred between two patients in the course of a session in an analytic group. Suddenly, one of the protagonists broke off the argument to say, "I can't go on. You are arguing to have the pleasure of triumphing over me. At best you win an argument. At worst you lose an argument. *I am arguing in order to preserve my existence.* (Laing, 1959, p. 43)

Less drastic, but nonetheless vehement, defense of a point can come from people defending a shaky line of study, competence, or trade. If one can grant their point, one has a chance of getting onto something further.

But isn't this true of all of us? Do not all of us authors in a given field, upon seeing a new book in that field, first turn to the index to see if we are mentioned? After all, we are centers of our own worlds. If *our* point is not included by some new venture, why should we include *them* in our reading? We are all vulnerable:

The poet knows that, without the accurate record of art, people *subside*, as transient statistics, into the anonymous census of history. (Vendler, 1985, p. 13) (my italics)

We are poor passing facts warned by that to give each figure in the photograph his living name. (Lowell, 1985, p. 13)

Indeed, it is possible to be generous to those who leave us out of their proposal for a world. We can put our arm around them anyway. But it is hard, sometimes. For those who stand upon points of reiteration do not see lines, figures, or shapes, such as interest *us*. We are often on our own in their company.[4]

No doubt there are many readers who are not at home in spatial references such as I have provided for finding one's way into a group. Don't give up. All of this freely translates into dimensions of time.

We like to say on our family therapy team that the interviewer must do her own interview and that the composer of the final message to the family must compose her own message. The two teammates only play accompaniment. This is because the interviewer-and-message-giver is more likely to be in tune with the prevailing music of the family than two teammates who have had so much less interaction with its members.[5] But it is also probable that the interviewer-and-message-giver will not be able to put in all the crucial notes and rhythms. Family polyphony is very difficult to compose. Now, while it is true that the interviewer may get the family to sing many different possible songs, which may be equally clarifying, and the message-giver could compose many different messages, which assemble the family equally well, there are certain musical errors which will be so dissonant or so lacking that the family gives up listening to us.

Therefore, the job of teammates is to notice certain musical elements in the interview or message of their lead colleague which could get her disqualified. She may not take care of sounding the dominant theme and its ground bass, of the danger of too much excitement and strange dissonance, of the lack of balance between the competing themes, and of the inaccurate recapitulation of the different voices. The teammates must content themselves with pointing to one or two of these elements, which could be troublesome or missed, leaving her to decide whether or not to work these elements into her interview or composition. This allows us outsiders to get across to her and her to listen to us.

Getting New Variations, Fresh Departures, Out of Intolerable Regions

Now, while it may be difficult to bring news of difference from outside to people inside cages, it may be even worse to be inside the cage where one is trapped like all the other group members. The "group" often degenerates into worse and worse states, as follows:

By relating to "the group" the individual of course renounces major attempts to relate to many of the individuals present as well as any prospect that they can make personalized relations with him. This withdrawal from *personal* relations means that the individual is alone in the group and much in resort with his own inner world. In this state of increased narcissism he is now liable to use projective processes to rid himself of unwanted aspects of his personality, and because he relates now not to individuals but to "the group" it is mostly into "the group" as a single entity that these unwanted and aggressive aspects are projected. "The group" which is somewhere around but not located in any persons thus becomes endowed with unpleasant aspects of the self. It is felt as uncannily alive and dangerous, while the individual, weakened and depersonalized, is no longer in possession of his full mental resources. The perception of the group can eventually get so distorted by cycles of projective processes that all the *others* may become felt to be authors of a developing group malignancy, in vague, inexplicable fashion. The dreadful belief may arise that in some inexplicable way all have collectively created an intangible monster to be appeased or hidden from. (Main, 1975, p. 69)

We may go from bad to worse rapidly. Should one stand out as an individual, one now is at considerable risk of the collective envy (of those who have given themselves up): "They will bring me to my knees." Therefore, most are apt to take refuge in their own class: "we" the faculty, or trainees, or staff, or whatever: "Many remarks in a large group thus appear to come from nobody in particular, to be about nobody in particular, and to be addressed to nobody in particular." (Main, p. 76) Those who can stand out in this climate may now imbue themselves, and be imbued by the group, with stranger powers: "A few may even vie for idealizing projections and seek to be regarded by the depleted majority as 'the only people who make the group worthwhile.'" (Main, p. 77) Dread of takeover by these "saviors" (very great in university faculties) now brings about a greater weakening: "Indeed the general fear of enviable distinction may lead to the election of harmless nonentities to important posts." (Main, p. 78) This too is unstable. And so forth. And so forth.

Fortunately, there are ways to break the downward spiral. First of all, your chances improve drastically if you can address those who have already spoken, taking up what they say, either to agree or disagree, giving your own perspective from where you sit, about the shared plight, tersely. Secondly, your chances improve further if you have proven allies who are likely to second your lead by declaring themselves (Skynner, 1975).

There are third, fourth, fifth, and sixth principles we will get to in entirely specific, everyday situations. I believe it may help, beforehand, to see the difference between feeling that an everyday group is intolerable, which is commonplace, and the most extreme situations of total, literal, physical terror. I often feel: "I cannot stay in there for one more minute or I will burst." The delineation of literal terror, as by Lifton in *Nazi Doctors* (1986), can help us to keep perspective on these perfunctory impasses of everyday life.

I do not want to presume to summarize Lifton's delineation of this monstrous history. Like the *Gulag Archipelago* of Solzhenitsyn or *Shoah* of Lanzmann, it cannot be grasped unless you are willing to ride through it, doubling back and forth many, many times. I only mean to take us up to the gate at Auschwitz.

So much has to go wrong at so many different levels that we may see a little from this about what to secure as best we can. First, we need to fear the kind of hopelessness when there is no future to build.[6] Being nobody with nowhere to go is to become open to recklessness:

The cultural climate of post-First World War Germany was compatible with totalism: a mood of extremity, of "often ludicrous immoderation" in literary and artistic expressionism . . . many artistic experiments came to be consumed by a death-saturated confusion. . . . (p. 471)

This only invited the desperation for cure of the deadly sickness of degeneration:

It was Hans Johst, an Expressionist novelist and playright and later head of the Nazi Chamber of Literature, who first used the phrase made later famous by Goring: "When I hear the word culture, I draw my revolver." That was the only cure for Germany's disease. (p. 472)

Such a cure required a vision of victims who posed "absolute danger" to the body politic:

Jews were equated with every form of death-associated degeneracy and decomposition. . . . When the threat is so absolute and so ultimate — where the struggle becomes "fighting between humans and subhumans," in Himmler's phrase — genocide becomes not only appropriate but an urgent necessity. . . . Once that . . . necessity is established, perpetrators can take the more casual tone of Himmler's suggestion that "anti-Semitism is exactly the same as delousing." (p. 477)

But the murder of a people needed agents who were ready to carry out the "biocratic" vision: what Lifton divides into the educated "killing professionals" — "physicians, scientists, engineers, military leaders, lawyers, clergy, university professors and other teachers — who combine to create not only the technology of genocide but much of its ideological rationale, morale climate, and organizational process" (p. 489) — and the "professional killers" who make up the "hit men."

Finally, the scale of the atrocity required the "success in rendering their most murderous actions into technological problems" (p. 494). For this, bureaucracy was indispensable:

The combination of relative silence and organizational reach puts the bureaucracy in the best position to plan the details of genocide. The original involvement in planning contributes in turn to the bureaucracy's normalization of a genocidal universe. Mass murder is everywhere but at the same time (through the efforts of the bureaucracy) nowhere. There is only a flow of events to which most people in the environment (as Dr. B. said of Auschwitz doctors) come to say yes. To say no would take one outside that flow, outside of normal social existence, outside of reality. One seeks instead the most "humane" path within the going project. . . . The faces are there, even if hidden and merged into a mass. (p. 497)

In summary, total human degeneration seems to take, at least, the absence of a future to build, reckless loosing of culture, desperation for an ideology of "cure," which poses "an absolute danger" (of subhumans) to the body politic, "the half-educated men" (killing professionals and professional killers) willing to be its agents, technology, and bureaucracy that can be coupled to any (however murderous) project.

The opposite direction to all of this is what I hope to get across. As we discussed about all large groups, there is a prevailing tendency for becoming impersonal, anonymous, arrogant (saviors), or harmless. Lifton proposes some of the way forward:

The professional does well to prepare for such exigencies by maintaining a balance of what I call advocacy and detachment, of clear ethical commitment and technical skill. A physician's "calling" would include commitment under all conditions to Hippocratic principles of healing. The embodied self requires both constant critical awareness of larger projects demanding allegiance and equally pervasive empathy, fellow feeling, toward all other human beings. (p. 500)

IMPASSES OF EVERYDAY LIFE

The balance described by Lifton is extremely important for being able to help ordinary groups out of their impasses. Robin Skynner (1975) wrote of this balance in terms of three capabilities: first, "a capacity to tolerate silence," to ride in a group with "trust in one's own essential buoyancy"; second, the willingness to stay oneself "despite the destructive envy this arouses in others, which is experienced as greater and more terrifying as the size of the group increases"; third, the ability to "demonstrate to the group that it is possible and desirable both to lower defenses and become one with the group, while at the same time maintaining individuality and standing against it (or rather for oneself despite it)." With these capabilities you may tackle the shared plight, speaking for yourself, which is likely to be seconded by others, who can also bear the burden of self-revelation and will declare themselves as well.

Notice how these capabilities are secured by the balance of a tradition of critical awareness of large projects and empathy for fellow human beings, as proposed by Lifton. Not only is such a person involved in the trouble of the group, but he or she also can step out of the horizontal into the larger world of a tradition bigger than the group, and into the smaller worlds of individual beings who matter, no matter what they mean for the challenge of the group.[7] Such a vertical freedom uncouples a person from being swallowed up, from envy and from defensiveness. Lacking this buoyancy, leaders preside over commonplace meetings and classrooms, which are mostly tedious, with occasional breaking out into open hostility:

If the designated leaders fail in this, then at best there is defensive functioning where they lead an orderly retreat into limited problem-solving within restricted boundaries, usually intellectually focused; at worst they abdicate and allow "mad leaders" in the group to push it towards more destructive ends. (Skynner, 1975, p. 248)

Although the danger of intolerable regions is greater in large groups, they are often found in couples, trios, quartets, subgroups and small groups. There too you can find yourself in flat boredom which runs on and on. In mean digging at one another. In going round and round in circles. And so forth.

We turn first to such a region in which we found ourselves sinking in the trio of our family therapy team. Here is the kind of situation which can feel intolerable unless you can stand back far enough to keep it in perspective. Nearing the conclusion of an hour and a half with a couple, my colleague was hearing from the wife that she could never tell her husband how she felt about being slyly hated by his son, her stepson. She complained that her husband always disqualified her by saying, "Now what did he actually *say* that made you think he hated you?" "Are you sure he used that tone?" "Maybe he didn't really intend to offend you?" And so forth. Only my colleague, trying to conclude the interview, could not get her to stop her narrative. Complaining of a denied coalition against herself, she pulled for a denied coalition against her husband (the most common of marital pathologies), a so-called "perverse triangle" (Haley, 1966). As she kept barging on, my colleague lost patience like the husband, and made a hostile remark or two. The wife was taken aback. My colleague knew at once that she had made an error and asked me to join her behind the mirror with our third teammate to discuss the situation.

How she recovered her bearings in the next half-hour is interesting as a clear sequence of steps. First, she held to her instinct that this breach with the wife had to be repaired at once, disregarding my advice that we would take our usual half-hour break before giving a final message. We went back and she made a joke about doctors who know everything, which was gladly received by the wife. Sitting across the room from both of them, I could see them leaning forward towards each other in a clear mutual gesture of reconciliation. I was glad she hadn't listened to me but to herself!

This is an overriding truth about getting out of these intolerable regions: If you stick to your own feeling, you've got a chance. If you lose your own feelings, your position becomes irretrievable, no matter how much so-called help you get.

Therefore, she continued to take counsel with herself in our half-hourlong break from the family to work out her own message. She did this before hearing from us two, her teammates. If she had her own bearings, she could make use of small suggestions from us.

Then she turned to our third teammate to hear what was important to her. I tried to sit back as far as I could, to watch what happened between *them*. What I witnessed was our lead interviewer proposing her message in an urgent, hurried way, while our third colleague was counterposing a highly rational exercise to be prescribed to the couple. This only made our lead interviewer more tense. The strange loop of the husband and wife, of frenzy begetting rationality, begetting more frenzy, begetting more rationality, and so forth still had our team in its power. My colleague appealed to me to do something.

I told her I sided with her terse message. After all, she was just getting out of a big snare. I would only suggest she take care to use their particular words, carefully.

She settled down right away. Interestingly, what she said was: "What I'm hearing is your tone." I think she meant that I had set a rhythm which was outside the strange loop. This helped her to step out of that oscillation of frenzy and rationality.

But there was one more step. She said: "I feel there is still something wrong. You two are so quiet. Are you holding back criticism?" I said, "No, but I can see how you would think that I am critical from the past (about your acting emotional). I am *not* critical of you now. 'I think that making mistakes . . . is less important than the ability to recover from them'" (Rice, 1965, p. 49). She understood at once my admiration for her. She went in to the couple and gave a very good message, centered well in her own feeling, reaching across well to the husband and wife in their very own words.

I believe my contribution to getting out of this intolerable region, set up in us by the pull into the strange loop of the couple, was threefold. I backed her instinct. I was terse. And I did not get drawn into the strange loop of frenzy and rational criticism, although she enacted it with our third teammate and enacted it towards me by thinking me critical.

I do not think I could have helped in this way without the vertical clarity about levels that is built into method as a team. I am four levels back from the interaction: viz., from the couple, from my colleague who is interviewing the couple, from her interaction with our third teammate, from watching myself in relation to the three previous levels.

If I can stay clear of an intolerable region by these vertical, spatial possibilities, I may also stay clear by having different horizontal, temporal possibilities. The simplest way to move horizontally out of a hopeless loop is to follow what de Shazer (1987) calls the principle of minimal elegance. The gist of this small but decisive movement is to say something as follows to those who are badly revolving: "All right, this is the rule. What is the exception to this rule? *When* are you not like this?"

There are also complex variations. Two of them are especially important in large group situations or organizations. It is astonishing, but true, that large groups or organizations cannot tolerate trade-offs (Steinbruner, 1974). Therefore, they oscillate in large discussions between the several options, until everyone is seasick. In the context of the present, no one sees a way out.

Several years ago, my department had a single faculty position open. In a two-day-long retreat, we began to discuss whether this new faculty member would be sought in the area of psychopharmacology, in the area of drug and alcoholism treatment, in the area of child psychiatry, or in the area of psychosocial treatment. This discussion oscillated between these four possible areas for many hours. The group became so weary that many were on the verge of leaving the room, giving up altogether, while others seemed increasingly frantic in their reiteration. I was able to break the spell in a few sentences, as follows: "We will fight forever this way, since one position is not four positions. But there is a way out. If we agree to four positions over the next five years, then all four interests can have their way. I can give up my insistence that this be a psychosocial position this year if I know I can get what I believe to be all important next year, or the following, or the following. I believe you all may feel this way as well about what you are defending." I was thinking that a game which is insoluble in a single play becomes soluble once there are many plays.[8]

This year, we began another one of these discussions about the child psychiatry position. Again, the trade-offs were very complicated: "We might offer the opening to one of our own bright residents. But then we might offer the position to a woman from another training program. But then we might seek a senior child psychiatrist from elsewhere to come be in charge of our child division. But then he would take a very long time to woo and we might lose the two junior candidates. But then how could we decide between them? Didn't we have to have a woman in the child sector? But then didn't we have to have a researcher?" And so on. And so on.

Several colleagues later told me they felt they were on a boat that was rocking wildly, from left to right, fore and aft. Some literally felt sick. Another said she needed a stiff drink. I was able to break this spell again in a few sentences, as follows: "We can oscillate in this way endlessly. The only way that organizations get out of these spells is by having a procedure in time, a sequence in which the decisions will be made. I propose: (1) We see the senior psychiatrist next week as planned to see if we want to consider him further at all. (2) We see the woman from the other program the following week, to see if we want to consider her further at all. (3) We take a straw vote now on our own inside candidate to see how close or far apart we are on him." There was unanimous accord. I was only following Steinbruner's rule (1974) that large organizations cannot tolerate simultaneous trade-offs. They need to move out of the present into a sequence of yes/no decisions. This is the freedom from the present, generated by a horizontal set of temporal possibilities.

LIMITS OF TRANSLATION

Free passage in and out of enclosing groups is much simpler for oneself, alone, than for an entire group. If the reader thinks I can usually bring a great deal into my department's faculty meeting that will carry us along, or that I can often carry us out of miserable hours, he or she is greatly mistaken. My influence is occasional. I see three major limitations.

The first great limit is that some kinds of music will not interest professors. They believe in numbers of grants, research subjects, published papers, and in money.[9] If their numbers are threatened, you will be esteemed when you can repair them. Otherwise, they are apt to stop listening.

The second great limit is that department meetings can wear you down, unless you can give them a small, brief place on your map. Notice how A. R. Ammons gives the modern machine two lines in the history of the universe:

> A bit of the universe's
> business slopped
> over and, strung
> out of the way,
> cooled and lode-slow
> gave rise
> here and there to
> a quickness like
> shade, protoplasm,
> a see-through
> coming and going of
> dots and pulsing veils
> that soon enough filled
> the bit seas:
> the veils and cauls
> toughened, curled
> into rolls, centralized
> backbone: taking to

> the land and coming up
> into us, our agency,
> they milled the
> green continents white.

I have noticed that many of my colleagues, like Ammons, or like senators in the drone of the Senate, give an ear only occasionally to the proceedings. They bring stacks of work and look up occasionally. There is a great limit to what you can do with an extremely redundant milling machine. Better to enjoy your own preoccupations and listen occasionally for a change in the gears and look occasionally at the faces around you.

The final great limit to translating into groups and out of them is that the infrequency of getting across means you are on your own. Vertical shafts of delight flatten fast in broad daylight: the excitement of the seminar is over as if nothing happened at all. As Vendler (1988) wrote about Ammons:

. . . consciousness must be a center unto itself, no matter what its position in the universe. (p. 100)

You may have free passage if you are willing to be on your own. The only great comfort is that fellowship can come back. I like how Ammons puts this too,

> a light catches somewhere, finds
> human
> spirit to burn on, shows its magic's
> glint lines, attracts, grows, rolls
> back space and dark . . .
>
>   it dwells:
> it dwells and dwells: slowly the
> light
> its veracity unshaken, dies but moves
> moves
> to find a place to break out elsewhere . . .

PART V

Counterposing

8. *Time and Timing*

OUR SOCIAL LIFE EXISTS within many different time frameworks. Some situations demand our focus on the future, others expect us to be relatively present; some situations move like a whirlwind across time, others plod along slowly. Because time is so prominent, it becomes one way we can express the unworkability of a situation to ourselves and others: There is a lull in the situation, nobody knows what to do, or nobody wants to do what is needed now. Time stands still. We are obsessed with the past or the future to the detriment of the present. Another's time frame overshadows our own. The central strategy offered in this chapter involves movement that can be triggered by working in contrasting time frames.[1]

There is a wide range of possible ways that time becomes manifest as a social obstacle. Three forms will be described here, ranging from the relatively simple lull in ongoing activity, to the moderately more complex experience of two contiguous systems with antagonistic pacing, to the even more complex situation of two differently paced situations in which one of the time frames is largely invisible. It is important to be able to stand back and consider the different possibilities on this sprawling territory; there is often little urgency.

One of the authors (Jim) was supervising a trainee in individual psychotherapy. The case involved a young man who was terribly inhibited and unsure of himself, and the therapist's inclination was to barrel ahead, structuring the conversation during the first hour so that the interview had the flavor of a press conference. As part of the regular procedure of the clinic, Jim then interviewed the patient, uncovering a tremendous amount of isolation and passivity; the patient felt unmet and unable to make an impression on people. The trainee watched the interview and got some coaching on the kind of person he was dealing with. He started the next therapy interview by saying that he realized the patient needed to feel more in control, so half the interview would be open-ended and he, the therapist, would conduct the other half. The patient was visibly disheartened. Should (Jim as) the supervisor have intervened with a quick time frame in mind, meeting the patient's more immediate needs for this therapy to work, or should he have responded to the slower time scale of the trainee's learning? To jump in immediately to save the treatment could easily have undermined the therapist, but to take a longer time perspective risked losing the patient. In fact, that is what happened. The therapist got a hard lesson about the bad effects of being controlling, and the patient came back a year later to the author to get a more suitable trainee. Such are the dilemmas of conflicting time scales.

In the middle and later stages of group life, having secured organization, appreciated a coherent picture, and overcome obstacles to moving, one must face certain specific challenges best seen from a well-placed viewing position or platform. Since one is forced to make decisions about when to enter, it is useful to be able to see various controls or dimensions interacting.

Experiencing difficulty staying in the present is common. How often have we all sat around in a group chatting in a friendly way, only to be cast into a mindless pall when the designated leader enters or starts the meeting? There is a whole change of feeling from outside to inside the group. Once inside the group, all too commonly we drift within ourselves to outside territories — other groups, other moods, other concerns altogether (from ill spouse, to sprained muscle, to waiting chores, to sexual fantasy, etc.). We are constantly drawn into larger or smaller enclosures which integrate for us individually what the group will not allow. The small group is always in danger of succumbing to these lulls of attention, and the resultant tension makes the group hard on the spirit of the participants and leader alike. The group feels like the preserve of small minds, riddled with windows of escape to the more appealing, the more profound — at least the more compelling. It is impossible to judge the meaning and importance of one encounter without observing the time context in which it occurs.

USING THE LULL

The simplest story of timing is making the right move at the right time. One very clear spokesperson for this simple plot is Balint, who states the cardinal intervention rules: Do not enter too soon (and intrude), do not wait too long (and abandon). In describing his method for working with general practitioners in group seminars:

As long as the mutual identifications of the members are fairly strong, any individual member can face strains because he feels accepted and supported by the group. His mistakes and failings, although humiliating, are not felt as singling him out as a useless member; quite on the contrary, he feels that he has helped the group to progress, using his failings as stepping-stones. *It is a precondition of our technique to establish this kind of atmosphere in the group, and it is only in such an atmosphere that it is possible to achieve what we term "the courage of one's own stupidity."* This means that the doctor feels free to be himself with his patient, that is, to use all of his past experiences and present skills without much inhibition. (1954, p. 40; italics added).

To intervene successfully is to create an atmosphere of safety for self-exposure. The irony of using the lull, that is, just letting peaks and valleys develop, often means doing some very active watching and waiting. Balint explains further:

. . . the technique we advocate is based on exactly the same sort of listening that we expect the doctors to acquire. By allowing everybody to be themselves, to have their say in their own way and in their own time, by watching for proper cues, *i.e., speaking only when something is really expected from him* and making his point in a form which, *instead of prescribing the right way of dealing* with the patient's problems, *opens up possibilities* for the doctors to discover some right way of dealing with the patient's problems, the leader can demonstrate in the "here and now" situation what he wants to teach. (p. 41; italics added)

Again, Balint guides us to the importance of being there when needed, not prescribing, not being intrusive. Balint's conditions for safety involve timing congruent with what he believes individuals need to learn from their mistakes.

Working in Balint groups with an eye to the emergence of problems endemic in the surrounding institution suggests another importance to the lull: giving room to fail. In jumping in vigorously to solve the problems of a specific medical case presented to the group, one obscures other crucial events in the group, such as low attendance, the substantial noncompliance the physicians feel towards their supervisors, etc. By letting failure unfold, one has an opportunity to bring a larger issue into view, an issue that may stay invisible when one burrows into the case-by-case struggles.

As I am using the term here, lull refers to periods of slowing down, quiet, silence. The lull could last years where efforts are diffuse, little gets done, and time weighs heavily. Or the lull could be fruitful in the available time set aside for the interviews.

In discussing his family work, Skynner (1981) talks about timing from a slightly different angle. There is the sense that he adheres to the lull by waiting to become part of the system and seeing what he must do and where he must do it. Time must be extended for the proper moment to emerge. When issues as potentially touchy as sex within a family are being raised, it often takes time to read the impact of an intervention, knowing whether one should push ahead or make a tactical retreat. Time becomes a clinical instrument that the whole system plays in its unique way. One is reminded of Whitaker and Lieberman's (1964, 1978) incisive timing in groups, aiming interventions precisely when restrictive solutions are about to be reached. The challenge in timing (for Whitaker and Lieberman) is keeping the dialogue open and deepening the conversation. As with Skynner, correct timing adds material to the discussion and provides the basis for new ideas to be considered.[2]

In discussing their view of "clever satisfactory (communication) competence" Pearce and Cronen (1980) emphasize moving "with unusual effectiveness and originality within a system," sensing the right moment and "playing" with pacing. One wonderful example they use is the exchange between Valvert and Cyrano in Rostand's *Cyrano de Bergerac*. Being slapped in the face by Valvert's verbal assault, Cyrano leaps into the breach, pushes insult to farcical extreme: "You are too simple. . . . why waste your opportunity?" He then proceeds to intensify the pace, cracking open the insult by intensifying it, redoubling Valvert's challenge ("Your nose is . . . rather large!") and counter-challenging all at once ("You are too simple. Why, you might have said — Oh, a great many things!") Not only is the verbal expressiveness crucial in such a "competent" reply, but the timing is all important. Cyrano seized the opportunity with vigor.

Studying rhythm and tempo is another immediate way of looking at time (Gustafson, unpublished manuscript, b). In the context of individual therapy there are rhythms that must be respected and can be used. The lulls give time to see "dangerous currents (building). . . . Unseen in places that seem not to move at all." The lulls give time to prepare for the fast periods. They are not just times of rest and retreat, but natural ebb and flow which can be used. A wise analytic technician appreciates "the judicious use of waiting in silence" as an important tool for "facilitating the development of the transference" (Greenson, 1967, p. 269).[3] So more traditional analytic thinking about technique offers the story of waiting for the right moment, and there is clear merit to this position; people cannot be expected to move forward relentlessly. I believe that it is a common enough experience for us all that we have natural "tides" and tempos as individuals and as group participants. As in sports, it is impossible to imagine no rest periods built into the structure of the game. Sustained forward movement is too much to expect.

The simple story line has its two cardinal rules: don't intrude and don't abandon. Kathleen Leverick (personal communication) wittily summarizes this pair of rules as the Lull Hypothesis. This hypothesis runs certain risks of error. For instance, as Gustafson (1987) describes, certain schools of brief and family therapy have been very successful with very focused attention on the present. Certain strategic approaches (de Shazer, 1985) offer ways out of difficult vicious cycles by exclusive negotiations in the here and now. History does not enter into the picture. Insofar as "securing the present" becomes a method or part of a method in and of itself — what Gustafson (1987) calls the "convention of the exclusive present" — appreciation of a certain depth and repetition is not evident; thus the possible risk. The timing of the past may be different from that of the present and require longer to come over the hill and into focus. While knowing history can sometimes be used to guard against repetition, some misfortunes have to be dissociated to live in the present. The reentry of history may be slow compared with the activity in the present. This is yet another perspective on time: In family work (and this would be applicable to group work also), while we are busy discovering and securing the present, sooner or later the past reenters. It may reenter as new information, new emotions, or even a reversal of direction.

Gustafson offers a bridge in looking at time. On the one hand, the simple story line continues: Follow time as it unfolds; time has its own valuable pacing. There is also the notion that different dimensions of time have different paces. While focusing on present time, we will be riding at a rate often quite different from past time (history) but dramatically influenced by it. From our present position in time we are looking through a window onto another experience of time moving at a very different speed and experienced very differently by the individual. At times, lulls serve as windows to different dimensions of time. However, insofar as one chooses to secure an exclusive present, the lull must simply be dealt with directly.

The usefulness of the simple story line is not to be underestimated. For example, I had been participating in a small group planning a presentation on substance abuse treatment for a scientific conference. Time was very much on our minds. There was so much to say in a limited period of time. Our planning meetings had a fascinating (and all too common) rhythm. When the meetings started, we all had ideas about how to divide the time into segments. Each person was assigned a period of time and then there was a discussion of whether the allotments were fair and what would be done with the segments. This was all fine and necessary but tedious, and soon it would get boring.

The plan, in general, was to present the psychoanalytically oriented outpatient program for drug treatment, which this group sponsored. In the planning group, members rotated in signaling the boredom threshold, as when someone said, "This audience is going to be unfriendly to our approach because they are politically committed to other modes, such as AA. We are representing a minority view in the field and we'll get slammed for it. How can we address this during the presentation?"

Gone was the boredom as we were all tumbled into an anxious future. Everyone was excited by this challenge and ready to take on the challenge at the presentation. Soon this line of discussion got lost in nebulous debate about the form of the unseen enemy. Little more could be done in anticipation, and again the discussion died on its feet. Someone would then say: "Where on our current agenda can we address those issues?" This led us back to case material, integrative statements, and the nuts and bolts of the presentation. We went back and forth, managing the time frames to enliven the discussion, and using neighboring fields of time to control the downturns and reversals of mood and tone inevitable in trying to stay on a straight line.

The simple straight story line may be real and continue to mean something, but the story line may also become more and more convoluted. One must be ready for complications as one prepares to appreciate what is in store as different time frames are juxtaposed.

NEIGHBORING TIME

When Stevenson describes the lantern-bearers, the youngsters' moment of delight was the "essence of . . . bliss" (1892, p. 215), a timeless, idyllic state which seemed from inside to have no beginning, middle, or end. However, he walked into the moment through the adult time frame: "Toward the end of September, when schooltime was drawing near . . . " (p. 213). To fully appreciate the specialness of the moment, one must be sure to read the time frame around it; otherwise one risks getting lost, in this case with the burden of unending bliss. The larger neighboring parental control protected the specialness. This reminds me of a children's book in which one child is granted his birthday wish to have a birthday party five days in a row. By the third day, the party is tedious for all; by the fifth day, it is hateful. The idyll quickly sinks without protection from overindulgence. Enjoyment of the moment is sometimes best appreciated on a neighboring time scale framing it.

Another example from literature also reads the center of a situation best through a level of time neighboring the present. In Galsworthy's (1916) "The Apple Tree," the hero's knee gives out on a hike, when he and his friend are way off their beaten track. They come upon a farm, where they are taken in, and our hero slowly becomes filled with a wonderful love for a young woman living there. As his knee gets better and he can walk again, he returns to his life, wanting desperately to have this woman come with him. Tragically (if predictably) she can't and they separate, each to his or her own path. For me, the time to include here is that of his recovery from injury, not just the immediate course of their feelings for each other. For all of us who have been in a hospital and suffered intense love affairs (in fantasy) with our nurses, only to leave cured of ailment of body and heart, this story captures a familiar theme. The straight line of the love affair is more accurately a loop from a life course, fully influenced by a neighboring big picture in which it is imbedded.

In discussing the strengths and weakness of the Roman Empire, Fisher (1935) makes the point that centuries of dominance and conquest went along with (complacent) protection from invasion at the perimeter of the Empire. But one can't fully appreciate the downfall in focusing only on the increasing strength of the Goths, because in fact the Romans were successful at defense for quite a long time. A more satisfactory reading of the situation is gained by looking at other internal workings of the Empire occurring over a long period of time — slower and less dramatic, and covert, but very telling. Consider, for instance, the deterioration of education: Its drift to hollowness and loss of creativity left "nothing in the ordinary education of the Roman clearly calculated to direct his mind to the grave social and economic problems which lay around him" (1935, p. 105). Impoverishment of science left politicians, for instance, unequipped to manage the sanitation problems of large cities. The tide of economic reversals could not be stemmed. The richness of Fisher's presentation is the reading of the sweeps of events surrounding the army — events moving so slowly they could be missed. By the time the Gothic armies arrived full force, the outcome was no longer very surprising.

In discussing bureaucracies, Jules Henry (1973) brings Fisher's approach to our modern life. The strength of bureaucracies to routinize and break down complex tasks begins, over time, to serve other functions, such as perpetuating themselves and preventing internal change. Change is difficult to introduce into the system; the very strengths of the bureaucracy fail to prepare it for changing environmental conditions and thereby increase its vulnerability over the long run. When time is taken into account, the straight line of progression in growth of bureaucracy creates its own reversals and perhaps leads to self-destruction. Fortunately, progress is rarely a straight line, and there are loops along the way which reflect influence by the neighboring environment moving at a faster pace, the forces of transformation.

An example also comes from the neighboring field of education. Within the current intensity of curriculum development for the humanities and social sciences at major universities, it is easy to lose sight of the downward spiral of science education (Westheimer, 1987). Brief statements by Koshland (1986) and Carey (1986) in *Science* magazine show the disastrous results of political decision-making about allocation of money for science. As with Rome, survival insists on continual evaluations of the bigger picture in educational directions (as in other areas). When the long-term perspective of balanced education is overly influenced by quicker transformation pressures of the moment, curriculum is shifted too much, too quickly. The surge of intense rapid movements can be overly influential, hard to resist.

Let us turn to a more mundane example from group life related to the questions about society raised by Fisher, by Henry, and by *Science*. We have all had the experience of working in the excitement of the present and then feeling that develop into a stultifying atmosphere of boredom and sameness. The surface drones us into a misleading dullness. At those times especially, having a position from which to notice the lulls everywhere, to invite an outside view, makes survival possible.

Often, it is through the judicious experimentation with correct timing that the curtain is slowly pulled back to reveal other dramas on other time scales. I am familiar with an organization, functioning in a large university setting, that was taken over by a program director who was well versed in group dynamics. It was a work group of manageable size, but its members had had difficulties working together in the past. He took them on and worked with them tooth and nail, trying all kinds of interventions and outside consultants to coax, encourage, force, and persuade people to work together.

After months and months of the group's stubborn unwillingness to cooperate, which was often painfully obvious, he was exhausted. What became more and more apparent, as he searched for a reading of the situation, was the drag of the group's history, which was quite long and preceded his arrival on the scene by many years. Internal antagonisms were intense and unspoken; when verbalized they were often filled with venom.

The movement of this process was so heavy and had accelerated over so many years that turning it around was impossible in the time frame of several months. The director decided (wisely) to disband the group, work with individuals, and meet only infrequently with fixed agendas. Only after *several years* of working this way could he win the allegiance of many of the individuals; some never could be won over, and the group could only have marginally satisfactory work sessions on very specific topics.

How are we to understand this situation? Starting from the immediate level of the current group, the new director's experience was that he had to work with the group members to win them over to his leadership, and he fought long and hard in his attempt to do this. Their collective capacity to get a job done was decimated by forces unaccessible to the new director. His time frame was intensely present and future oriented; he wanted to get them to work together to conquer the challenges of the current program and develop future programs. His interventions involved wrestling with the present vicious intensity and bringing outside resources to bear on the problem.

Over the months it became clear that he wasn't getting where he wanted to go. Why? He began to look at each individual and the history of the group and realize that these were long-time employees, each committed to his or her own view of the work, simmering along on a low burner that had been ignited — for some — twenty years earlier. Loyalties were deeply rooted, subterranean, and unuseful even when surfaced. As this encrusted, overheated stew was increasingly exposed, he could appreciate the enormity (indeed, impossibility) of adding new ingredients. The freedom here came not in direct victory, but in the ability to face "terminal lull" with a different kind of understanding of the process, intrude on it, and emerge with another strategy for getting on with the present and future jobs. The program director was able to protect and sustain his own intensity, surviving what could have been thoroughly a demoralizing (and it *was* disappointing) experience while continuing to move ahead. When the usefulness of the simple story line was played out, further movement came from looking through the window into a thickly viscous history and suggesting a way of breaking up the group.

The Swirling Seminar

A clinical case seminar I have taught for several years is like a bumper car ride — it is continually hitting up against its neighbors in a way that throws it off course — or threatens to. From the moment the class starts, there is unevenness. Some people come late, while others register late and don't appear until the second or third meeting. I try to set my own pace and announce at the very beginning when I will start the class. I refer all late-comers to other members of the group for catch-up information. After a bit we are all momentarily within the same time frame. We have gathered around our common antagonist, the course content.

There are two typical early disjunctures that abruptly shift the pace. One comes from a student having a clinical crisis, commonly at the beginning of the seminar (and the training year). She has an agency emergency, can't get to the on-site supervisor fast enough, and just has to tell the class about it to get some support. The tempo of the crisis bumps us hard. It is good to listen to the crisis because it usually captures students' interest. Most often it is impossible to solve the problem with the agency's time frame, so one must instead instruct in the pace of the class and refer the student back to the agency for intense speed.

Another typical early challenge comes when I announce the course out-line: I want to fit a lot into a semester; the students feel like they want to dilute it and slow down the amount of work because of other commitments. I wonder whether I am being unreasonable. Students feel pushed from all sides (other courses) and dig in their heels to slow things down. I usually make some compromises.

At the middle of the semester, I almost always find myself frustrated when the school suggests that it is time to have a mid-semester evaluation session with the students about the course. I realize that I have drifted into feeling that there is a lot of time. My experience slows down; the school reminds me that time is moving along relentlessly and that I must attend to it. This is always paralleled by students' frustration that their clients aren't changing fast enough. Here students are a significant way through the train-ing year with clients who either don't stay in psychotherapy or don't change easily in spite of students' following to the best of their ability what I and the agency teach. I am under the gun to make things happen quickly or admit that my approach is improper for their settings. The time pressure comes to them from their own desire to be effective, and they are impatient with my looking too far into the future.

Often the best I can do with these frictions is to teach about brief therapy vs. long-term therapy and other intervention possibilities. I can't let myself get caught up in the pressure, but if I wall off *their* neighboring pressures I lose my connection with them. I must stick with them and still pull back enough to be able to teach. The most common dilemma here is their feeling that they are being asked to do short-term therapy with long-term therapy techniques. The two just don't fit together as they experience it, and my credibility rests on being able to be helpful with this swirl of pressures.

Again, the school imposes itself directly in forcing students to think about their future in the midst of the present seminar. Students must begin to choose their clinical placement for the following year. The future pressure is viciously abrupt because the competition for "good" placements means that fragile cooperation and positive morale are threatened in the class by painful comparisons among peers. I try to cushion them by putting the pressure from the school to choose their fate for the following year into the context of their long-range career plans. We switch temporarily to a broader conversation about career development, and I try to project my sense of time into the future in a more regulated way, to derail some of the panic. Again, I must connect with some of the friction they pick up from the neighboring future focus of the school, compared with feeling totally engrossed in the present. If I ignore it altogether the class becomes an anxious cauldron and the students' clinical concentration is undermined.

The seminar's last brush with the tension of time is at the end when it comes to student evaluation; the school context imposes itself. Is the evaluation for the betterment of the students; is it a useful guide for their development? Or is it a permanent record that will make or break them in their future career?

The challenge is to end the seminar and in a sense bracket our time together, while communicating that their learning goes on, that time extends continuously into the future. There is a temptation to be too finite, as if to say through a clear ending that the topic has been learned. Stretching out the time is a bit scary, in that it continues ignorance into the future. It is helpful to be realistic about what has ended and what continues, not be falsely clear or unnecessarily open-ended.

When the seminar is seen in its context, it has a particular time frame and pacing of its own, but is exposed to multiple neighbors with their differing speeds — like asteroids flying through space and crashing into each other randomly. The ride can be uneven, if not rough. It is best to be prepared to know when and how to hold on when there are abrupt moments. Like an amusement park ride, the surprises can be thrilling even when unanticipated, but it is a little easier to keep one's stomach in place if prepared.

"DEEP TIME"

Gould argues that to fully appreciate time we must have a linear concept (time's arrow) that sees movement as progressing through a particular period ("History is an irreversible sequence of unrepeatable events" [1987, p. 10]). This is a view akin to the simple story line I described. To get from point A to point B in the life of the group, the leader directs the well-timed intervention at or near the right place on the line — neither blocking nor deflecting. In addition, however, we must also hold a belief that "time has no direction"; rather, we are seeing motions of repeating cycles of creation and destruction (time's cycle). "Deep time" takes arrows *and* cycles into account, making historical sense of literally deeper layers of rock (using Gould's [1987] geological context) as reflecting cycles of creation and destruction in the depth of time.

In a fascinating discussion of this problem from an ecological perspective, Allen and Starr use a metaphor of interacting holons to get across the idea that sometimes the information coming from the holons is different in scale, i.e., different in "the period of time or space over which signals are integrated or smooth" (1982, p. 18). In the simplest story, the information from two holons can be readily integrated if information signals from the two move at the same rate. Speed of a neighboring car is easiest to figure out if that car is traveling at the exact same speed as we are. But more usually, the information comes to us at different rates. The window to a neighboring holon reveals time of a different (past or future) scale, and it is the distorted (relative) signal that becomes "the firm context for any responses the receiver might subsequently make" (1982, p. 22).

From inside a group, we are most connected to the experience within the bounds of the present. Sometimes, however, this does not provide enough information—especially when the events in the group are being dwarfed by other levels of time. A platform or perspective that permits a deeper view of time can both increase appreciation of just how complex the situation is and also sharpen the choices for action.

I am reminded of an example of a case conference in an agency working with domestic violence. A student therapist presented an individual therapy case. The man had sought treatment after his wife left him because he hit her; this incident had been preceded by several months of nonviolence. He had also been thrown out of a support group that required nonviolence. Within a matter of a few sessions he was stirring up more and more dust in the therapy: He wanted to be in group therapy and couples therapy, he felt that the clinic was not responding quickly enough to his needs and was thereby endangering him for future violence, he wanted a letter to the group he had been tossed out of saying that he was recovered and should be readmitted.

The presentation itself stirred up a lot of dust (in the present) in the conference. Involved discussions took place about what to offer, what clinic policy was about various treatment combinations, etc. Lots of uncertainty erupted about whether this person was "appropriate" for the clinic because of his disturbed character. The discussion was completely captured by the present. It was very clear that taking this present slice of time, a current moment of crisis could be addressed—and to some extent had to be addressed, for this person to continue to have faith in the clinic.

It was also true that, at another level, what was being revealed in *this* scene of *this* act of this person's life was really a patterned scenario of long duration and many cycles. We knew that because it had been described in the case history, yet there was no connection of one part of his drama with the other. Past incidents were dissociated from present; the past seemed quite opaque in the crisis moment of blame, confusion, and demands.

I suggested that, along with the management decision, this man be told about his pattern, specifically, that when he failed (to contain his violence, for instance) he felt so humiliated and rejected that he decided to spread it around wherever he could. His misfortune was too much to hold inside. It was not necessarily so that this was the truest story abstractly, but it was a way of relating two dimensions of time—current moment and constant pattern—for the case conference group. It was in *this* group that the broader sweep had an immediately calming impact on the mood and sense of pressure. Subsequent discussion about the case offered some therapeutic strategic planning.

If one is captured by the present, the technical rules (of linear timing) can at times be difficult to figure out. Another platform is needed. A case appears to be in a crisis. The staff group, not wanting to abandon, gets very busy giving, offering, supporting—so much is needed that intrusion seems impossible. In the present moment the staff loses track of its own cyclical history (deep time), namely, that in working with a crisis-prone population there is nothing more frustrating than coming up with plans that never materialize because the patient decides that he or she can't follow through on the recommendations. On the other hand, to remember and weigh history so heavily that the staff members take the position that they should interpret all this as transference and not offer anything concrete is very likely to be seen as a discouraging abandonment. What is one to do? Responding to only one of the time dimensions can make one feel not as smart as one would like.

From the present group moment, one gets some power in the situation by looking across a broader sweep to a level of recurring patterns. In this situation the staff also lost track of other current cases which offered the same lesson. The pressure and intensity of the present chaos do not create a useful ambiance for thoughtful case planning, and the level of one specific case is in a sense moving too fast for a group of thirteen staff and trainees to keep up with; the pace must be slowed down. The case may, however, fly right out of the window of time into another treatment setting. This is a common experience in agency work, especially agencies that attend to crisis-prone populations, such as adolescents, domestic violence couples, and people with substance abuse problems.

Deep time in our social life is a metaphor for a pattern which is recurrent and operates automatically. Individuals have their character, organizations have their culture, and in both contexts the current experience often moves at a different pace and feels more immediate than character or cultural development. The intervention challenge is most complex in this situation because crucial influences on the present are out of view. There is no urgency in seeking solutions; one must patiently unravel the parts of individuals or social situations that need to surge forward from the knots that delay them.

The Case of the Reformed Mother Rooster

A man came in for a consultation about his company. About a decade prior to the consult he had begun to manufacture a craft item on a small scale. It was a unique product and slowly the business began to grow. He kept his hand in all steps of the manufacturing, marketing, shipping, etc. One ready way he experienced his "hands on" was in the kitchen, where people had their coffee breaks and socialized informally. He had originally loved this space. It was his place to set the atmosphere he liked in the company. He got to know his employees, and they clearly looked forward to their boss's making them coffee and being their "den mother." As the central person in the company, finally entitling himself as president, he had decided early on not to socialize outside work with his staff, but in the kitchen he could foster a closeness which he thought was key to the success of the manufacturing process. For many years he vigorously attended to the present and the future.

As (inevitably) began to happen, the company got beyond his ability to control individually. He hired more and more people, working completely on instinct about how to organize and structure his shop. By the time he sought consultation he had fifty employees who were organized loosely into several departments and had several factory sites within walking distance of each other. The organization of the business had lagged so far behind its expansiveness and success that he was no longer able to operate with a full sense of the future because he was so bogged down in the present with his "hands on" duties.

As he expanded, several things began to happen, especially around staff he hired to assist him. Since he felt reluctant to delegate clear jobs to them, they were constantly in his office asking for approval for doing this or that. He couldn't get work done. This all came to a head for him when he noticed his own growing hatred for the kitchen. He didn't want to socialize in that kitchen anymore. At first he had the urge to move it to another building so he didn't have to see it. He had to walk through the kitchen to get from his office to other parts of the building, and he began to feel trapped. Whenever he heard people laughing and having fun in the kitchen he was pleased they were enjoying themselves, but felt a distracting pressure to join them. They would expect him to join in and manage the kitchen activities. Between that and his floating assistants, he felt more like a "mother rooster" than a company president.

He felt trapped in his own (past) time perspective, which had become part of the company culture. The present experience was dominated by the past slowness of family life—the mother hen and her chicks working together in the cozy coop producing and reproducing and having fun together. As the enterprise grew, however, he found that facing the challenges of expansion involved more time away from the shop, more vigorous attention to future (such as the possibility of foreign manufacturing contracts, foreign markets, etc.). Whether or not this kind of expansion was a good thing, his sense was of his future being infringed upon. Direct recommendations as a consultant, such as clear delegations to assistants, were received as intrusive and as underplaying his ability to see the obvious, and made him anxious about the desertion of the past in the present culture. To suggest that this was a personal issue for him at present was received as overlooking the real management problems — an abandonment which left him unsure and nervous about finding a solution. A good number of both of these mistakes were made.

His situation was restated as follows: given the value of the atmosphere he had initiated many years ago and which laid the cornerstone of the company's success, he was understandably reluctant to give it up. He had also made the company grow successfully by attending to and anticipating future needs at every step of the way, and it was clear that only he could do this. Could he hold onto a vigorous future perspective since he had decided that he wanted the company to keep growing? It would have been a different situation were he comfortable with the current level of the company, but he wasn't. The question was posed: What in his current situation would bridge past with future?

What we worked toward in talking about this was directly teaching his "mother rooster" skills to others and making sure they were doing them correctly before he let them go. He began to hire department heads who were young and vigorous, and paid special attention to how they treated other employees. He greatly preferred promoting from within, so he felt secure that people had already been exposed to the culture. He took on the specter of the kitchen by establishing monthly potluck company lunches. He was able to bring his dish, spend a few minutes with everyone, then leave to his office. He became able to work behind a closed door and enjoy others' socializing without him.

Making the delegation in his own special way was the first sign of the future opening up. He spent more time hiring consultant specialists to do things like set up financial systems. He began to inquire into foreign manufacturing contracts. Probably the most telling switch was beginning to focus on expanding his personal horizons, striking out in new ways in his personal life, leaving day-to-day business to skilled employees. The movement here came after putting the time perspectives next to each other, adjusting the scale of the past, which had gotten overwhelmingly large and slow, so that it could fit with the expanding (indeed terrifying) future. Because of his personal style, this president could experience the company's dilemma inside himself. While there were different pieces of the time problem in different employees, as new managers (future) compared with original production workers (past), he could embody the two scales of time himself and articulate them without going off the deep end.

There is another compelling way of understanding time from this example. Holons have their own natural ebb and flow. The oldtimers in the company were moving along at a pace that had been established through the years and had a rhythm quite different from the newly hired go-getters, who were at different points in their careers and unrelated to the company's past. For this company president one way to break out of the constraints of the past was the very hiring of these new people, because it highlighted the different frequencies of movement. In ecological terms, the new people set up perturbations in the established culture that could be used to change it. It wouldn't be long before new employees became oldtimers, so the moment had to be seized.

The culture of the company was very slow moving. For this manager, it had all but stopped. As he faced the company's future, however, he wanted to accelerate his pace. To do so he had to disconnect from the sluggishness of the culture without wrecking it, since he could also see its value. Besides, it was too scary to risk destroying a culture which had obvious benefits. Small but secure bridges could liberate him as long as they respected and preserved the culture. His sense of what needed to be preserved was crucial; smooth transitions were essential.

CONCLUSION

In this chapter we have traversed the territory of time and looked at some nonlinear effects of time taken at varying extents and grains. We have also tried to point to some of the interactions between time and other dimensions taken up earlier in this journey over group landscape.

9. *Defensible Territory*

So MUCH OF WHAT BEFALLS us in the social world has little or nothing to do with us as individuals, only with the postures we show, only with the nature of the territory in question. For instance, there is a natural history of small teaching or therapy groups that runs its own course if we give it just a little help (Skynner, 1987; Yalom, 1975).[1]

First, everyone is anxious to be included and welcomes a calm, firm posture in the leader. Second, there is fight over who is more dominant and so the leader cannot avoid being tested. Leaders who can refrain from showing their necks or from being harsh will find themselves with comfortable groups that settle down into some comfortable hierarchy, as with dogs after some display of ferocity. Third, there is some unburdening, which will bring everyone closer if the leader can be friendly, easy, and even off-handed himself.

All too often leaders take all of this personally, so they are carried away when the group responds well to their posture, thinking they are loved as individuals. This is not likely to hold up! Then they take attack personally as well, when it is but the time for testing.

Who can accept that individual being is of so little importance in most affairs of our fellow men? We are shocked when a faculty member who seems important is hardly mentioned a week, a month or a year after leaving. Her vacated territory is much more important. In this respect, we are like the songbirds.[2] Most of us are "floaters," who range in the middle of a social situation, neither too big nor too small, ready to swoop into bigger places when vacated, ready to back into smaller places when necessary (Gustafson, 1987).

In any population there are more timid animals biding their time, and changed circumstances may yet give them a chance. This was shown in territorial songbirds that hotly contest territories with the most abundant resources. Males arrive early in the season and contend for space, singing both to warn off neighbors and landless rivals, and to attract females. That timid but fit male songbirds are being excluded from the breeding population was found in a gruesome shootout experiment that few scientists would conduct today. When resident territorial breeders were killed, new "floater" males promptly took over. Indeed, floaters arrived nearly as fast as the experimenter could create vacancies with his shotgun, which suggests that the population of disenfranchised timid males was very large, very watchful, or both. (Marks, 1987)

No doubt human "floating" has widely different origins from that of song-birds and is mediated by entirely different structures. The analogy troubles us, nevertheless.

Even more difficult to accept than this Darwinian perspective of pos-turing and territory is the martial metaphor[3] evoked to meet the needs of defense, such as in the following passage from Machiavelli:

Philopoemen, prince of the Achaei, among other praises bestowed on him by writ-ers, is lauded because in times of peace *he thought of nothing but methods of warfare*, and when he was in the country with his friends, he often stopped and asked them: If the enemy were on that hill and we found ourselves here with our army, which of us would have the advantage? How could we safely approach him maintain-ing our order? If we wished to retire, what ought we to do? If they retired, how should we follow them? And he put before them as they went along all the contingen-cies that might happen to an army, heard their opinion, gave his own, fortifying it by argument, so that thanks to these constant reflections there could never happen any incident when actually leading his armies *for which he was not prepared*. (1527, pp. 54–55, my italics)

Only the modern businessman lives like Philopoemen: When he is not strate-gizing, he is keeping fit at sports. Teachers, social workers and doctors generally dislike a martial metaphor like that of Philopoemen, as if they could ignore the modern contest. They prefer to be comforted and even lulled by the civility of art and science and help, until they are rudely pushed aside or much worse. I am counseling them to prepare for such armies to appear suddenly. Of course, this takes vigilance that I would rather not have to continue around the clock. The more internal spaces or compartments of play and of solitude with one's own being give this freshness for what Lampedusa calls the "indiscretion" of friendship.

We have to make some kind of trade-off between the virtues of vigilance and the virtues of indiscretion. The first unremitting makes for an overly harsh, if not paranoid, person. The second unrestrained makes for an easy mark. I propose that each is a suitable posture in its own fitting compart-ment, in its own depth. Much of wisdom is adopting the right postures for the right occasions (extremely important in a game like tennis, as most expert players know). We turn to the subject of different compartments, external to internal, in Chapter 11. For now let us assume that the martial metaphor has some advantages in the modern contest, even for the helping professional.

It not only has competitive advantages but is also enlivening. Left to their devices, people nowadays tend to pull back into very small segments, both geographically and personally, into what Tuan (1980) called "segmented worlds." Privacy has much to be said for it and gains continually in the ways we house, feed and entertain ourselves. But it can be isolating, dull, bureaucratic, and lacking in challenge. Everything can be settled, which is as close to being dead as we can arrange in this world. What pulls us fast out of such private holes is some shared emergency: "The town is burning! The enemy is upon us!" Children are very obvious about such thrills: they love a rotten fight (if they can manage it well) (Steig, 1984). Dull, one-dimensional adults can be more interesting when they've got to fight for themselves (if they can manage it well), discovering new sides of themselves, doubling in interest when upside down (Lobel, 1988). The bit player becomes a some-body in the fight of a lifetime (Conrad, 1897, 1900, 1912) (Melville, 1951): Commercial war can provide us with the best adventures.[4]

A successful captain has to know the different natures of the invading armies. I will delineate the most prevalent armies: the oblivious middlemen, the desperate troops of the weak, the occasionally overpowering squadrons of the most powerful. To defend himself well, our captain also must know his own nature, especially how his very strengths become weaknesses.

The fit of the military metaphor with social worlds is an experiment anyone may conduct for him or herself. For me, it clarifies many of the vicissitudes of marriage, friendship, seminars, departments, hospitals, uni-versities, and much larger terrain still. I am more apt to see when my soldierly friend falls away from me into his own campaign, when he even enlists me to agreements that hurt one of mine. I learn to place our little interactions on the larger fields in which they belong. We are but captains in different campaigns, who may ride in the same direction often, but not always.[5]

This outlook on the social terrain is not peculiar to just Machiavelli and myself, but will be found as well in many other modern writers, especially Nietzsche (1872, 1878), Gramsci (1957, 1973), Bourdieu (1977), and Foucault (1980), but most succinctly Foucault (1980, p. 90).[6]

. . . This reversal of Clausewitz's assertion that war is politics continued by other means . . . [the] hypothesis to the effect that power is war, a war continued by other means. . . . The role of political power . . . is perpetually to re-inscribe this relation through a form of unspoken warfare; to re-inscribe it in social institutions, in eco-nomic inequalities, in language, in the bodies themselves of each and every one of us.

If this hypothesis is a reliable guide to the modern world, then the "unspo-ken warfare" of everyday life is best construed as disguised warfare itself, and managed as such. For me, this means going over the fields of battle, first to read the lines along which attack will come, second to propose the terrain that is defensible. Once you discover that some sitting down with colleagues to supper is an occasion in an unspoken war, you may manage yourself accordingly.[7]

LINES OF ATTACK

Teenagers are thought to be mostly oblivious to all but their own preoccupations, so that we expect them to tune us in only as we are willing to be audiences for what they sing. So we may humor them, as it suits us. They sweep by, but we are usually untroubled by them when we do not let them corner us.

If we do not recognize that the vast array of peoples in the middle of life are only better disguised in their selective inattention (Sullivan, 1954, 1956; Gustafson, 1986), we are wide open to being walked in on from all sides by the armies of the oblivious. This is a very extensive subject. I hope the reader will exercise patience for the next several pages, for mastering the breadth of obliviousness is excellent preparation for daily life at all levels of modern society.

Most people in the middle of life have learned to pretend broad interests, while actually attending very narrowly to their control operations. Like trout, they are almost always facing upstream, in wait for the flies to touch the water. They will not leave this subject, although they are likely to pretend otherwise. Trouting works best when it is not broadly announced.

They can be dangerous in groups, because oblivious search parties trample over everything that is not their concern. In general, the modern world is a huge, loosely connected set of such search parties, controlling one or another boundary or distinction (Rice, 1969). This is crudely recognized by university faculties when it comes to promoting assistant professors to tenure. They advise their young colleagues to forget about everything except publishing papers in the "refereed journals" carrying the prestige of the field, saying, "Deans can't read, only count" (the number of papers in such places). This, indeed, is highly reliable advice, insofar as the young faculty member otherwise appears to be agreeable with students, patients and senior faculty. But it is misleading, in that it projects being oblivious to everything that young professor stands for (except his numbers) onto the deans when it is the chief characteristic of faculties altogether! They may never read the actual work of one another, almost never. By and large, they would gain very little by doing so for their own specialized niches.

But this group, perfect in its simplicity as a group controlling access to the privileges of professordom, is dangerous thereby to any worthwhile content or line of study or fertile tradition. It can be counted to pass on such traditions weakly, *only* insofar as the tradition augments local power.

I struggled for a year to bring on a younger colleague whom I believe will contribute mightily to the great and broad tradition of psychotherapy. His worth was granted by my opponents; it made no difference in their vote. His coming would weaken their hold on their territory.

A faculty of psychiatry is no different from any other controlling group in the enormous, oblivious middle of American civilization. In general, you don't notice them and they don't notice you, until you run afoul of some boundary they are controlling: if you go too fast on the highway; if your eyesight is not up to par at the drivers license bureau; if you build onto your house; if you do not pay your taxes, and so forth. Any such transgression makes you visible, but otherwise you are not.

This organization of power was carefully observed at the turn of the century, as follows:

The "objective" discharge of business primarily means a discharge of business according to *calculable rules* and "without regard for persons" (p. 215). . . . The more complicated and specialized modern culture becomes, the more its external supporting apparatus demands the personally detached and strictly "objective" *expert*, in lieu of the master of older social structures, who was moved by personal sympathy and favor, by grace and gratitude. (Gerth and Mills, 1946, p. 216)

In other words, bureaucratic organization is oblivious to persons, but also to all purposes, higher and lower, than present themselves. They simply do their assigned technical job, never seeing the persons or purposes that happen to cross their path. This is why the defender has to be ready for these monocular machines cutting a line right across his terrain every hour, every day, every week, for they are simply everywhere and will insist upon your reply and will find you acceptable or rejectable in terms that they alone will define. So you might want to pay attention to them!

They are what Foucault calls the "vehicles" of power. If you want to go anywhere, communicate with anyone, buy anything, study anything, you must meet their terms. They do not care who you are or what purpose you represent, so long as you have the correct sign for their apparatus. This is their surveillance, for the correct versus the incorrect.

Bureaucratization is no longer a sufficient term for this organization of power, which includes bureaucratization but moves outside the bounds of bureaus, companies, departments, and other formal modes of organization. Yes, there is the surveillance of all of these formal organizations. But notice how surveillance achieves a momentum of its own beyond the formal bounds, as Foucault explains, utilizing the example of "pastoral power":

And this implies that power of the pastoral type, which over centuries — for more than a millenium — had been linked to a defined religious institution, suddenly spread out into the whole social body. (Foucault, 1980, p. 215)

Nearly every social relation comes to involve a pastoral "concern" for the "individual," which means someone who will fit into the story line of the concerned party. This is a highly "disciplined" event in which:

. . . the operation of technical capacities, the game of communication, and the relationships of power are adjusted to one another *according to considered formulae, constitute* what one might call, enlarging a little the sense of the word, *disciplines.* . . . They also display different models of articulation, sometimes giving preeminence to power relations and obedience (as in those disciplines of a monastic or penitential type), sometimes to finalize activities (as in the disciplines of workshops or hospitals), sometimes to relationships of communication (as in the disciplines of apprenticeship), sometimes also to a saturation of the three types of relationship (as perhaps in military discipline, where a plethora of signs indicates, to the point of redundancy, tightly knit power relations calculated with care to produce a certain number of technical effects). (Foucault, 1980, p. 219) (my italics)

Thus, Foucault arrives at his term for the organization of power in the modern period: "disciplinary power." This will be the ordinary shape by which we can expect to be invaded: If the discipline involved finds us a threat to its "considered formulae," we will be attacked or dismissed. If we augment their story, we will be applauded and asked to join. If we do neither, we will be ignored altogether. Any author will be familiar with these three possibilities. This is why one's reviews are predictable in advance, depending on the discipline of the reviewer. But the same fate awaits us in the hands of the "disciplines" that come across our territory on any kind of business. It has almost nothing to do with us, and everything to do with them.

A final word on the oblivious concerns their longevity, which is not great:

Art . . . is often found "ahead of progress," ahead of *history, whose main instrument is* —should we not, once more, improve upon Marx—*precisely the cliché* [the "considered formulae of Foucault"]. . . . A political system, a form of social organization, is by definition a form of the past tense that aspires to impose itself upon the present (and often upon the future as well). The real danger for a writer is not so much the possibility (and often the certainty) of persecution on the part of the state, as it is the possibility of finding oneself mesmerized by the state's features, which, whether monstrous or undergoing changes for the better, are always temporary. (Brodsky, 1988b, p. 28) (my italics and reference to Foucault)

Since the main instrument of history is the cliché (the considered formula) and since the vehicles for these clichés (considered formulae) are individual beings, the chief danger for nearly everyone is emptiness, whose chief signal is boredom (and drug use). Who can retain enthusiasm for the cliché for very long? These careers do not last well. These are bored invaders, who will soon pass.

If I have spent so long on the nature of the armies of the oblivious, it is because they are everywhere and because careful attention to their methods will indicate very clear lines of defense. Before we reach to defense, let us briefly consider the other two kinds of armies, infrequently seen in the university world where I dwell but terrifying in their frequency in some streets in other parts of the world.

The armies of the desperate can be found in two conditions, either demoralized into complete disarray or making desperate comebacks. When they are in the latter mode, they can be extremely dangerous because they are unwilling to be stopped (fearing to fall back into their disarray). Depending upon the cause that organizes them, they may be helpful or harmful: helpful, probably, in Alcoholics Anonymous; helpful and harmful on the religious right; fully destructive in something like National Socialism in Germany.

I see a relatively harmless group of the desperately weak in the university world every year: these are the first-year residents, who are desperate about the distance between what they actually know and what they might know to do a good job. They tend to cycle from the edges of panic to conversion to some method they have just seen and then to contempt for some weakness that threatens to come back on themselves or others. Then back into panic, and all over again.

The squadrons of the great powers are not seen very often in the university world either. The hegemony of the disciplines will ordinarily do, to keep most of us in line, most of the time (Foucault, 1980; Gramsci, 1973). Only when departments are on the verge of falling apart, only when regimes are collapsing, do I see the meanest, crudest outbreaks of what is still only the killing of careers. No, there is one other occasion: matters of money and matters of recruitment will bring out our hatchet men for routine scapegoating. In contrast to the oblivious, these squadrons make highly personal attacks.[8]

The outcome of any campaign of (unspoken) war depends not only upon the nature of the invading army but also upon the nature of the defending army and then the way in which the attacking and defending armies come together. Before we tackle the subject of optimal engagement, I want to place my own army upon the field. Like most other armies, it is apt to be undone by its conceit. Its very strengths are its own undoing. My three favorite conceits are about being colorful, confident and generous. All of these get me in trouble on a regular basis.

I understand that other captains may prefer a discussion of other conceits, namely their own, for the purpose of discussing defensible terrain, but I only know my own well enough to be of any use.

In the segmented worlds of the disciplines, being colorful as a leader or group is usually trouble. A little is entertaining, but more than a little is risky, for it makes people feel insecure, envious, or stupid. The reverse is true with the overpowering. Sometimes you need to color up more than they or they will walk all over you; other times you should appear to have none at all, until they pass by.

Confidence is worse than color for arousing envy. Most who have it pretend not to have it among the oblivious. But for the desperately weak, you are nothing without confidence. They read the least falter, almost catching their breath when you catch yours.

Generosity is a great danger with all invading armies, for many, many reasons. One is that those whom are given to get rotten when little is asked of them in return. Two is that giving has its own physiology, where the more you give the more you need to get back (Skynner, 1983). You open yourself to being hurt. Three is that giving may get you to show some unguarded delight in what you bring forth. This invites injury.[9]

How then are we to locate defensible terrain for color, confidence and generosity? Where does it have its best chance to win the day, hold out and retreat when prudent? How do we defend against the chief lines of attack of the unending oblivious, the desperate, and the occasionally overpowering?

COUNTERPROPOSALS

The Armies of the Oblivious

Once you look at the world as (unspoken) war (by other means), you are better placed to accept that your fellow captains will be oblivious to your purposes, except insofar as they imply cooperation with or defection from their campaigns. For this they will be entirely alert. A very selective reading of yourself! How then are you to conduct your own campaigns in this darkness, to get as much help from them as possible and as little interference?

Fortunately, the game theorists have been working out the logic of these situations since the 1960s (Russett, 1983). The infamous game which has been most appealing as a paradigm is one imagined between two criminals "being held incommunicado in a police station after an armed robbery and murder have been committed. Each person is presented with a pair of unattractive options, and each is questioned separately and given a choice by police officials" (Russett, 1983, p. 100). Isn't it interesting that we can learn a great deal about negotiations with our fellow captains by thinking of us both as criminals held incommunicado by police! Being otherwise oblivious to one another could hardly be stated more baldly.

The "dilemma" propounded to the two "prisoners" by the police is the following:

I'm pretty sure that you two were responsible for the killing, but I don't quite have enough evidence to prove it. If you will confess first and testify against the other prisoner, I will see that you are set free without any penalty, and he will be sentenced to life imprisonment. On the other hand, I am making the same proposal to him, so if he confesses first, you will be the one to spend life in prison and he will go free. If you both confess on the same day, we will have a little mercy. But you will still be badly off, because you will both be sentenced to twenty years in prison for armed robbery. If you both want to be stubborn, we cannot convict you for a major crime, but we can punish you for a small crime you committed in the past — one that carried a one year prison term. If you want to take a chance that your fellow prisoner will keep quiet, go ahead. But if he doesn't — and you know what sort of criminal he is — you will do very badly. Think it over. (Russett, 1983, pp. 100–101)

The first urge of every player must be to defect and get off free! Go ahead — betray one's fellow thief to life in prison! The second surge of the mind is usually in the opposite direction, towards reconsideration: Oh, wait, he will have the very same urge to defect — we will both get twenty years! The usual third drift is towards contemplating cooperation: If we both cooperate, we only get one year each for small crimes of the past. The usual fourth reaction is again in the opposite direction: Oh no, if I cooperate, while he defects, I go to prison for life, while he gets off scot-free. Thus, the player comes full circle to his first urge to defect.

Many of us might go around these strange loops for a while, but most arrive at a strategy. Those cynical players who are determined not to be suckers will always defect, ensuring themselves of either freedom or twenty-year sentences. Those idealizing players who are determined to be coopera-tive will get either one-year terms when met by other cooperatives or life in prison when meeting the cynical. Such a life either way! The trade-offs are quite unhappy for both.

Fortunately, the game turns out very differently once it is no longer a single play, but reiterated. The latter is more like what we all see with fellow captains with whom we are obliged to live on a long-term basis, as in a department. We have many, many chances to cooperate with them or defect from them. Axelrod's tournaments of the Prisoner's Dilemma revealed a strategy much superior to cynicism or idealism:

Professor Robert Axelrod conducted a tournament among 13 social scientists to see whose computerized strategy for playing repeated prisoners' dilemma games would be most successful. Of all the strategies played, he found that *tit for tat* (cooperating after the opponent cooperated, defecting after a defection) was most successful, especially when *coupled* with *optimism* (opening with a cooperative move) and being somewhat *forgiving* (punishing once, then trying again to cooperate). (Russett, p. 111) (my italics)

When you have to live with fellow captains for a long time, through many episodes of possible alliance versus possible antagonism, be optimistic, rough and forgiving. Open in a friendly way and continue with friendliness when you meet cooperation. Punish decisively when let down. Forgive soon and be friendly again.

If I provide some unusual chances to see my work from behind a one-way mirror and get friendly discussion, I continue. If grousing starts, I stop, giving the responsibility for the next week's clinic back to the residents and fellows. Yet I forgive easily and resume my role.

If I provide a great deal for the department overall in bringing in a great teacher for a week, yet get no thanks, I simply take off from the Clinic for the next week. They respond right away (while never commenting), by taking more responsibility, bringing in new patients, suggesting new reading, etc.

If I get help back from my political allies in the department, I help them. If they let me down, I let them down sharply. Then I respond to their new friendly offer with my own friendliness.

Any reader who has brought up kids, especially teenagers, any reader who has stayed married for more than a few years, will be asking him or herself just now: "What is new? I have been doing this all along. I encourage my family. When one of them lets me down, I put my foot down right away. When they set the letdown aright, I resume my encouragement of them. I do not rely on words. I rely on these actions, which speak much louder."

What is new and different for me in the terrain outside my family is that I expect them to behave no better than my family. I suppose I have had that common illusion which one of my teachers (Reider, personal communication) called "positive paranoia": the idea that the world was out to help me. I am prone to think that rivals, colleagues, and students actually are of such a mind. Balint put this illusion a little differently, calling it "the depressive position":

. . . the patients leaving analysis before the depressive state could be resolved usually complain a lot, try to raise guilt feelings in their environment (and in their former analyst) by exhibiting and flaunting their shortcomings, but they hardly ever want to make real efforts towards a basic change. Apparently they cannot renounce their right to expect miraculous help from their environment. (1952, p. 256)

That Reider and Balint have seen this continually gives me comfort. I am not the only one. Red Auerbach, longtime coach of the Boston Celtics professional basketball team, also gives me comfort, for he has come to the very same conclusion in his own down-to-earth language. He said that a good coach knows whom to kiss and whom to kick (Leston Havens, personal communication). Actually, Red knows even better than that, which is *when* to kiss and *when* to kick. Listen to him:

Basketball ain't no democracy. A coach can talk a lot, even yell. All that matters is what is absorbed by the players. All I liked to say was, "We're uptight." [kick] I'd tell them that, then add [kiss] that was how I liked them. Then, I'd ask them to think about that other team. They're playing the Celtics. (1986)

Red would not expect athletes to understand him or even to help him. No, he would just be friendly when they did what he wanted. Decisive when they didn't. Forgive when they did again. With a few complicated, simultaneous moves like the one quoted just to make it interesting. After all, they catch on to you after a while. It is best not to be too predictable. They start taking you for granted. Surprise them. Then be your usual self again.

There are many cul de sacs in the social terrain where you cannot get people to notice what you want. One bad one appears innocuous to most people, who walk into it like sheep. This is the formal dinner party for six, with handcuffs at each place setting.

This is usually an unspoken contest. The hosts may have taken you prisoner for demonstrating their largesse. The other couple will thrash a little in their places, until they see the hopelessness of their situation. Then they join the hosts in tripping up anything that may interest you as a subject of conversation. You may kick and kiss all you like, but you will get nothing but kicks back. Often, a very warlike couple will declare war on their hosts and guests by showing enormous gusto about their mutual thrust. Sometimes, they blank out their poor hosts. I have seen such victories: in particular, a pair of determined monologists, or a pair of purveyors of gloom, can break the backs of the defenders. More often, the hosts plus guests overturn the thrust of these invaders so many times, by (smooth or accented or) abrupt transitions, that the barbarians finally tire and go home. Unfortunately, it is exhausting for all concerned, as the invaders keep having to restart their monologues, while the defenders have to keep undercutting them by changing the subject. Anybody else who attempts a fresh turn gets cut off (leveling of all is the price for subduing tyranny).

One way to reduce casualties is to counterpose: either a different get-together where there is more freedom of movement (such as going to a movie or cross-country skiing together) or that you can only come later, as for dessert. By that hour they all will be glad for relief and actually listen to you!

The Armies of the Desperate

If you must lead a desperate army, however small, you must arrange early success, and continuing challenge — if you do not want to be immersed in their misery with them, if you do not want to get their contempt.

I lead two ragtag outfits. The first is a group of medical students interviewing psychiatric patients. The second is a group of first-year residents in psychiatry reading about the psychopathology of everyday life. Both are rank beginners, up against the largest, most complicated problems, which can rout them at any moment.

How are we to set upon such dangerous foes? How can we even stay in the field? How retreat suddenly? The attack must be defensible, against the swiftness and sureness and overwhelming force of the counterattack that these patients will mount with their very difficult problems. My strategy is quite simple. It works about equally well for the two small armies.

First-year residents are similar to medical students except that they *think* they should know what they're doing. They hardly do. So when we read about depression, anxiety, obsessive-compulsive disorders, phobias, hysteria, and so forth, they are full of fear and anxiety — fear I will show them up; anxiety that they themselves cannot bear their own performances without thinking themselves worthless. This is trouble from both the external and internal critics (Havens, 1986).

How am I to lead this green troop into the field of psychopathology, which is so daunting that most of their teachers distance by means of relying upon psychopharmacology! First, I arrange an early victory. They will succeed in outlining the official portrait of the disorder of the day, portrayed in the bible of the profession. They also are better than I am on this score. Second, I offer a continuing challenge. They attempt to take their understanding of an essay against the complexities of the disorder of the day. They get so far — freshly! admirably! — until difficult questions set in. They frown. They get restless. They prepare to hit or run. Third, I come in with reinforcements and admiration. What a terrific question they are entertaining! How much they have understood! Let's see where they are stuck. So we rally to a success and leave the field.

But one, fourth, complication. They are uneasy as we wind down. How can they go back to those inpatient services "where we throw drugs at patients and stay as far away from them as possible"? They need help with the retreat. I say, "Oh my, you are quite right. I could be making your life much too difficult. Here you see you might understand these patients. Then you might try up there and get yourself in one trouble after another. You might get someone thinking you understand them, only they've got to leave you in a single week. You've got the next twenty years to get to understand people." I quite agree with them that their job is more to close out subjects of conversation than to open them.

The more experienced residents and fellows talk better, but this is not to be overestimated. Patients can back them into a corner and make them desperate every day. So can their teachers. Even their peers. So they are scared all too often. And they have better days. The challenge of leading this recently desperate sort of army is to know when the soldiers are in danger of losing all confidence. When they are in trouble, they are more than a little dangerous, because they resort to contempt. This is dangerous. Contempt makes its object feel "small," unless its object is adroit. Feeling "small" leaves a lasting wound (Sullivan, 1954). So they can really injure each other. And they do. They can really injure me. And they have.

Several measures defend the field of roving contempt. One is to see it coming from afar. This allows time to gather oneself. This is why residents and fellows coming out from behind a mirror are especially dangerous. The place back there is a kind of sewer for difficult, helpless, hostile feelings. Everything the patient dissociates from his or her narrative builds back there. Everything successful can build envy back there. I and the patient dance freely together, while they are going nuts having to watch. Who wouldn't!

So around the corner they come into the room to discuss the interview before I know what they are going to slam me with. In such situations just expect trouble. Gather yourself.

They are just as dangerous when they have seen an amazing guest or read a great essay. They find some weakness in the guest or the essay with unerring accuracy. This critical insight may be a truly independent discovery, but it can take over the field, dismissing the guest or essay altogether. Contempt mounts as it is shared. This drives a few among them to back the disqualified work. Since this looks like currying favor with the teacher, it only drives the contempt of the independent. The recently desperate struggle so hard to keep their own heads above water that they are obliged to drown visitors who could make them feel inferior. Just like the faculty.

So you mustn't allow them to go on, if you can get in their way. How to do this? Without losing your temper! Leveling gets worse when you get defensive of something of so-called importance. Not even currying of favor will come to your defense. If you do not remain a gentleman, you are in big trouble.[10]

But there is a way forward, right into the teeth of this enemy. Only it takes three sudden turns in quick succession. It relies on taking them by surprise.

First you join them against their feared, hated, threatening object (even though you love that object as dearly as yourself!). You have to join them to shake them. Yes, the object has faults. Secondly, you turn it from contempt to skepticism. Wouldn't anyone be skeptical! Havens is the master of the first two turns:

. . . contempt is a difficult attitude to share, especially when it is directed at you. The empathic task becomes easier if the contempt is aimed at outsiders. This last can be utilized psychotherapeutically once the therapist acknowledges and puts outside himself a characteristic of himself or his profession that sane people would regard with skepticism. Skepticism, in turn, has many uses and is readily preferred to contempt as hopefulness is to overestimation. Now we are on our way. The possibility of empathy with skepticism is in place. The therapist should be able to identify something about his professional work which evokes skepticism (such as being paid royally for listening). It only remains to pick up these two points and give them a slight proverbial shaking. . . . "God heals and the doctor takes the fee". . . . (1986, p. 114)

When you share their skepticism, they are likely to drop the subject. "Oh no, let's not stop here!" I insist. I take the third turn: "In our skepticism, what *could* we be missing which could help us?" Now they will ride with me hard in the reverse direction from which they came at me!

Here is how it went when they read one of the most useful essays in the last hundred years on how to work with dreams, Jung's "Dream Analysis in Its Practical Application" (1933) — which they found greatly wanting.

Unerringly, they went straight for its weakest place. Although Jung argues for the dream as a *complement* to the waking perspective, as the night watch which sees what is missed by the day watch (and the day is the complement to the night, conversely), he still proclaims the dream to many of the patients in the essay as truth:

The dream gives a true picture of the subjective state, while the conscious mind denies that this state exists, or recognizes it only grudgingly . . . but simply tells how the matter stands. . . . The patient must be prevented from going full speed ahead . . . (p. 4)

Without any hesitation whatsoever, I joined them in their criticism. But I wasn't sharing contempt of him. I shared skepticism of someone who tells patients the truth that *he* divines, which they have missed. Yet I insisted they did not go *far enough* in their skepticism. Concerning the man dreaming of a train going out of the station full throttle on an S-shaped curve, Jung may have driven him to run violently off the track of his career. Telling a stubborn German Swiss the night truth of his dream that he *has* to halt often gets him to steam ahead even worse. Concerning the man who dreamt of such elation that he could mount right up into space off a mountain top, Jung may have driven him to fall to his very death. Telling him never to go alone hiking again may have determined him to climb even more wildly! The man stepped out into the air one day, dashing himself and his friend off a cliff to pieces far below. He may have wanted to show this Jung that his day watch was better than Jung's night watch. The students are not skeptical *enough* of this fellow Jung. Telling people the night truth missed by their day truth is like everything else in psychiatry: half right. Half the patients it may have helped. The other half it may have worsened!

Now I could take the third turn, as they were entirely prepared to drop their Jung essays on the floor, dismissed, forgotten, and go home and do something worthwhile. "Hold on," I said, "Now about this trio of dreams about a woman crossing a frontier the night before seeing her first, second and third psychoanalyst . . . of course, the night truth Jung propounds for the first, second and third are just possibilities. Let us suppose you were one of these doctors. Your patient is telling you something as she walks into your office about her experience of crossing boundaries into another country in her dream of the night before. How do you proceed?"

I could not believe it. Several of those most vehement about Jung's dogmatic weakness had *never once* analysed a dream! They hardly even knew how to begin! I was floored. If they had been able to keep up their contempt of Jung, we would never have gotten to their desperate weakness in the face of patients coming to meet them with a dream. And so we set down to work. Now they were eager to be helped.

There was a final, fourth turn in this story of roving contempt. With five minutes left in our afternoon, one of them said to me, "Yes, but . . . (I said, "Go on, please."). What if the patient says to me, 'I want to tell you, doctor, about a vivid dream I had last night, but it probably means nothing. Do you really believe in dreams? Are you one of those Freudians?' The patient sneers." God, I thought, they are *most* afraid of the contempt of their patients for themselves! Now they were asking me to help them defend themselves against what they had inflicted on Jung (me). They feared to be made utter fools of if they professed to believe in something important. So I decided to come to their defense.

I said, "Oh terrific. Let's tackle this. You play the patient (we've got less than five minutes left). I'll play you. . . . So the patient comes in and says what?" "The patient, me, says: 'You see, doctor, I've got this performance anxiety . . . when I go to the piano, I cannot play. Now I had this vivid dream about it last night. But it probably means nothing. Do you really believe in dreams? Are you one of those Freudians?' Sneer." (Aside to audience I say: "Oh my, this patient dreads to perform. Am I such a fool as to drag him to the piano? to the dream?" "Could this dream be important?" (Aside to audience (Sullivan, 1954): "Some patients expect the psychiatrist to be a perfect genius or a perfect ass").

My reply: "Could this dream be important? Oh my, I hope so. Otherwise, I am in the wrong profession!" And so they all burst out laughing. . . . "and so would you like to discuss it?" "Yes, I think so." "All right, we can begin by your telling me what you were doing yesterday and last night, before you went to sleep." And so the work was defended from an army of the recently, desperately weak.

The Armies of the "Overpowering"

I wouldn't have much of a chance fighting for Jung's dream work in an open field of the entire department's monthly case conference. My colleagues would not think much of the essay, preferring their own superior knowledge. I would be outnumbered. We are nothing if not prudent in gauging strength arrayed against us. Not just the nature of the force, but its magnitude. Machiavelli notes this, like most everything else, as an opportunity:

. . . I think it may be true that fortune is the ruler of half our actions, but that she allows the other half or thereabouts to be governed by us. I would compare her to an impetuous river that, when turbulent, inundates the plains, casts down trees and buildings, removes earth from this side and places it on the other; everyone flees before it, and everything yields to its fury without being able to oppose it; and yet though it is of such a kind, still when it is quiet, men can make provisions against it by dikes and banks, so that when it rises it will either go into a canal or its rush will not be so wild and dangerous. So it is with fortune, which shows her power where no measures have been made to hold her. (p. 91)

There is little standing room in the conference to build *any* barrier against contempt.

Where the tyranny of the majority (Madison, 1787; Vonnegut, 1961) is in full force, daily, weekly, year in and year out, you must stay out of the way. Skillful minorities in danger of persecution have always known about living behind a dike while riding the turbulent river in company with the most unlikely and unsteady allies. Sit in the middle of the boat. Push sharply back when shoved towards the edge. Occupy the center. As Galbraith (1986) put the matter, "Remember that you speak for the great majority" (which is also excluded from power). If a junior faculty member or resident presents, I can come to his or her defense against all-knowing senior faculty—and get the crowd on our side. But it would be unwise to present there myself, since everyone would get a say on the weaknesses of my work before I got a chance to reply. Only in a lecture can I prevail against such odds, because I can take on questions one at a time.

Sometimes you do wrong to occupy the center, for the center is evil. To go along or to be silent is to abet it. Archbishop Tutu (1988) discussed a strategy against such an overwhelming evil as apartheid in his own country. The gist of what he said was that Christianity could overthrow such a regime, because it professes that God is in every man, woman and child. You wrong God Himself when you debase his tabernacle, which is every person.

Tutu builds a moral world showing how far off center the apartheid regime has gone. A militant church helps him. Sometimes, however, one is so alone and outnumbered that it will take more than the evoking of a better world, as Brodsky wrote:

Let me remind you that we are not talking here about a situation involving a fair fight. We are talking about situations where one finds oneself in a hopelessly inferior position from the very outset, where one has no chance of fighting back, where the odds are overwhelmingly against one. In other words, we are talking about the very dark hours in one's life, when one's senses of moral superiority over the enemy offers no solace, when this enemy is too far gone to be shamed or made nostalgic for abandoned scruples, when one has at one's disposal only one's face, coat, cloak and a pair of feet that are still capable of walking a mile or two. (1986, p. 390)

Brodsky tells about a prison situation in northern Russia, where the guards challenged the exhausted prisoners to a contest to chop the amassed lumber in the prison yard. While most of the guards stopped early, the prisoners soon after, this man kept a rhythm of his own right into the evening until he staggered to bed. Brodsky tells us that this is Biblical strategy, not just the first line of the famous triad:

> but whomsoever shall smite thee on thy right cheek
> turn to him the other also

but continuing without either period or comma

> And if any man will sue thee at the law, and take
> away thy coat, let him have thy cloak also.

> And whosoever shall compel thee to go a mile, go
> with him twain.

Brodsky summarizes the lesson for unseating the armies of the overpowering:

Quoted in full, these verses have in fact very little to do with nonviolent or passive resistance, with the principles of not responding in kind and returning good for evil. The meaning of these lines is anything but passive, for it suggests that evil can be made absurd through excess; it suggests rendering evil absurd through *dwarfing its demands with the volume of your compliance, which devalues the harm. This sort of thing puts a victim into a very active position, into the position of a mental aggressor*. The victory that is possible here is not a moral but an existential one. The other cheek here sets in motion not the enemy's sense of guilt (which he is perfectly capable of quelling) but *exposes his senses and faculties to the meaninglessness of the whole enterprise*: the way every form of mass production does. (p. 389) (my italics)[11]

I recall a minor but more familiar incident showing how to make evil absurd in the ordinary life of professors. A friend in another university told me how his opponent had misreported the judgment of the most eminent man in the field about the work of his assistant, which would be tantamount to getting his assistant dismissed. Confirming the misreport with the famous man over the telephone, he then thanked the opponent in the next meeting for drawing the most qualified person in the country into the discussion: His letter would arrive the next day to give his recommendation in black and white. Not only was evil exposed but the colleagues of the opponent were deprived of the opportunity to come to his defense. If my friend had attacked him for his evil act, his faction would have gotten hot.[12] This way my friend was saying that his reporting colleague was really helping them all out by his misreport, by helping the report to be spelled out exactly.[13]

But with all the prudence in the world, huge troubles can get to you. I am thinking of the experiment we did of showing Helen Caldicott's grand rounds on the subject of nuclear war, where she compared the world to a patient in mortal danger. We showed a videotape of this terrifying speech to two groups of interested people, who then had our services for three periods of an hour and a half to discuss their responses. They were mostly stunned, demoralized, and anxious for the groups to be over. At the time, I felt very little, except helpless to do much about the groups. Behind the mirror, once, I felt like I was in the cockpit of a B-52 looking down on the poor world, even a little gleeful that Lowell was down there in his group. A warrior glad (just then) he was not a victim (Gustafson, unpublished [a]).

Lowell and I talked between groups, but this didn't help either of us to be of use to the groups, although it may have allowed us to go on at all. Perhaps a year later, I took an edited tape of this work to London to show it to some colleagues at the Grubb Institute. They were not impressed. This started some hurt going in me, for I thought we deserved some applause for our courage, if not for our performances.

It was not, however, until Barry Palmer and Bruce Reed kindly took me out to supper, afterwards, that I burst out with my grief for the world lost. They fathered me just enough, so that I finally let go of what I had carried around about that group for an entire year. In war, you may only drop your chin when you are fully away from the field of battle, in very reliable hands. I think I scared them, however. They didn't write me for years. I see why wounded soldiers have to be extremely careful back in so-called civilization, telling about their experience of being overpowered. Who wants to know? They can tell their story only if they do not overrun their listeners. Brevity is important. So are tact and understatement.

Brodsky (1988b) is right about the place of retreat that is our solace, in flight from the armies of the overpowering:

One of literature's merits is precisely that it helps to make the time of his existence more specific, to distinguish himself from the crowd of his predecessors as well as his like numbers, to avoid tautology—that is, the fate otherwise known by the honorific term "victim of history" . . . history, whose main instrument is—should we not, once more, improve upon Marx—precisely the cliché. . . . (p. 28).

. . . the book . . . is a means of transportation through the space of experience, at the speed of a turning page. This movement, like every movement, becomes flight from the common denominator, . . . flight in the direction of the "uncommon visage," in the direction of the numerator, in the direction of autonomy, in the direction of privacy. . . . Otherwise, what lies ahead is the past—the political one, first of all, with all its mass police entertainment. (p. 29)

In language is our home, our lines of retreat which suddenly throw open doors for us. John Bayley follows the blinded Gloucester, led by his son Edgar disguised as a fool, up Dover Cliff, where they just soar out over that occasion:

Edgar apes a cheerful working-man's relish in the way things are. In the midst of tragedy we briefly glimpse the daily round of hazard and accident—fires, floods, falling off ladders—and with Edgar we rise to the pointless occasion of them. . . . And we have got there at least, to the cliff's edge, for whatever purpose . . . But there is no purpose, only the sudden sense of freedom and exhilaration. . . . (1981, p. 8)

Delight in oneself as an individual, local being in literature and in nature not only puts the armies of the overpowering behind us, but equally well the armies of the oblivious and the armies of the desperate. It is well for us to follow our own songlines (Chatwin, 1989) as much as we can and stay out of the clutches of armies of all kinds! We need to mingle in them, skillfully, to secure our own territory, but not too much.

PART VI

Complex Counterposing

10. *Changing and Staying the Same*

LIFE SOMETIMES SEEMS besieged with daily floods and high winds; there is more change than one wants or can control. At the same time, some randomness is useful; it can upset and revitalize rigid and outmoded traditions. On the other hand, certain traditions are worth defending. How then are we to have transformation and tradition complement each other? Being devoted to transformation can trigger efforts to hold the line, and attempts to stay the same can lead to surprising transformations. Bateson (1979) discussed this problem in relation to the University of California during one period of its history. Parts of the system that should have been conserved were tampered with, while other structures were protected without regard for their obsolescence.

What changes should we resist? What traditions are to be defended? Looking from the other side, how do we correct for obsolescence without the fear that coherence will be lost? Bateson argues for a platform; he calls it a perspective about perspectives.

What we need is a strategy that protects us from the foolishness of transformative invasions and holds onto valuable traditions. On the other hand, being sealed off from transformations and only holding on can also be deadly and so it is useful to have a strategy for "airing out" sealed chambers of tradition.

TRADITION RESPECTED AND PROTECTED

One of Bateson's operating principles is "to bring to the reader's attention . . . two or more information sources . . . to give information of a sort different from what was in either source separately. . . . The evolutionary process must depend upon such double increments of information" (1979, p. 22). He called this process double description, a conceptual platform from which to introduce new points of view into a system.

Following Bateson through a biological metaphor clarifies the time dimension of tradition. He makes the point that the somatic/genetic aspects of our lives require a long-term reckoning and represent a very conservative tradition which stands apart from environmental learning. The environment, on the other hand, is relatively faster moving and requires shorter time reckoning from the individual. Our chromosomes, however, are protected from the environment; their own pacing can be maintained. Tradition can be purified and refreshed by chromosomal changes over long sweeps of time, changes which keep biological creatures related to their outside environment. But these changes in tradition will not affect any member of a species in his or her own life time.

Tuan (1980) speaks passionately against a historical trend towards segmentation in many areas of our lives. While pointing out this drift in some quarters, he also notes how we have been countering this notion of how life should be lived, with its emphasis on individualism and privacy, with communal and connective moves, what he refers to as integration. He doesn't refer to tradition as such, but talks more about discovering or rediscovering constancies in experience: return to nature, social wholes of utopian or egalitarian communities, and activities or places that endure over long periods of time. There are many dichotomies here: freedom/constraint, individual/group, individual/community, rural/urban, enduring/short-term, and others; Tuan's platform is the constancy of lasting social connectedness as a solution to the transformative segmentation of everyday modern life. Tuan extends Bateson's biology to our social life.

Literature abounds with stories of what one risks in making extreme choices that are anti-tradition and pro-transformation. In spite of our worship of the plastic culture, our emphasis on faddish connections with an environment built to be obsolete, some strong moral fiber warns against this trend. Howell's "The Rise of Silas Lapham" (written in 1885) continues to be part of some high school and college curricula as it was 30 years ago. This is a moral tale about a dreadful reversal in a narrow, transformative, short-term perspective. Lapham was a good man, moral in many ways, a decent husband and loving father. But his business dealings were another matter. "Happy is the man forever after who can choose the ideal, the unselfish part" (1963, p. 47); when it came to money matters, he lost sight of his ideals. He pursued luxury and social status, turning his back on his own moral traditions. His social ambitions were thwarted, however, and when he suffered major material reversals life was without coherence. In spite of the opportunity to return to his rural home, he was a broken and lost man. This very moral tale ends with Lapham being redeemed through admission of his errors and reconnection with his old traditions. It was no doubt comforting 100 years ago to be in a world in which one could reverse the tide of transformation and restore oneself through timeless traditions. In this respect modern life seems increasingly cruel, as the transformative thrust threatens to obliterate some traditions altogether.

Social systems are not as well protected as genes. Tradition deteriorates more quickly and can be interpenetrated more easily by environment. Aspects of American life, for instance, seem prone to obsolescence, anti-traditionality. Objects are not made to last; improvements are for the short-term (Forrester, 1971). One quintessential American problem, seen in groups and organizations, is the loss of constancies that should be defended against meaningless, continuous revision. For instance, even in religious life shifts are as rapid as the development of media and marketing. One aspect of the crisis in higher education is the active moving away from a broad-based humanities and science education toward packaged units appealing to smaller and smaller trade interests. Since there is nothing inherent in the social system to protect the tradition, system coherence can be pierced by environment on the one hand and dominant forces of accommodation from within on the other.

A very common way of using tradition, along with securing connection with the environment, is as a force of self-protection against an invasive common antagonist. Freestanding professional training schools in psychology provide a good example of the vulnerability of social forms to transformative invasions. For instance, the graduate tradition is rooted in the academic pursuit of a broad-based understanding of how the mind works. While there has always been considerable debate about the balance of research, teaching, and applied components of the training, the university provided some protection from the immediacies of the marketplace. While the balance is often an uneasy one, various elements of the field most often coexist, if not prosper.

The private, freestanding institution must attend to the marketplace. It must attract students, whose tuition pays the bills. The institution must attend to public image — how to attract an adequate number of students in a competitive market. The traditions of the field must yield to fast changing forces in the environment and to students who say, "If you want me to pay large sums of money to get your training, I want some clear promise of a job. Can you prepare me?" Well, academic traditions are protected; they can't directly answer questions of employment. Consequently, programs must be focused and packaged to address much more immediate needs; they often become obsolete quite quickly, when a reading of the environment says that the jobs have dried up, or a new vein seems richer. The complicated part of this debate is that the logic of it is valid. It is really true that the training culture demands the protean institution, with the character of an amoeba, because at the level of future survival in the guild, applicants need the packaging. The school is accurately reading its environment and would doubtlessly go under if it ignored the demands of the marketplace. Where is a platform on this dilemma, when it is clear that to defend tradition is to go down with pride — but dead nonetheless?

How is one to detach from the local levels of the two perspectives to see issues of overarching importance? In fact, faculty and administration are able to keep a grasp on some issues. There are attempts, for instance, to develop structures for quality control of aspects of applied (skills) training, to test for some mastery of a large body of technical knowledge. But these structures are vulnerable to pressures, and it is very difficult to let a student go; exams and minimal levels can become lower hurdles over time. Students have their lawyers in the wings, *making sure* they get their fair share for their substantial financial investment. Double descriptions posing the enduring aspects of curriculum and applied training against the responsiveness to environment are a part of the continuous steering tension.

A couple of points are noteworthy. First, a functional platform must encompass both sides of the debate; it must be aware of the double description of the given situation, appreciative of both sides. The strength of the tradition is best seen in the context of proposed alternatives.

Secondly, looking for the constancies in the larger professional environment — the enduring aspects of the culture — gives the institution some way of standing against the invasion and its ephemeral pressures. This point of view keeps one looking through windows onto the outside world and at details within. In other words, it is important to stay connected to the ecology during the debate. It immediately inclines one to a longer and wider perspective. In the school example, the ecology consisted of both the student constituency and the larger professional community of practitioners, academics, health service providers, etc. The ecological perspective enhances odds of success in searching for deeper constancies.

Thirdly, getting to a platform must be encouraged by participants who represent both sides of the debate: people who are interested in seeing the training as part of the fabric of a larger environment and those who will resist being captured by the merely transformative.

The platform is vulnerable, if for no other reason than the people on it are both the developers and carriers of tradition when wearing one hat and the transformers when wearing another. They are vulnerable to the outer world of pressures, student demands, and an important desire to stay connected with a more conservative tradition.

Counterposing is an immediately useful strategy for the survival of an institution in the face of tradition-transformation struggle. At a member level, counterposing also helps support individuals' morale as the institution goes off into deadening resistance or whirling transformations. While it is possible to be in the center of the debate, arguing one side or the other, one might decide defeat is too likely and demoralizing. Stepping back, one can counterpose one's own position to the position in the debate.

My own temptation, for instance, is to be intolerant of institutional mindless insularity or overzealous transformativeness. But if I can counterpose with my own position, I feel and stay connected. If I am heard, I feel validated. Insisting on change as a condition for staying connected is not essential. Even in the fight for change, I have a better chance of surviving if I can counterpose my own, controllable turf. Defining and holding a turf, I can expand to fill it as I challenge neighboring territories. As a faculty member, the classroom, not the total institution or the field (of psychology) as a whole, is my immediate domain of effectiveness. I must find a level for counterposing which is within a controllable domain, where movement is possible for me as an individual.

On Others' Turf

As an outside intervener I am drawn into many different territories of an organization, but always to defend *both* transformation and tradition.

The following example is an ensemble of proposals and counterproposals drawing together a consultation in many parts over many years. The central actor in this drama was an administrator driven to change his institution as quickly as possible. Some people weren't like him; they were slower moving. Rather than risk his own morale by slowing down, he hired consultants to do the slow work for him, thereby protecting his own morale *and* the morale of subordinates. The experience, however, was a bit like being a Keystone Kop. It is a story of small and large oscillations, of attempts to make adaptive changes in some parts of the structure while holding large constancies. It was an especially good lesson in a simple truth: One must connect with the part of the organization offered and work within that part to do whatever is possible. If one has larger horizons, the future is open, but the present can only be what it is. When the fluctuations are rapid, one must hold on tight to stay with the ride.

It was even difficult at times to decide who the client was. I met the professional administrator running this medical clinic when he was trying to expand the services offered by the clinic and wanted consultation about how to design the expansion. The expansion never occurred, but the meeting set up an interesting tension. The administrator was very enthusiastic about change and new program implementation; I felt more cautious and thought that certain areas of planning should be pursued first. We agreed, but then various events in the clinic blocked the program, we stopped meeting, and soon afterwards the administrator moved on to run a large, regional health services organization with many service sites.

Months later, he called. Again he wanted to change a particular unit; although the morale was horrible, he saw this as a golden opportunity because the unit leadership was undergoing dramatic change. Again, he was for rapid transformations in a system that was notoriously ossified. I took on the project of the subunit, analyzed the situation, and submitted a long report (as requested) detailing a program of change, especially leadership development, requiring considerable time. I was very modest about how quickly I would suggest moving. This process took several weeks, during which the staff was somewhat heartened by the attention and some small suggestions I made for clarity, such as job descriptions for a couple of crucial positions.

The proposal was received warmly, but again, circumstances intervened to prevent long-term programming from getting going. The administrator, very vigorous about change, got engrossed in several major political battles, and it wasn't until many months had again passed that he called me for more work. If any gain could be said to have come out of the subunit work, it was in lifting morale and supporting the hard work of some dedicated bureaucrats. Some clarity and learning about meeting management, unit goals, and conflict management had been accomplished within the allotted time. A larger direction was mapped, but the work actually done was smaller, preparing people to work together into their collective future.

He called again. This time he said that he wanted to deposit his assistant and righthand person in my office so she could work on certain issues, and change (read, change *quickly*), so he could count on her to support him in his push for change. He was not averse to veiled threats under pressure, and he made it clear in no uncertain terms that he wanted her to change, become more commanding and capable of representing him as strongly as he saw himself. It was easy to imagine why the two of them were at odds. The more demanding he got, the more cautious and anxious she became. His request was (not surprisingly) one for transformation. They had been working together for several years but, as the institution was now entering a period of particularly hard political haggling, she needed to be more assertive. It was quite clear that he wanted her to be there as his right hand, but with some changes.

When I met with her and posed some questions about changing or remaining the same, she was clear about wanting to change in some specific areas. From her point of view, she and her boss were tuned into similar areas, and as he began to move out more and give her more autonomy, she was able to feel empowered to move in directions they both desired. Basic tradition was maintained, but adaptive transformations were permitted and encouraged. We agreed that our contract was not a psychotherapeutic one, standing against the personal intensity of her boss's attack. We were able to connect around some areas where she wanted to change, to take command of her role more autonomously. She felt stronger, and he felt he had a better partner.

Another chapter began several months after this one. It must occur to the reader (as did to me) that I was being integrated into the tradition *and* the change process in this organization. This time, the assistant director called. It seems she had hired a new program chief from within the ranks and wanted to use me to provide him with essentially inservice training on management. He had been very competent in his former line staff job but hadn't been able to find his ground as an administrator. This new employee was very much in agreement about changes to be made, but he needed some other way of thinking about his administrative work because he was walking around former peers, feeling on the spot, watched, and generally uncomfortable. This complement — supervisor-subordinate — became the central working metaphor for looking at his position, others' reactions, and how to think about what the new job entailed. There were very specific ways in which he would have to take charge. The efforts at transformation stayed quite close to what was a constant for him, his relationships with former peers and his desire to get the job done. While the position he was promoted into was a new one, the larger organization was working within its own structures; I was expected to appreciate pacing differences wherever they appeared.

I could accept the role of transformer only under the condition that I adhere to my own pacing. So while I could embody the central spirit of change, an opposing current which slowed it down added balance to the organization. When the forces of transformation are fast, as social influences can sometimes be, there isn't time to evaluate what should be retained and what should be discarded. Paradoxically, systems can be anti-adaptive and keep the unuseful traditions while throwing out their creativity. Connecting with the situation on its own terms may offer the possibility of a platform for evaluating constancies. Change may or may not be possible, but it is crucial for us as individuals to have our own bearings.

"RESIGHTING" TRADITION

What about change of dysfunctional traditions (from family patterns to groupthink)? Is counterposing useful when taking on traditions that are so entrenched as to be outside awareness/control of group members and blind to the current of group life? One line of argument is that change is inevitable if the counterproposal connects the group to a new context—as with the therapy endeavor (de Shazer, 1985). At another level counterposing is at the base of "resighting" tradition, opening it to possibilities of time and space of which it had lost track (Havens, 1988). It can be a tactical move in a strategy of "purification" of tradition; randomness is introduced.

When the curtains are drawn around tradition and there is nothing but darkness and being stifled, fresh moves are not possible and the system just dies on its feet. Such a death stirs radical solutions. Borges suggests in fiction the possibility of introducing "the lottery in Babylon" in the form of randomness—so much chance that "one abominably insinuates that . . . the sacred disorder of our lives is purely hereditary, traditional. . . . Babylon is nothing else than an infinite game of chance" (1962, p. 35).

Sometimes family and group traditions can have such a long time reckoning that they operate unseen, the roots hidden in past generations but exacting prices from living progeny. Selvini Palazzoli et al. (1978) tell a story about this with the Casanti family. The family myth was "one for all and all for one." It had survived three generations, two world wars, and the move of the family from a rural to an urban setting and business. The authors note that the myth represented a "detachment of the group from reality" to a "pathological" extent. The family was blind to the changes in its environment as the changes affected the myth. While individuals within the family had had some difficulties participating in the myth, these difficulties had been contained. It wasn't until anorectic death threatened one of the family youngsters that treatment was sought—a major admission of the outside world.

The power of the myth was frighteningly unveiled when soon after the termination of a "successful" treatment the recovered anorectic almost killed herself. It was revealed that the family had been against treatment, and the *status quo ante* had been restored. The curative interaction finally involved a family ritual which "united the participants in a powerful collective experience" (1988, p. 283). The prescription involved special kinds of family interactions that both challenged the myth and capitalized on aspects of it.

The myth was almost killing people. Tradition was being guarded by family members who were clannish and hateful of outside meddling of all sorts, while the victimized member who was ill and needed help represented the desperate need for change. The perspective which made the ritual possible was one which encompassed the whole system under the power of the myth. The myth itself, with all its destructive force, couldn't be attacked directly. The ritual arranged the platform. Enactment within careful rules and regulations drew both factions of the family together in a third pattern which, paradoxically, challenged the myth. The curative interaction occurred at "secret" dinner meetings which excluded the outside world but included the suicidal Nora as a full-fledged member. The myth was "aired out" by the ritual expression of feelings in the nuclear family members about the extended family.

The proposal in this situation was the family's presentation that, while there was one sick member, this was a family that believed "one for all and all for one." This myth could not be attacked directly, nor could the sick individual be cured, because that would mean acknowledging a possible flaw in the myth. The counterproposal was embodied in a ritual of specific instructions about conversations in which the individuals would tell each other what they felt and observed regarding other clan members. The counterproposal was the therapy team's belief that there *could* be critical family interactions (directed by outsiders) which wouldn't destroy extended family cohesiveness, and that the sick family member *could* be reaccepted back into the nuclear family.

The counterproposal wasn't the cure, but it laid the conceptual basis for the ritual platform. In other words, realizing the myth, appreciating the basis of the family unity and what was required to maintain it, opened the door for the paradox. Finding the right level with which to stay connected won the cooperation of a basically xenophobic family. The intervention "aired out" the myth, i.e., secured in the present and future what had been a family captured (if not imprisoned) by their past. Nuclear family members discovered they could (together) be secretly critical of the clan without destroying the family unity. Family coherence gained more current meaning. A transformation (Nora's cure with the revitalized, critical nuclear family) could occur within the tradition (the clan which had to appear to stay the same).

Sometimes finding the right double description of a situation takes some trial and error, clinical experimentation. Their initial anti-myth stance seemed to win a partial victory, but the family regrouped and returned to zero with a vengeance. The therapy team had unwittingly triggered a complementary process in which the solution eventually became a problem (Watzlawick, Weakland, and Fisch, 1974). It was useful to realize that there was some experimentation here in the search for the right level of counterproposal to the family presentation. There is no magic about it; in fact, a congenial level of double description often involves an interactional search. What Watzlawick, Weakland, and Fisch emphasize, which is implicit in Selvini Palazzoli's work, is that seeing the other's situation accurately *as it is* can possibly lead to change. Whether or not such accuracy promotes change directly in any particular stance, it is a necessary condition.

Family and group traditions operate with variety and power. At crucial transitions, the weight of a family tradition becomes obvious. For instance, when children begin to leave home the parents, after 25 or so years of family life, have to find a way of rewriting their relationship to account for being a dyad with grown-up children. If this task weighs too heavily, they could well enter the consulting office with a child unable to leave or a marriage in crisis.

In a case I supervised, a 17-year-old girl entered individual psychotherapy for an eating disorder. What unfolded was that the mother was very critical and undermining and father had recently left to live in another part of the country, though the parents were not getting divorced. Mother was to join him when daughter, the only child, left home. But how could daughter leave when she was so inadequate and symptomatic, mother worried? When this story emerged, I suggested that the focus of treatment be the mother-daughter pair, because there seemed to be a critical piece of the story missing.

Mother proved a worthy adversary, taking the position that daughter was indeed a terrible girl. When confronted by the therapist, mother turned her attack on him. The win-lose combat revolved around whether the girl was indeed "bad." Mother and daughter each wanted the therapist to take her side. It was clearly a no-win situation at this level. Looking at other levels gave some leverage in the situation. At the outside (mother-daughter) system level, it was clear that the parents' getting back together was doubtful; father was away to stay. Mother was heading right into a life alone; the family breakup was imminent. While daughter couldn't make strong connections with the outside (adult) world, she had thrown out life lines which she then reeled in — she had gotten a job, she had occasional boyfriends, and she was doing well in school. It also became apparent quickly that when mother's attack could be focused on the therapist, the daughter would almost immediately flower. The therapist could see this, but not mother. It also seemed true that mother was able to take symmetrical steps, so that she and daughter moved forward together; mother considered school herself, got a job, etc.

One kind of constancy here was the movement of time. This constancy could be played with rather nicely by counterposing mother to daughter and vice versa. When the daughter moved forward and mother became attacking, the therapist joined with the mother in how hard it was to see daughter getting prepared to leave. When daughter worried about mother and held her own reins too tightly (became symptomatic), daughter was joined at the level of her concern about the mother's future. Each joining move gave mother or daughter a chance to inch forward, but never too far—neither was to outstrip the progress of the other—until their paths slowly and gradually diverged. One might say that they were able to use the therapist as a temporary transitional partner, taking tentative steps over unsure ground.

Another way of seeing tradition from a platform is to keep track of disavowal, part of a strange loop which downplays unbearable emotions and intolerable change (Gustafson, 1989b). The loop goes something like this (using domestic violence, an important family matter, as a concrete example): There is a battering incident that both parties will acknowledge but downplay; it occurred but wasn't terrible, since the woman was not forced to go to the emergency room. Here is the disavowal. Either nothing legal is done about the incident, or the police are called but then charges are not filed. The violence triggers the disavowal, so the treatment commitment is most often desultory. The reversal from violence to disavowal is very rapid: contemplating the full force of this experience is too horrible.

Treatment is recommended. A very active therapist might stir things up a bit and push for changes: a restraining order, separation, more intensive therapy of one sort or another. The forces of transformation are mobilized. Sometimes during this phase a change is made (usually a small one, like the threat that if it happens again the woman will leave). The efforts here crest for some period of time and there may even be a sprinkling of optimism. Separation moves, however, spur tremendous terror of incoherence, either at the system level or within the individuals, and there is a reversal, i.e., an argument which escalates into another battering incident, to complete the cycle.

The reversals are both crucial nodes of transition. The disavowal keeps the system intact, but as a public statement it arouses rescuers to arms and there is a mild flurry of symmetrical outrage and maybe even intensive action. The danger of loss in the form of emotions or behaviors, the terror of separation, triggers its own disavowal.

Therapists who stay in the cycle and follow in the wake of each phase can get extremely frustrated. A constant attitude here keeps both the disavowal and loss together as the couple or family travels through the cycle: being for change in the face of the seriousness of the problem, while appreciating the terror of separation. Only the couple can break up the system, and only the individuals can change their violent patterns. Being in the cycle is like riding a circular bobsled course: Once the ride begins there is no window out until the sled stops. The therapist has to suggest windows and then point out when they are approaching.

Existing at either transition point in the cycle is perfectly acceptable — stopping the violence or leaving the relationship literally or figuratively. Forcing people out of relationships doesn't usually work, but joining them in either loop sometimes does. Shelters, for instance, join in the separation loop, but may not deal with the terror of being independent. Therapy may deal with the terror of independence, but termination of the relationship has its own form of terror. Some of us would perhaps prefer to stay out of certain very strange loops altogether. Counterposing from various stances in the violent cycle is a way of connecting with this kind of group problem (or family tradition) as a basis for hope that the cycle can be broken.

Bly insists that one thing that makes tradition hard to break is the belief that we must take it as a whole or not at all. She advocates "dividing a subject into its components and treating the several components differently" (1982, p. 52). You can save the barrel by taking out the rotten potato. We don't have to take the entire Christmas ritual, but can enjoy pieces of it, whatever suits our fancy — food, relatives, the "vision." What makes tradition stale is having to take them as a whole. She calls for thinking as critically as possible, even something as "radical" as thoughtful conversation, as a way of "recognizing the bad fraction of sacred wholes" (p. 55) — bad for each of us that is. She is in favor of neither "sacred-cowism" nor random idol-smashing; rather, she prefers polishing up traditions and institutions by cutting through falseness.

A platform allows considered evaluation of the whole and its parts in the context of larger beliefs, aspirations, and ideals about the way life ought to be. This is another kind of coherence problem. The larger questions are attempts to be clear about what really makes sense of how things work socially and politically in everyday life. One must look at neighboring holons and other group dimensions. How bold to believe that critical thought and good conversation (!) could attain the "singular playfulness that goes with not lying to oneself any more" (Bly, 1982, pp. 57–58).

Bly's argument is in some sense exemplified by Fisher's analysis of Rome's final inability to protect its empire. He doesn't dismiss the whole system, but looks rather at where the rotten potatoes were, or might have been. He suggested, for instance, that the department of education had died, secured to the past but disconnected to present and future. By being cut off from or unresponsive to the new demands created by larger urban areas, larger boundaries to defend, etc., education became hollow. A tradition of innovation had turned to dullness and empty routine. Without removal or refreshing of complacent or blind parts of the inner workings of empire, the whole barrel inevitably rotted.

Apropos of overwhelming tradition is the work by Freire in combatting the "director culture" under which the peasants he worked with had lived for years and years. In seeking generative themes he found a tunnel out of the peoples' mental oppression. His platform was built on his belief that peasants were capable of knowing and working on learning, literacy, and control of their own fate through collective efforts at heightening awareness of their own mundane experiences. This was an assumption which the ruling class had heretofore only applied to its members. The assumption of humanity gave him the means for proving its existence. To the ruling class's disdain and hateful treatment, internalized over many generations by the peasants, he counterposed possibilities of literacy, thoughtfulness, and hope. What he awakened was a realignment of what was the barrel and what was rotten. The posing of this new possibility evoked a current of strength against oppression.

CONCLUSION

There is a tremendous risk in taking on tradition. For every Freire, there is a cemetery full of outspoken idealists. Faiths have avid defenders. One stands against the tradition, fighting being swallowed by a nonthinking mass or broken by the rigid strokes of the ruling class. The experience is one of standing for oneself while still inside the frame of the system. But one must have a place to move when and if the attack comes. The constancy is the sense of connection, but the chain of proposals and counterposals covers widely disparate locations: some close up, right on the battleground; others off at a distance, looking at the larger picture with an eagle's eye. One must nimbly move back and forth over great distances to discover the counterposal that keeps one connected with the situation in the long run.

11. *Gathering Strength*

REDRAWING OF MAPS CAN ONLY be attempted in well protected quarters, where contemplation will not be rudely interrupted, where deep commitments can be entertained in fresh ways. Ancient, Biblical tradition provided for such quarters by dividing the secular realms from the sacred. We will be proposing to divide the world further, placing more compartments between the external world and the internal world. We start from the contrast of ancient versus modern strategy. Then we march from the external through the middle and conclude in the most protected compartments: war; contest; the central compartment of the modern world; civility; play; solitude.

ANCIENT VERSUS MODERN STRATEGY

There have always been several advantages to taking to the hills before the arrival of one's adversaries. One is to save oneself from mortal wounding. A second is to study his forces which sweep in under your eyes. A third is to be able to reduce vigilance, to become refreshed. All of these gather strength for the counter-strike.

The Western version of local self-defense bursts forth in the book of *Psalms* like this:

> Jehovah, how are mine adversaries increased!
> Many are they that rise up against me!
> Many there are that say of my soul,
> There is no help for him in God . . .
> I cry unto Jehovah with my voice,
> And he answereth me out of his holy hill . . .
> Arise, O Jehovah; save me, O my God
> For thou hast smitten all mine enemies upon the cheek bones;
> Thou hast broken the teeth of the wicked. (3: 1,2,4, 7)

There is extraordinary strength that can flow from dividing the world in two: between the inviolate and the wicked, between the sacred and the profane, between the black of the church and the red of war. This kind of vitality flows down from Jahwist writer of the Old Testament through Christendom and runs through us still.

> I will lift up mine eyes unto the hills
> From whence shall my help come?
> My help cometh from Jehovah,
> Who made heaven and earth (121: 1,2)

But let us see what strength flows from dividing the world further, placing more compartments between the terrible and the inviolate.

Imagine the compartment of war farthest to the right. Every war seems to have its own code or conventions, but the aim is destruction.

Still to the right, but one compartment farther in, imagine the compartment of the contest. Resources are commandeered, training is rigorous, the fighting is fierce, but short of killing — to win rather than lose, to profit rather than fail, to establish innocence rather than guilt, and so forth. We see contests of every ilk, athletic, commercial, legal, and so forth.

Next we come to the center compartment of the modern world, where help and taking advantage come in all proportions. This has been the compartment where we have placed most of the action of the world as we know it in daily life.

Left of center, we locate the compartment of civility (Tuan, 1986) which allows art and science. These ventures may have the martial aspect of contests, certainly no less fury. Like legal contests, they have rules for how testimony may be introduced, challenged and judged. But here many possible imaginative proposals may be entertained, all of which fit the available testimony (Bloch, 1953). Some may be more appealing, some less. Some have greater parsimony, some less. Although competition may be profound, the challenge is to bring out something of nature. Anyone who can abide by the rules of the conversation may contribute as well as benefit (Bloch, 1953).

Next in, we come upon the compartment of play. Here testimony may be shaped as it pleases. Challenges of shape are allowed only if playful (St. Exupery, 1943). Winnicott (1971) called this "transitional space," because it is undecided by the players whether their constructions are in their minds or actually in the world. My eight-year-old daughter prancing on neighboring Fox Hill is riding a horse neither in her mind nor in the world. There is no such distinction there.

Finally, we reach the compartment which is most protected from the world. It has many names, such as the sacred, the province of God or religion, of deepest beliefs or commitments, love, loyalty, or solitude.

War. Contest. The center compartment of the modern world. Civility. Play (transitional space). Solitude. With six compartments, in place of two, what advantages are ours?

There is a better chance to map what is otherwise confusing. Contests become wars. Science can turn into a grim contest. Play may be taken over. But there is great calm in knowing where you are in the six compartments. If

I am struck from behind in a contest, I am extremely agitated, until I recover my bearings, facing up to the war at hand. Then I wage war cheerfully.

There is much more room for invention, because each compartment farther in is an opportunity to fall back, to watch the other compartments for the movements of one's rivals, out of their reach. One can gather strength for the counter-strike of war, of contest, of art or science, of play!

There is much more room to take defeats, setbacks or reversals if the war is only a contest . . . if the contest is only a finding for art or science . . . if art or science is only the play of an antic disposition . . . if play is but a shining forth of spirit. Then all of this can go wrong without mortal wounds. No one has laid a hand on me, myself. Yet I have entered the world with great feelings. Vitality so well defended lasts long.

How does one gather strength for each of these six compartments of the world? Each has its own challenges.

WAR

War is more terrifying for those caught by surprise. Immature people — that is, most of us until middle age, many beyond — are not apt to see it coming and cannot quite believe it when it has arrived. Because mankind can be fair and just in the lulls between new outbreaks of warring, we forget the ferocity of this creature, until it may be too late.

How do we develop a nose for war? The hard way is to fall victim to war parties, any number of times. By middle age, the nose ought to be connected to thought (Gogol, 1836). But thought has to be able to face what is cruel. Let's do that.

There are at least three terrible truths about our species. The first seems hopeful until you track down its implications. This is the way in which the "niche" works for human beings:

"Niche" describes an animal's or plant's role in life, or its profession. As a consequence of living in its niche the organism collects the resources of matter and energy needed for life. The niche of each species has been fashioned for it by a natural selection that requires that every individual of a species conforms to the species norm. The niche of every non-human species is fixed and cannot be changed without the act of making a new species. Over the last 10,000 years, people, however, have been continually changing their niches without speciating. This is something wholly without precedent in evolutionary history. It is the essential human quality. (Colinvaux, 1983, p. 2) (my italics)

Let's be more specific, following Colinvaux, comparing the profession of "trouting" to the profession of "professing." First the trout:

The idea that a niche is fixed for all species other than our own gives a useful intuitive grasp of the problems of limits to number. There cannot be more individuals of any species in any place than there are units of niche space. There cannot, for instance, be more trout than there are *opportunities for hunting trout food, in the trout way*, in water that is both relatively cold and of high oxygen content. The number of opportunities for the narrowly defined profession of trouting *sets the number* of trout that may live, a number that is quite unaffected by the breeding strategy. (p. 3) (my italics)

Now the professor:

The profession of a university professor may be thought of as a niche, just as the profession of "trouting" is the niche of a trout. Opportunities to profess are fixed in any human community; we say that the *number* of professor jobs is limited. If we train or graduate more students in the arts of professing (reproducing professors) than there are professorships, the surplus graduate students will not be able to profess for a living however *cum laude* their degrees. They may have to take to honest work. Anyway, they will change their niche. Enforced change of life-style when there is no room in the traditional job market is a direct consequence of our having learned to change our niche at will and it is a powerful driving force of historical event. (p. 3)

Trout who lose contests for occupying a niche die. Would-be professors need not. Contests for niche are cruel for us, but not mortal, because there are many possible niches in which we might reappear.

But this very maneuverability of the human being is what allows the cruelty characteristic of him. He will seek allies in order to take possession of the most favorable niches. God help anyone who gets in his way:

The lives of the organizers, whether merchants, bureaucrats, kings, or priests, were wide ranging. These people had broad niches. But for the mass there was a constricted way of life. These people lived in those narrow niches that we call "poverty." Power in human societies is granted to leaders who promise to *maintain* the traditional niches or even to *expand* them. In this endeavor, two strategies are open to leaders that might be called further changes in the niche: Technical ingenuity, that produces more goods and services, or trade. When these eventually fail to satisfy . . . only a single stratagem remains, that of taking land from other peoples. (Colinvaux, 1983, p. 3)

This is our *first* terrible possibility: Why not find allies and occupy the most favorable niches? This has been a tremendously attractive idea for the most maneuverable of creatures. The most favorable niches are always possessed, secured, and expanded by war, or through "war by other means," namely technical ingenuity or trade. This is a cheerful prospect for those who can get in on the alliance or the discipline but a gloomy, cruel one for those excluded.

If alliances are for war, then some alliances are relatively cold and some relatively hot, as Levi-Strauss explains:

. . . the societies studied by the anthropologists are in a sense "cold" societies rather than "hot" societies, or *like clocks in relation to steam engines.* . . . Our modern societies . . . structurally . . . resemble the steam engine in that they work on the basis of a difference in potential, which finds concrete expression in different forms of social hierarchy. Whether we call it slavery, serfdom or class distinctions is not of any fundamental importance. (Charbonnier, 1969, p. 33)

Here is our *second* terrible truth: The engines of merchants, bureaucrats, kings, priests and professors derive their ferocious momentum from their very inequality. Social engines based on relative equality go to sleep. Social engines with great disparity between top and bottom get extremely hot. Cruel differences get us going.

To do what? To govern, as Foucault suggests, which " . . . is to structure the possible field of action of others (1980, p. 221). Or to strategize: " . . . to deprive the opponent of his means of combat and to reduce him to give up the struggle . . . the means destined to obtain victory" (p. 225):

A relationship of confrontation reaches its term, its final moment (and the victory of one of the two adversaries) when stable mechanisms replace the free play of antagonistic reactions. Through such mechanisms one can direct, in a fairly constant manner and with reasonable certainty, the conduct of others. (p. 225)

Our *third* terrible truth: Order is that lull when opponents have been induced to give up their means of combat.

In short, we should expect *regimes*, with their terrible strategies of war or war by other means, to (1) occupy the most favorable niches, (2) derive ferocious momentum from inequality, and (3) deprive opponents of their means of combat, which brings about lulls from war.

Children, immature adults and subordinates are the most likely to be fooled by order: by contests that are civil, art and science that seem gentlemanly, and play that is fair (Eliot, 1871).

A few months after I joined my department fifteen years ago in a beautiful summer of thunderstorms, a grim cohort of professors met in my living room to discuss — supposedly discuss — what to do about the inpatient service. Little did I know that they had already agreed to put me in charge, perhaps destroying my career by placing me where my career would be impossible. This was convenient for them. In war you destroy lesser powers as necessary. Young people are usually ill prepared to protect themselves.[1]

Now, fifteen years later, in another civil war in the department, I tell the younger people how to gather strength for such warring occasions. Most of them cannot believe the outbreak of personal attacks. They tell me it ought not to happen. I tell them this is indeed what happens when the previous order is going out of power: The defeated are savage in their futile thrashing, while the rising order will have its revenge. I do not go out into the hall without looking both ways for who might be bearing down upon me.

I gather my own strength carefully in such a long, mean fight. First of all, I do not care to be taken by surprise. I keep in mind the image of a certain boss, who always listened for what was coming down the hall to his office. He would turn his back to the door, staring out his window, preparing what the assailant would get of him. Angry subordinates would soon leave, glad to have their jobs at all. Despondent ones would leave with more hope. Someone said of this boss, "No one ever laid a hand on him." I do not believe this is an end in itself, merely a way to last in war. Very little is gained by allowing personal injury to yourself. It is better for them to get a very small slice of me, when I suddenly turn around.

Second of all, I am very deliberate with my allies. If they help me, I help them. If they let me down, I am punishing back. If they correct themselves, I am forgiving. I do not expect them to care a whit for my cause (which they do a little), but only that they act like my allies. Mostly, they do.

Third of all, I am prepared to lose battles. Those who always have to go forward in the justness of their cause will overreach, such as Charles XII, the "Swedish Meteor":

With a speed which seemed miraculous the young Swede broke through the circle of his enemies and had them beaten on every front. Even Marlborough was prepared to salute him as a great master of war. Unfortunately, he lacked sanity. While Marlborough was always as cool as ice, Charles was in a constant blaze of excitement. . . . A fatalism, born of early success, carried him buoyantly through every vicissitude, while Sweden, bled white through his obstinate ambition, descended swiftly in the scale of power until she forfeited forever his place of command and usefulness in the affairs of Europe. (Fisher, 1935, p. 797)

Thus fell the greatest power of the 17th century, Sweden, at Poltava on June 28, 1709. No sense acting like that in these minor, minor wars of an obscure department.

Notice that all three measures I propose for myself in this tiny war step back out of that compartment of war into the compartment of contest. Thereby, I do not take the battle as all important, I can watch my adversaries coldly, and I can come back with fresh initiatives. When war is but a game, my chances improve: I can actually enjoy waiting for what comes down the hall, with my back to the door. I feel some relish in my strategy with my allies. I can take lost battles as a chance to come back harder at those who have *taken* their victory too far.

CONTEST

I do not care, however, to act like society is merely what Hobbes (1651) claimed, "a war of all against all." Sometimes, it is just that. But it also settles down into the order imposed by the discipline that is victorious (Foucault, 1980). Then we get contests, whose rules are strictly given by that discipline.[2] Two such contests I must manage every day are those with students met in seminars and those with families met by our family therapy team.

By the late hour in their careers as students, when they reach my seminars as postdoctoral fellows in psychology or residents in psychiatry, these young adults know all too well how to shine over their peers. If they didn't they never would have ascended so far. They meet in me someone who is not interested in such displays, per se. I hope to get them to deploy their combative skill in the service of art or science, specifically, to meet the challenge of the seminar for that given day, viz., to probe the richness of an essay we have read, to discover the range of a patient one or two of us have interviewed.

Sometimes they respond directly to the challenge, moving quite beautifully in concert. Of late, I have had to contend with their most miserable performances. In a civil war, they degenerate towards the level of the faculty. They dare not attack openly. They become experts in disqualification of strength. They learn to disarm power.

This is understandable as a strategy for war, for those in the weakest positions. It is terrible for the civility of seminars. The game that they play there is relatively simple: Any reading, patient or interviewer which shows strength will be found to have weaknesses as well. If you go straight for the weakness, announce it, and run on and on about it, there is a chance that the contribution of this author, patient or interviewer will be forgotten and thus destroyed. This used to demoralize me. Once I was demoralized, soon the seminar was as well.

But once I knew their game, I discovered the counter-game. I allow for the weakness, stating it more fully, loudly and persuasively than they have dared. I draw out the *insinuation*, which is otherwise as chilling as an iceberg moving into one's snug little harbor. I want to haul it out on the wharf — piece by piece. Left in the water it defeats me. Then, I say: If we *stayed* on this weakness, what would we miss (from this author, patient or interviewer)? This allows a richness of discovery to flow into our conversation, in the service of the art or science of the work at hand.[3]

Families are similar. They come to us, invariably, in a state of war, by which I mean that some of them are driving others of them into terror or despair, attempting to " . . . deprive the opponent of his means of combat and to reduce him to give up the struggle . . . the means destined to obtain victory" (Foucault, 1980, p. 225). Of course, the losers strike back, perhaps regaining higher ground. If about equally matched, they take turns winning and losing, inflicting damage, which slowly widens the fault line between them, until the marriage or family is destroyed, and the parties must all leave the family territory.

Almost always, our family team gets called in when one party is in grave disarray. The opposite party has struck so hard that the party in question has felt "deprived of his means of combat . . . reduced to give up the struggle." Someone feels his dignity has been nearly destroyed, or her pleasure in life or her trust. We are the reinforcements called.

The contest for us has a beginning, a middle and an end. The challenge of the beginning is to win the acceptance of all crucial parties, to induce them to stage their battle on the field that we provide. We do this by backing all of them, but the temporary loser slightly more. The temporary winners accept this, because they want to keep the loser on the field. Usually, the consultation has been set in motion by a threat to leave the field, by separation or by worsening of illness. When we meet the challenge of reviving the temporary loser, they are glad to resume the war in earnest.

Now the war proceeds through many campaigns, before our eyes, once a month, on our field. The tilt of the field may swerve about wildly, from month to month, from hour to hour, even from minute to minute. Our inexperienced team members can get unnerved by this inevitable see-saw. How to stay calm! It helps to remember that their war is but our contest. We look for the turning point in the war.

This occurs when one of the contestants, coming in badly hurt once more, suddenly discovers how to cope with the thrust of the other party, without injuring him badly, without therefore, driving another round of revenge. We bring this discovery about, usually by reflexive questioning, occasionally by getting them to perform a ritual.

Very succinctly, here is one such turning point in a very long, terrible marital war. The young wife who called for our help spent ten years being held in contempt by her husband's two daughters from a previous marriage. The daughters were merely taking their revenge upon the new wife for the betrayal of their own mother by their father. Upon the field provided by us, the most striking, recurrent event was this strident young woman's lashing her husband into silence. We backed him just enough to keep him on the field, but he usually arrived late to show his protest.

The way out of the war, out of the rule of one or both feeling despised and helpless, was to discover the exception which already worked (de Shazer, 1987): How did he *help* her not to feel despised and helpless? How did she help him? The discovery was minimal but decisive, shown by a sudden turn into calm, from a terrible rending of each other. He helped her by simply keeping his daughters away, out of the house and out of the marital conversation. She helped him by letting him finish, without waving her arms, "no, no, no." For the very first time in many sessions, he could find his calendar to arrange the next appointment. This is the kind of turning point in a long war, which takes the family or marital war into the calmer compartment of a friendly contest.

The end of our contest with them is to help take them out of war like this a number of times, until they can do it for themselves (however imperfectly). It is more precise to say that they learn to do it sooner and more decisively (for they have always had truces, the exceptions to the rule of war from which we take our cue).

THE CENTER COMPARTMENT
OF THE MODERN WORLD

If we have witnessed a war becoming more of a friendly contest, we have had it staged in this central compartment where taking advantage and help are very difficult to distinguish. We have been loyal to their cause, but we have expected them to act terribly, as if they were not loyal to their own cause, as if the family therapy were merely an occasion to take fresh advantages, as if getting help were a mere pretext. Our job is to help them overcome what is awful about them.[4]

We have not come to our crucial decisions out there. They have come to us in the useful and profound ambiguity of the center compartment of the modern world. It is impossible to say there whether the family is out to injure or even kill each other or to sustain each other. Since we do not want to get drawn into such an awful ambiguity ourselves, we can look out for our own constructive civility by interviewing them for brief intervals and then retiring to our own civil compartment.

Behind the mirror, our lead and second interviewers have thought out loud with their third, anchor colleague, hypothesizing freely, entertaining certain striking findings, preparing the next line of questioning. Here we dwell in the more protected compartment of art and science, the interviewer gathering him or herself with the help of thoughtful colleagues, for another experiment with the family games of taking advantage/help.[5]

I have been brief about this center compartment as it is wholly characterized in Chapter 1, organized for in Chapters 2 and 3, anticipated in Chapters 4 and 5, moved in freely in Chapters 6 and 7, and defensible time and terrain in it are located in Chapters 8, 9 and 10.

CIVILITY

Here we discuss ever so briefly that compartment of the world so well characterized by Marc Bloch (1953) and Yi-Fu Tuan (1986), where testimony can be arranged many different ways, so long as it stays within the rules of evidence or form. Yet the most interesting works of art and science even show cause for extending and revising the rules of procedure, in the name of a better disclosure of nature.

I limit myself to my theme, which is to show how life in any given compartment of the world gathers its strength in the compartment farther in. I see art and science flowing out of the preoccupation of play (transitional space).

I go every week to the department of medicine to help two professors think over their groups for medical residents, which are concerned with the difficult relationships of the residents with patients, families, nurses, other doctors, and faculty. The professors are usually worried about getting their groups unstuck.

Last week one of the professors reported a group of four residents who seemed very lively about the subject of bucking authority: Several weeks previously the residents had been impressed by a faculty physician who had dared to protect a poor patient against the hospital administration. This attending had ordered the nurses to start an intravenous line, so it would be too late to get rid of the patient for lack of funds. Now they were interested in protesting against the faculty themselves: about the faculty using actors to simulate illnesses to test the residents in the clinic.

The trouble for our professors was that the four residents in the group would go no further than this. They were lively on the subject noted. But they presented no cases of their own, thus defying the working procedure of the group. They were friendly enough with her, kidding her in their usual jocular way. She felt reluctant to confront them about their lack of work, which might worsen her relationship with them. She felt reluctant to play along as if this standstill were acceptable to her. Indeed, she felt helpless and angry. Civility, once achieved, was once again threatened (with a return into covert contest, with being drawn back into the center compartment of help as taking advantage).

My advice came out of her evident preoccupation and that of the group. I wanted to ride both of those streams, which propel the work of such a group as this in the art of being a doctor. I told her that she had begun to help them by naming their interest, that is, in bucking authority. She had not known how to ride it further. Indeed, confronting them about their lack of work might have worked to dam this flow. I shared her reluctance to do that. How to take it further? Well, there were several ways I could think of. One would be to say to them: "Oh, how interesting, this bucking of authority. You must have done it several times today already!" She could ride their momentum into the channels where the specific cases were apt to lie!

But, I said to her, you would be likely to say this differently, in your own way. I carefully marked just how she was following their preoccupation, just how far she got, what might take her further, in her own way. After all, she must work from *her* preoccupation. I do not want to get in the way of her current, any more than I want her to get in the way of theirs! If she is stopped cold, she could take weeks to recover. The most brilliant consultation is destructive when it loses or stops the person to whom it is directed.

The same respect is due to preoccupation in the residents and fellows in my brief therapy clinic. I tell them that each has to take his or her cases in his or her own way. I and their peers will try to help them with their own inclinations, concerns, fears and doubts.

PLAY

When I say such things to the residents, I ride a deep current of my own out of my childhood. I was once the general of a little army whose fort was in my backyard, but which ranged freely to the south, two doors away, to the pickle factory, continuing to the mysterious destroyed factory we called the Sonora, east to the grocery market and the railroad line we could hear all night long, north to the Illinois Shade Cloth factory down the block, and west to the elementary school. We dug tunnels under our whole backyard and built roads between the trees with bailing wire from newspaper stacks, using Christmas trees as our planks. We wore union buttons in our caps and feared no one.

The clinic group rides this deep pleasure of mine from the past, drawing as well upon the like in themselves (Stevenson, 1892). It is difficult to find such deep play among adults, who become lost in practical matters.[6] The great problem of adult play is to find mates and to tolerate their loss when voyages have to end. Fortunately, I have had Lowell as my friend, colleague, partner, and fellow captain for twenty years. This kind of relationship, which reaches through all the compartments of the world — from play, to civility, to contest, to war — is the greatest comfort in life. Jean Renoir (1974) said this well:

For, after all, I have been happy. I have made films that I wanted to make. I have made them with people who were more than my collaborators; they were my accomplices. This, I believe, is one recipe for happiness: to work with people you love and who love you.

Fortunately, I have my team members on our family therapy team for the last five years. Fortunately, my clinic often becomes a year's sail together.

SOLITUDE

All too often, there are no such companions of play. There may be no one to tell what one is full of:

> At night, when I go out to the field
> to listen to the birds sleep, the stars
> hover like old umpires over the diamond
> . . .
> and I realize again that our lives pass
> like the phased signals of that old coach,
> the moon, passing over the pitcher's mound,
> like the slowed stride of an aging shortstop
> as he lopes over the infield . . .
>
> I remember

how once, sliding into second during a steal,
I watched the sun rest like a diadem against the
head of some spectator, and thought to myself
in the neat preutterance of all true feeling,
how even our thieveries, well-done, are blessed,
with a certain luminousness . . .
. . . It is why, even then, I loved
baseball: the fierce legitimacy of the neatly stolen . . .
that boy still rising from his theft to find the light
        (Blumenthal, 1980, p. 3, "Night Baseball")

The responses to such as this may be uncomprehending: points of contact, perhaps about a common interest in baseball or verse, but no coming close to "the fierce legitimacy of the neatly stolen" which I would glory in with my friend.

Better then to depart from the surprising landscape of group life to find inscapes, as Hopkins (1953) wrote, into worlds where one finds a home in language for oneself (Margulies, 1989). I like to take off with my dog following the ridge, which is like going with a ship headed westward across the plains, like Ammons, who wrote:

but I like the ridge: it was a line
in the minds of hundreds of generations
of cold Indians: and it was there
approximately then what it is now
five hundred years ago when the white
man was a whisper on the continent . . .
        (1987, p. 10)

I believe we all need such places beyond the reach of the world, beyond the pattern that connects the world, beyond the modern contest. It may be a ridge, or a hill, or the sea (a couch, a book of poems, or a mass).[7]

It is where I dwell when the world has gone to sleep (all of us take our leave from the world every night to be on our own). It is where I dwell when I have not won or been recognized or understood (there are these intervals to be borne, between the fortunes which turn up as the modern contest will allow). There I am glad for myself and for what I propose to give to the world, and for the tradition from which I come (eventually, we will take our leave altogether).

There I am glad we have taught devotion to become more astute about how the world is put together. Once we can sketch in the highly likely set of events from a small arc of what has only begun (Holmes, 1858, pp. 8–9), we have the perspective necessary to anticipate the movements of the modern contest. Then we can give ourselves intensely and playfully to the thrills of the sport, in the most commercial of contests. Then we can be at home in the world.[8]

It is no longer the world of 19th century causes in which we could enlist under a grand banner and feel solidarity with masses and do huge harm to our antagonists. We can no longer charge forth like Tolstoy's (1869) characters into the struggle against Napoleon. It is no longer the world of 19th century commerce, of trade empires stoutly put together and ferociously defended. We can no longer charge forth like Melville's characters into the struggle against the whale. No, it is the world of the late 20th century, in which there are endlessly shifting commercial contests, a ferment so powerful that it dissolves the old dichotomies of communism and capitalism. The leaders of those two empires fear to fall behind the fluid enterprises which prevail over the old causes. This is the new world of the modern contest in which we want to be fully at home. So we must be ready to fall back into our own modest solitude, stealing bases in the moonlight and following the ridge in the morning.

PART VII

Taking Our Bearings

12. *An Attitude for All Seasons*

T HREE BROAD STRATEGIES help secure and sustain a positive attitude for prospering in the modern contest. First, one must be able to see and evaluate victories. Victories occur frequently but can be overlooked or underestimated; the challenge is to find them and keep them in proper perspective. Second, one must be able to hang in for the long haul to open the possibility of victory. Third, we must have a strategy for finding and loyally holding onto our own sense of what is moral and responsible. This third strategy poses the value and possibilities of self-awareness.

CAPTURING VICTORY

If victory is total, it is not likely to be overlooked. It is uncommon to win all the battles *and* the war, but it does sometimes happen. There are those instances in which a disturbed family leaves treatment having made a major realignment, so that all are winners and there is agreement by all that the clinical interventions were central curative factors. One can also be a victor on the family field in being well served, as a couple headed into deep trouble, reaching out, and being convinced that the relationship has been fundamentally altered and saved. This is no less a victory than being on the intervening side. Everyone wins; cooperation and help were available.

There are times as a teacher and mentor when one influences another's life dramatically. Both parties in the relationship see and feel the substance of the victory as a career direction is influenced, an inspiration emerges, and an almost parental bond is experienced and acknowledged.

Inspired business leadership, small group leadership in the therapy room, business setting, and consultation arena also offer the possibility of major victory. The group can emerge as a vital force with the capacity to accomplish certain goals, be they goals of building a house or helping each other overcome some heroic personal obstacles.

What is one to make of total victory? It is such a heady experience. One must feel able to enjoy and relish it, and protect it from being qualified, reduced, or canceled. Perspective is essential in this situation. If one can be clear about the terms of victory, one's vigor and outlook can be enhanced. However, insofar as one is going to reengage in another social challenge even on the same field, i.e., another student, another family, another consultation, one is best advised to celebrate with an eye to tomorrow. One's victory is *protected* by perspective. It is useful to be prepared for newness and surprises, unanticipated challenges, and excitement about new learning. If one tries to repeat the victory too slavishly, disappointment could invade the specialness of the victory — as if one were saying, "It worked once, so I'll try it again exactly the same way." Rarely are conditions exactly the same. In other words, even if victory is total one must have perspective in how to use it in future encounters, even on the same field.

It seems to me that the enduring gain of major victory is going to be the learning in it. If one can repeat the victory exactly, little new is learned. While there are other important benefits, like the elation and increased sense of power as a participant in the highly changeable social field, one is best advised to accumulate useful ideas and tools as well as self-confidence and buoyancy. Total victory deserves total celebration, but perspective keeps clear upon what field the victory actually occurred. A sense of steadiness and self-reliability is the goal of this strategy.

By far the more usual experience is to experience partial victory which is difficult to find and/or difficult to hold on to. Here an attitude that adjusts one's lenses to see the field of success clearly is crucial. One can easily be discouraged as a teacher if some of the students are critical. A family or organizational consultation can be dispiriting if only some progress is made or only some people are improved somewhat. There is a relation here to the old saw about whether the glass is half-full or half-empty, but there is more to it.

To see what part of the glass is full does not just deny the negative; it also asks the question of what was done right and enjoys where territory was won. It also permits clear focus on the side of the situation where there needs to be more experimentation and new learning. One small step enables one to know what one knows and how to expand this territory.

Perspective in this broad strategy for relating to victory involves adjusting one's lens to see the vertical or horizontal field on which the victory occurred. If one is getting critical reviews from one set of students, where are the satisfied customers? What has one done well for others that didn't work for some? Do the complainers represent a particular subset of the group, while there are also less voluble others with whom one is consistently successful? Is one particularly victorious teaching one subject as compared with another? Critical discriminations on this horizontal plane can be where to look for information about victory and new learning.

Sometimes a perspective for victory must be sought on the vertical terrain. What looks like a local defeat may have victorious elements at other levels. In one of my first consultations, I was quite surprised when the person who had hired me decided to end the consultation in the middle of things several months later. I was very unclear about what had happened until I realized that a defeat at this higher level in the hierarchy had been precipitated by success at the level of the small group with which I had been hired to work. I had been able to get connected with the members of the small group and had gotten them to be more questioning and thoughtful staff members (participants). At that beginning point in my career, being useful that way was a good bit of learning to have acquired. The group was working well together, we made inroads on several important work issues, and we had become quite connected with each other. I was very naive, however, about how systems worked, and the man at the head of this institution was upset by the changes. There is where I had to focus my next learning. I would not consider this kind of naivete acceptable in myself now. Yesterday's perspective doesn't work today, but that makes yesterday's victory no less uplifting.

Bateson offers a classic example of this problem of perspective, and solves it with his usual elegance: finding the best question to ask. He saw hopeless muddles in observing and participating on the U.C. Board of Regents in the 1960s. If he stayed on the field of his own direct impact on the Board, it is arguable whether he would have felt very effective. On the other hand, it was a vital laboratory for his discoveries about the replication of institutions; he was able to illustrate how institutions work in a backwards way, how they hold onto what is not adaptive and give up what is useful and creative. Through his writing he was able to use this experience as a piece of his attempt to figure out how systems work. His capacity to see clearly in the face of the Board muddles offers the possibility of thoughtful tactical planning. As is often true of gifted writers and teachers, Bateson's victories were not necessarily on the action fields, but in his capacity to think, see, and communicate via direct instruction and/or through the written word. This is not a victory to be overlooked, but to be kept in perspective.

This kind of victory is no less powerful than those of many artists who overcome possible or actual defeat through clear thinking and the written word. Their victory is best enjoyed and used by their readership.

Without clarity, one risks spoiling one's victory by taking actions outside the limits of real expertise. The so-called "Peter Principle" exemplifies just how devastating this kind of unclarity can be. Persons who do well in one kind of organizational position are promoted until they eventually move outside the field of expertise. Personal and organization muddling reward success by taking such persons *out* of their strong area. If this process gets out of control, employees are victimized by a bureaucratized reward system under which they are promoted until they fail. They are in danger of losing their true strengths.

This is a good transition into a broad strategy for protecting oneself from despair by lasting for long hauls. While at times we are powerless to directly influence and control our social circumstances, by enduring and keeping an eye on events all around us in the environment—attending to vertical and horizontal scaling—victory can be found. Possibilities of success can be created.

THE VICTORY IN ENDURING

When one has really been treated badly by conditions one cannot hope to control, but can only hope to survive, perhaps one's best victory is the survival itself. It is extraordinary if, in addition to survival, one is able to endure for the long haul, until a more successful face of the situation becomes apparent. There is also victory in being able to inform others of the dangers and to engage them in a conversation that enlists their help against a common antagonist. The capacity to survive adversity for the long haul opens up the opportunity for further victory.

Conviction about the value of enduring, resiliency of spirit and mood, and good humor about one's mistakes are an important cluster of survival skills. Bayley, in discussing Auden and Brodsky, sees that "civilization, in this sense of it, is an affair of basic humor, a humor which naturally pervades their being and their works" (1987, p. 3). I believe he refers to a resiliency of spirit and mood. One must prepare to go back into the classroom after having had a bad day, to see a family in therapy again after having made a *faux pas* like forgetting someone's name or saying something dumb, to face a group after having done something foolish. The humor is in the attitude of "well, you got me there, let's play another match." For me this is like what Gass (1988) describes — that one must "make inwardly aimed adjustment," no "spray of sparks" or hand-wringing, just bold humility.

I have learned a tremendous amount about resiliency from watching resilient group leaders and organizational managers in action. I am most often exposed to them in consultations which span a broad territory and have many phases over a long period of time. There is much to be admired in vigorous staying power. There is always a characteristic form to combat disappointment and defeat; yet it is clear that individual styles vary tremendously.

In a situation I worked with over a several year period, the emerging style was very daring and risky, a pitcher with only a fast ball. On a good day, everyone but the batter had an easy time of it. On a bad day, watch out; the pitcher needed good backup and maybe an early shower. This was a person who saw a program need, called in an outside consultant, developed an intervention, and pushed it through by force of charisma. When the program was accepted, he became a magician, felt powerful, and gave himself a deserved pat on the back. When the program met opposition, serious opposition, he would gather his lieutenants about him. But often these felt like suicide missions: He would tuck the bomb under their arms and tell them to put down their heads and run straight through the opposition. He watched. If they made it, fine. If they didn't he would take defeat matter-of-factly, patch up his soldiers, extricate himself from the specific situation, and turn to another issue or person. Overall there was tremendous energy and devotion to a system which had so many needs that one could realistically go off in dozens of directions — and over time he did. I would get involved in consultations when he applied his style to staff. He would find a weakness, and I would be called in to fix it — the team doctor. It took considerable exposure to the style to realize its function and substance. He kept spirits up, always vigorous and exciting, but focused on the same target — improving his program overall. This kind of dedication offers yet another window to handling victory and powerlessness, with tremendous bounce.

Another major aspect of the resilient positive attitude it takes to endure and prosper in a social world often beyond our control is being able to hold one's ground with conviction, take a measure of combat and antagonism, and be open to influence — but ever at the ready to cut off their heads. In a humorous vein, Vosnesensky captures it in his "Antiworlds":

> Ah, my critics: how I love them.
> Upon the neck of the keenest of them,
> Fragrant and bald as a fresh-baked bread,
> There shines a perfect anti-head . . .
> (1966, p. 40)

From a more warlike stance was Field Marshall Turenne's response (in Havens, 1965) to his aide-de-camp, who wanted to flee as the army was being defeated, before all was lost. "Are you not afraid?" the aide asked. "If you were as afraid as I am," said Turenne, "you would run away." Havens sees how this applies to the "great challenges" of our work: "to stay with the battle and feel, not running from what must be borne" (1965, p. 406).

Lewin saw the importance of conviction from a more formal group dynamics point of view. In considering planned social action (and our plan is to stay connected with group life in the face of discouragements), he advised that "it is important . . . that . . . a plan be not too much frozen. To be effective, plans should be flexible . . . only in regard to the first step should the decision (for execution) be final" (1947, p. 148). I find Lewin very useful in reminding me to stay connected to action, move with conviction and sureness, but only one step at a time within a larger plan. His attitude was one of being unafraid and morally committed and at the same time fair-minded and step-wise. Look into the valley between mountains before heading downhill, but go one step at a time. The great victory in Lewin's attitude, it seems to me, is his quiet determination and frank willingness to make mistakes he can learn from and explore. There is no question but that he was in for the long haul.

Another angle on recovery and resiliency in the face of disappointment and defeat is described by Royce, who would have us ride defeats, but not be defeated, in order to rediscover strength.

Loyalty for the lost cause is thus attended by two comrades, grief and imagination. . . . The cause can no longer be served in the old way, and must be the object of new efforts, and so of some new form of devotion . . . human loyalty can never be perfected without such sorrow. (1936, pp. 283, 294)

Defeat, sorrow, loss, and disappointment all let us know our commitments and offer us opportunity for a new readiness.

In family therapy, no one describes better than Skynner the importance of holding fast to certain basic simplicities. His own search for the key to a family leads him to a rather intense connection, but the connection with himself saves him from total immersion. As he continually rediscovers this, he is confident in thinking that his own buoyancy will come through. The complexity of the family's situation is juxtaposed to his own "exciting simplicity" (1986b, p. 21) in getting involved with other people. From the resiliency he found in his own family's ability to bounce back from a family squabble, he knew he and his wife were ready to work together as cotherapists. Their (simple) ability to ride a wave together was telling, not their knowledge of theory or their ability to be correct. Sometimes humor saves the situation, sometimes being playful will do just fine. Skynner would have us be clear about setting up and holding onto the structure of the situation and even clearer about the importance of our buoyancy as individuals or work teams.

The appreciation of cycles and the importance of the right questions are endurance skills. Brodsky reminds us that "history, no doubt, is bound to repeat itself: after all, like men, history doesn't have many choices" (1986, p. 31). Yet, the morality of each situation demands of us that we take the full measure of the *current* case. Group literature is full of theories which explain a certain slice of the author's history, but stop short of appreciating cycles. A sprint during a marathon can end one's race prematurely.

Mann suggests a useful safeguard against giving in to the limits of history: "a useful theory is bound up with . . . questions" (1975, p. 237). Holding one's ground on the territory of the case involves a plan for questioning. One must stand in admiration of the elaborate framework for questioning developed by Selvini Palazzoli and the Milan school and greatly elaborated and clarified in a series of papers by Tomm (1984, 1987, 1988). The needs of the situation are not only exposed, but at times resolved by the questions. Michael White (1983, 1988) suggests that, with certain couples, confronting them with the question of why in the world they are together may throw a totally different light on their history and lead directly to a new perspective.

We all deserve our own recognition for social endurance. In a follow-up phone call to a stormy family I worked with briefly, I asked how they had been doing in the two-month interim since our last (of four) meetings. Mother told me how her adolescent son was still in a terrible state. He had made very unrealistic plans for his summer vacation, was studying fiercely for finals, and leaving parents out of his life more and more. Since they had come into treatment because of tremendous mutual parent-child punishment and the child's school failure, I asked how these new developments were going over in the family. She said that her husband had taken my advice to loosen up with discipline since he was too uneasy as a master and his son too uneasy as a slave. I said to her that it sounded like considerable progress had occurred on several fronts. Her friends had told her their teenagers were also doing what her son was, so finally her son had become normalized, he was like other teenagers. We had all endured the worst of their family life, and they were now (victoriously) emerging into "normalcy." What a relief! Though victory felt partial, they had begun to see the benefits of sticking with their son through his ups and downs.

How can one control the ride? When should we draw the line and give no more ground? How can we decide to pursue a farcical situation, risking drowning in it? There are many such questions that I find myself asking all the time in relation to sticking with group work. Finally, I must face myself, who I am and what I want from my group life. I must hold onto what I believe.

TAKING ON ONESELF AND GAINING GROUND

Robert Frost said it best: "I bid you to a one-man revolution. The only revolution that is coming." I propose that one is obliged to be loyal to the cause one can have most control over – one's own beliefs and loyalties. In a short piece on being fooled as a member of a search panel, Bennis (1988) writes of waking up to realize that he and his committee had been devastated. They had been taken for a ride by their favorite job candidate. In all humility, he discovered that they had to do something different next time, if they could. Maybe as a group they couldn't. He suggested that the best approach would be to change his own method. Take gains on the ground one can hold.

Allan Sillitoe (1967, 1949) had a lot to say about attitude in surviving life in Borstal as a "crook at heart." As a long distance runner representing Borstal "establishment," the hero took the preparation seriously, but did not *intend* to win, just *prepared* to win. He was perfectly ready, but then purposely lost the race. He had bigger plans in mind, plans for bigger and better crimes and showing up the establishment. Devoted to his convictions about his own survival in this institution, devoted to his hatred of the governor of Borstal, he remained honest about who he was. He bent for a while, played by their rules, but was tough to the end in his own behalf. From his point of view he had won the race. He made some concessions, temporarily, never conceding his own character and strength.

When I have to deal with my family, school organization, seminars, groups, and families depending on me in one way or another, that is a lot of "otherness" to handle. Add to this the larger world, the state of the country and its politics – this can all get me down. I can only take my own voyages on these terrains, captain my own ships. As with Bion, I can be clear about my own duty and be devoted to meeting the challenge of my cases (Winnicott, 1965). Some cases, however, are too terrible; it takes a good dose of cheerful hatred to find the farce bearable.

Even in writing this final section, I struggle to find my own voice. Do I make this a statement that captures my co-author's view and feel the comfort of the royal "we"? Do I try to defend my position by reference to others who have spoken in their own metaphor? Brodsky, Herbert, etc., use the tools of the writer with such humbling clarity and conciseness. I recognize that their inspiration encourages me to believe I have something in common with their experience. I know that others have had to come to their own measure of themselves — but what others want and are satisfied with will not necessarily be a good fit for me. I am thrown back into myself to make judgments about how to captain my ship over group landscape. I must appreciate my own niche, my own powers or lack thereof, and know what it takes for me to recover my robustness when defeated. Awareness and changes at this level are the one-man revolution.

My own inclination is to err in the direction of not being hopeful enough about group life, of not looking for opportunities to take on the odds. Knowing this, I must remind myself to stay connected with my own efforts to make things work and to stretch my perspective to see my success. Others may come from a position that drives ahead at full speed in the fog. Here, too, there are obvious dangers — hopefulness must be tempered with judgment or one's emotional insurance must be high. We are all inclined to our own position and attitude — some more inclined to the sublime, others to the ridiculous. My idea of a most useful attitude for me would be to take my own inclination into the contest, play hard at the game, and be ready to win big, lose big, or anything in between. Then be ready for another go at it buoyed by having been a vigorous warrior.[1]

Royce describes in detail the "beauty of loyalty" (1936, p. 103) in an incident from English history. The Speaker of the House of Commons was caught in a conflict between the privileges of the House and the royal prerogative, when commanded by the King to surrender members of the House to arrest as leaders of the opposition party. He was trapped, not knowing what to do when the King questioned him directly on the house floor. The Speaker responded as follows, after falling on his knee before the King, "Your Majesty, I am the Speaker of this House, and, being such, I have neither eyes to see nor tongue to speak save as this House shall command; and I humbly beg your Majesty's pardon if this is the only answer that I can give to your Majesty" (pp. 104–105). Royce emphasized the force of loyalty. What is also in this response is the location of ground this Speaker stands on, his sense of himself. He is forced to act in this vise of pressures; the transitional move is his loyalty to his role and constituents, as he sees it. The cause which one serves best — often highlighted under catastrophic circumstances — is rooted in a position that stands back and reviews and encompasses both internal terrain and connection with the social world.

We have been describing each of the twelve postures we have covered in our twelve chapters as control points. In this instance the construct is paradoxical, in that the degree of freedom to take on oneself is seen clearly from a position of little control. For instance, when I go through my day in the various social contexts in which I am embedded, I end up feeling like a whole series of pieces. What people want and expect usually flows from a combination of assumptions about who I am and what they want me to be. Sometimes I can enjoy the limited challenge, but I realize that this also means limited connection and impact. I must be good-natured about living life in pieces. As Coleman (1971) puts it, modern society is a matter of occupying roles. This is also true on the smaller scale of mundane social relationships — roles converging temporarily in common pursuit. How do we work against partial relationships in modern culture?

I have the sense that, again, I can gain ground on this by realizing that partiality gives me room for experimentation, opens up my degrees of freedom. If a specific seminar is especially rich and exciting, I can get more involved in it; on the other hand, if defeats heavily outweigh victories in other kinds of groups I must be in, I can survive better if I have only a small investment in them. I have the degree of freedom in positioning myself in relation to my world. I feel that I can use some amount of "naturally occurring" segmentation to my own advantage. I would hate to have too few social options, too easily to be disappointed and without backup. I also think it is true that relationships shift to greater or lesser involvement over time. One can have some control over the range of involvements. I can decide that, rather than many casual relationships, I will have fewer and deeper. One can realign social grouping at work for more informal support if the formal channels are too dry and ungiving. One cannot always control social structures, but the degree of freedom comes in how and where one positions oneself. If one has a light enough touch to see the farce and enjoy the humor in humorless situations, even the immovables and inevitables can be survived.

Bayley lets me stay with myself: "Dogs are also powerless, with that powerlessness which is the true fate of the individual . . . it links up with Tolstoy's curious observation that freedom consists in 'my not having made the laws'" (1987, p. 216). For me this is a tremendously liberating awareness. Realizing that I didn't make the rules, I permit myself just the position I need to see them clearly outside and around myself. I can inwardly adjust based on knowing them. I can join with allies to do combat, I can feel some degree of success in playing with them and enjoying what I manage to sequester for myself as increments of competence. The adventure is endless and my conscience is clear; I didn't make the rules.

It seems apt to end our effort with an attitude of embarking on another voyage. As in the extraordinary ending of Conrad's *Nigger of the Narcissus*, we will ship out again, the better prepared by our completed voyages. The new challenge and opportunity offer us further perspective on who we are and where we are going in our various social adventures. This makes each opportunity electrifying.

There is no point in going on further about the nature of things. Enduring depends on revisiting the landscape again, trying to understand it better, appreciating its "otherness," and operating more effectively. Ending is replaced by a renewal of vigor on a different field at another time.

Again: "I bid you to a one-man revolution. The only revolution that is coming."

Notes, Bibliography, Index

NOTES

*T*he notes that follow divide into three kinds:
The Footnotes clarify difficult points in the text.

The Practical Systemic Guide points to further reading in each of the practical systemic subjects: namely, individual psychotherapy, teaching, group therapy, group relations (group analysis, participant observation, sensitivity), family therapy, organizational management and consultation, and global problems. Courses in each of these subjects can be taught utilizing this book with each supplementary reading list. We provide the pagination of this book relevant to each course.

The Intellectual Systemic Guide directs the reader to the readings we found useful in constructing the postures for the modern contest: from the specific intellectual fields of cybernetic systems theory, sociology, anthropology, political science and history, biology and the philosophy of science, literature and religion, individual psychotherapy, psychiatry and psychology, group dynamics, systemic family therapy and theory, and methodology in social science. Our outlines of these fields could be considered the scaffolding from which the text was constructed. It is extremely important to understand that each academic field tends to allow seeing only arcs of the patterns that connect us in the modern contest. The terms peculiar to each academic field tend to restrict the view: viz., to the merely economic, to the merely group dynamic, to the merely biological, etc. This intellectual territorial behavior is absolutely typical of all groups in the modern contest which seek to stake out ground that they can hold and from which they can deny outsiders access, but it blocks the view of the modern contest as a whole set of patterns which connect us. Therefore, we believe it is of considerable importance to see how the crucial terms of each intellectual discipline are pieces of a whole picture.

I. Footnotes

1. The Modern Territory

1. In Bateson's language, by focusing on "short trains of causality" (1972, p. 145), "unaided consciousness must always tends toward hate" (1972, p. 146), from hoping for what is never going to happen, from the continual frustration of moving so often against the flow of swarming humanity, from being victimized. See especially the literary statements (Ian Gustafson, personal communication of this proposition in Porter (1935) and Hesse (1943). See also our own Chapter 5 for a full statement of the problems of defending morale. It turns out that good-natured hate (or what Winnicott (1947) calls "objective hate") can be very useful for helping us remember these problems and thus anticipate them better, even cheerfully.

2. It is important as dwellers *within* organizations not to forget how much we *still* remain in the dark. In the New Testament, this awareness is entirely explicit, as in the following passage:

> For now we see in a glass darkly; but then face to face: Now I know in part; but then shall I know fully even as also I was fully known. (Corinthians I, 13:12)

Modern science has been so penetrating of the mechanisms of control in nature that now we often forget how much is unseen by us. Take the following marvelous discovery about the channeling of rain:

> Raindrops that pass in random fashion through an imaginary plane above the forest canopy are intercepted by leaves and twigs and channelled into distinctive vertical space patterns of through-drip, crown-drip, and stem flow. The soil surface, as receiver, transmits the "rain message" downward, but as the subsoils lack a power source to mold a flow design, the

water tends to leave the ecosystem as it entered it, in randomized fashion. (Berry, 1982)

But once we call what is unknown to us "the random," we presume too much:

> [The writer] should have said that rainwater moves from mystery through pattern back to mystery. . . . To call the unknown by its right name . . . is to suggest that we had better respect the possibility of a larger, unseen pattern that can be damaged or destroyed and, with it, the smaller patterns. . . . Act on the basis of ignorance (which) . . . requires one to know things . . . —for instance, that failure is possible, that second chances are desirable (so don't risk everything on the first chance), and so on. (Berry, 1982)

What is so true of rain is all the more true of human beings in all their amazing arrangements. So much of them is hidden from us. Best to assume we see but a very small part, as they move " . . . from mystery through pattern back to mystery." We think we have a greater chance of respecting " . . . larger, unseen pattern that can be damaged or destroyed" *if* we have a potential space in the surprising landscape to imagine what we do *not* see before us just now.

3. Tolstoy's comments on writing could orient us about all local efforts:

> Judging by what I read I was convinced that Maupassant possessed talent—that is to say, the gift of attention revealing in the objects and facts of life with which he deals qualities others had not perceived. He was also a master of a beautiful style, expressing what he wanted to say clearly, simply, and with charm. He was also a master of that condition of true artistic production without which a work of art

does not produce its effect, namely, sincerity; that is, he did not pretend that he loved or hated but really loved or hated what he described. But unfortunately, lacking the first and perhaps the chief condition of good artistic production, a correct moral relation to what he described — that is to say, a knowledge of the difference between good and evil — he loved and described things which should not have been loved and described. (p. 852, Tolstoy)

4. See Royce (1936) for a rich discussion of loyalty beyond the family. Dante (Alighieri, 1314) put the betrayal of loyalty into the deepest depths of hell. This must be an abiding conception about what is most important in the world.

5. In his lecture of April 4, 1989, at the University of Wisconsin, "The Field of Power," Professor Bourdieu argued that familial strategy in the field of power depends upon family *positioning* in that field: for example, in France, some families are positioned to send their sons to schools and professions which emphasize economic capital, such as banking, while other families are positioned to send their sons to schools and professions which emphasize other cultural capital, such as in academia. Then, there are families somewhere in between which emphasize both economic and cultural capital, who send their sons into the civil service. Although this patterning is complicated by crossovers within families, and by the emergence of daughters into the field of power, the two patterns of dominance are still striking along family lines. We certainly would agree that the postures for engaging such a field are highly dependent upon positioning: Thus, all of us have to take up some postures concerning overall perspective, organization, reading situations, moving freely, counterposing and complex counterposing (we submit that such *distinctions* are useful, to use a crucial concept of Bordieu), but that all of these postures will be greatly altered by where one is sitting in the hierarchy: The *lower* one is in the hierarchy, the more indirect must be one's moving freely, counterposing and complex counterposing (suitable deference will be necessary!). Conversely, *marginal* positioning, such as occupied by psychotherapists, consultants, professors and so forth, allows a great deal more direct negotiating.

Gramsci (1957) is also interesting about this subject of positioning in the field of power, especially in the essay "The Formation of Intellectuals."

6. About the time we began writing this book I hung Bosch's Temptation of St. Anthony over the couch on which my patients sit. A year later, I put the sign in small capitals over my door: Exit to Nevsky Prospect (Gogol, 1835). Little did I realize at those times the theoretical significance of what I was doing in humor: that the line (panel) between the compartments of helping and taking advantage is one I and my patients must study ever so carefully. Most of them have protected themselves weakly there. Comedy and tragedy, the drama and the novel, literature and art, could be said to have taken this line (panel) between civility and taking advantage as their perpetual subject. Because double descriptions abound here, this area is rich in feeling, pleasure and story. From Moliere's *Miser* to *A Fish Called Wanda*, comedy loves to play the wolf and beat him up, to have it both ways. Somewhere there must be a Bosch who will paint the Temptation of St. Anthony of our time, the very center panel of the modern territory. I would love to place it across the room from the original.

7. The distinctions between war, contest, the center panel of the modern contest, civility, play and solitude are fully developed in Gathering Strength, Chapter 11.

8. The Health Maintenance Organization (HMO) is a typical institution, which purports to take care of patients, in the finest, lengthy promises, while being designed to give as little care as possible. Some HMOs represent fair trades, some go broke giving too much, some enrich their owners in the guise of help. You just can't tell from the gloss what help is actually being arranged.

9. For our full set of proposals on organization as readiness for war and disqualification, the reader may turn to the crude versions in Chapter 2, Us and Them, and to the subtle versions, in Chapter 3, Vertical and Horizontal Readiness.

10. Trevelyan's argument for the long phase of conservatism is interesting and relevant for our own times:

The outrages that provoked the Revolution had engendered an ideal enthusiasm for vested interests as such, because the action of James II had for a while identified vested interests with the cause of British freedom. And this ideal enthusiasm survived the occasion that had called it forth. The existing laws, which James II in his tyranny had over-ridden, became a fetish to Judge Blackstone and the men of the Eighteenth Century. (p. 378)

The great unrest of the late 1960s in our country has led, similarly, to a phase that calls for "strong men" in the presidency and which calls the status quo of vested interests the "middle road." Social justice in such periods is unusual.

11. In the terms of our own Introduction, we prefer to be Dr. De Soto, not the Fox.
12. Algebraically: Individuals can emerge freshly on their own terms $(i-1)$, meet the challenge of the case (i), and ride it into other domains $(i+1)$. Here are three fields of entirely different scope. See Platt (1970) concerning Deutsch's Theorem, and our Chapter 3, Vertical and Horizontal Readiness, especially the footnotes.
13. There are several ways to imagine territory which is free of the difficulties of the modern contest. One way is this imagination of a vertical set of realms, orthogonal to the horizontal stage of winning and losing. A second way is taken in Gathering Strength, Chapter 11, placing the more treacherous territory outward and the more protected territory inward. The first imagination has the virtue of slipping upward or downward in a moment, while the second imagination takes distance very carefully and deliberately by posing a set of compartments between the most painful and the most important.

3. *Vertical and Horizontal Readiness*

1. In the language of Deutsch's theorem (Platt, 1970), Reich's challenge to the "constant attitude" of the patient, the organizing element of identity $(i)_a$, weakens the hold of that confining identity, allowing the strongest component element, sexuality $(i-1)$, to resonate with the surrounding context, the political interest in liberation $(i+2)$, to bring about a new identity $(i)_b$. But this resonance alarmed the two establishments, psychoanalysis $(i+1)_a$ and the Communist Party $(i+1)_b$, which provided a more immediate context for Reich's work. These two shut him down. They had the power to do so, because his work was but a component in their fields, which didn't have sufficient resonance with a context surrounding these fields to bring about a transformation of them.
2. See Oliver Wendell Holmes (1858, pp. 146-147) for a similar spirit to that of Leopold: Holmes took personal command of all the waterways of Boston, while knowing all the while that Boston itself belonged to commerce.
3. Heilbroner (1989, p. 98) shows the great power of business in our time in an eloquent, opening paragraph:

Less than seventy-five years after it officially began, *the contest* between capitalism and socialism is over: capitalism has won. The Soviet Union, China, and Eastern Europe have given us the clearest possible proof that capitalism organizes the material affairs of humankind more satisfactorily than socialism: that however inequitably or irresponsibly the marketplace may distribute goods, it does so better than the queues of a planned economy; however mindless the culture of commercialism, it is more attractive than state moralism; and however deceptive the ideology of a business civilization, it is more believable than that of a socialist one. (my italics)

This has been a major victory in the modern contest on the global scale.

4. Examples abound. Many teachers and mentors see you only if you are talking about their line of contribution. Veer away and you disappear off their map or get rudely disqualified (flight or fight is aroused). This is simply a matter of territory (business) being first and last for them. If you want their friendly interest, you must talk to them in their world. Probably we are all like this, but some have small tents of hospitality and some have larger ones (Klein, 1959).
5. In tennis, the desired result is "fear free tennis" (Michael McDermott, personal communication) which allows the player to go all out, without being constricted by fear of losing.
6. See Gathering Strength, Chapter 11, for

full exposition of this strategy of keeping many compartments between what is most crucial and what is most dangerous.

7. Humor is vital to rendering contests less important (loosening their grip on us). Russell Baker (1989) puts political favor into perspective in his article, "A Low-Ranked Ball Can Ruin A Person," which begins like this:

I once went to an Inaugural Ball. There were five Inaugural Balls that year. The one I went to was No. 5. People who were going to run the government and make a terrible mess of the country during the next four years went to the No. 1 job. Their deputies went to the No. 2 and assistants to the deputies to No. 3. No. 5 was so far down the social line that people with tickets to it were ashamed to admit it. This was Lyndon Johnson's Inauguration in 1965. Knowing Johnson's talent for making distinctions, paranoids believed that getting a ticket to No. 5 was a kiss of death. Many refused to show up for fear they'd be ruined if seen there.

8. These three measures provide, in the language of our Chapter 2, a common antagonist: in terms of us against all our centrifugal obligations, us against the challenge of the case. The organization of the Brief Therapy Clinic is fully described in Gustafson (1986). See Chapter 23, "Autopoetic Students," for a description of the logic of consultations to the trainees by their peer group and myself.

9. Deutsch's theorem (Platt, 1970) is expanded by us from three terms or fields to as many as necessary. This allows us to write in shorthand form how four, five, six, seven levels or fields of entirely different scope interact, viz., regarding the clinic, we work together to "meet the challenge of the case" (i) (Winnicott, 1965), releasing individual members of the seminar $(i-1)$, to resonate with their larger life experiences $(i+4)$. The intervening level of the department of psychiatry $(i+1)$, which could dampen the freedom of this interaction by its highly competitive ethos, is excluded as much as possible by my emphasis on a sharp boundary between the clinic and other departmental activities. The intervening level of the medical school politics $(i+2)$, however, interacted with the department's opening of competing clinics to shut down the flow of patients to our clinic (i).

This obliged me to open up many sources of referral in the medical school $(i+2)$ and in town $(i+3)$ to the department $(i+1)$, so that I have the necessary flow to sustain my clinic (i). We are thus having to cope with a set of interactions that involve different fields of entirely different scope, from individual students $(i-1)$, through the clinic (i), to the department $(i+1)$, medical school $(i+2)$, town $(i+3)$, to the wider life experiences of the students $(i+4)$. This algebraic notation is extremely useful for keeping track of the relevant fields that impinge upon the field in question (i). I use it for vertical readiness in every field that I work.

10. In our algebraic notation all of this history can be summarized as follows: In the first Balint group $(i)_a$, three residents $(i-1)$ got free of their dreaded clinic $(i+1)$, their peer court culture $(i+2)$, their patients and their families $(i+3)$, and their medical faculty $(i+4)$ to be closeted with me. There they let loose their destructive component $(i-2)$ in a way that resonated with the task of the Balint group $(i)_a$ to change themselves $(i-1)$. In the second Balint group $(i)_b$, there was little closeting of the group from the larger dampening influences of heavy work schedules all over the hospital $(i+1)$, and an antagonistic peer culture $(i+2)$. Responsibility to patients and their families $(i+3)$ and accountability to the medical faculty $(i+4)$ worked relatively weakly upon the Balint group $(i)_b$, just enough to get it going and limping along.

11. Vertical scaling of our consultation to the psychiatrist of the Glue Team and the Crowbar Team can be summarized in algebraic form as follows: The challenge of the case is to respond to the predicament of the psychiatrist (i): namely that he is inadvertently driving the strange loop of the Crowbar Team $(i-1)_a$ by joining it against the Glue Team $(i-1)_b$. We stood outside this snare $(i+2)$ well enough to pose it back to him. But taking our presentation to our own colleagues $(i+3)$ in terms of possible missing levels, they helped us to see the missing levels: the developmental challenge of the parents' retirement $(i+2)$ and the need to address the patient herself who was left out of the party of the two teams after our message $(i-2)$.

Horizontal, temporal scaling of our team's entirely taking into itself the expected disturbances (perturbations) looks as follows in algebraic form: Let (t) be the rhythm of weekly teamwork. Then expectable disruptions (cancellations at the last minute) come less frequently, perhaps every two months (t + 1). Each of our three teams gets a chance for consultation from the other two in an evening meeting about once in three months (t + 2). Several times a year (t + 3), we provide observation groups for interested students and colleagues. Less frequently (t + 4) we present at departmental or national meetings. We arrange to be disturbed on these several different frequencies. This horizontal scaling has been superb for a relatively young team (Selvini Palazzoli et al., 1978, used a similar scaling to ensure their own autonomy in their early years) and is already changing as we become more confident.

12. It is always wondrous when we learn to look into smaller or larger, or faster or slower, holons. A simple device as a bird feeder brings bird worlds into view we never imagined there at all. Similarly, a doctor who leads a Balint group may see only the level of the group members banding together to back their colleague against a hostile consultant: he may be thrilled to see the smaller level of this individual person's experience of the event and the larger level of how this person will play his next round in the system with the next hostile consultant.

4. Gaining and Renewing Clarity

1. A dramatic example of a win-lose metaphor drawing together a highly complicated organizational consultation can be found in Selvini Palazzoli (1986).
2. Popper's argument against historicism is fascinating. In addition to Magee's summary, the interested reader is referred to Popper himself (1957).
3. Without Bion's clarity as to his duty, his sense of surprise would be diminished when faced with the actual events in his groups. Take the following quote: "I do not believe for a moment that the objective fact — namely, that I am merely one member of a group possessing some degree of specialized knowledge, . . . would be likely to be accepted. The forces opposed to this are far too strong. One external group — that is, the Clinic responsible for saying that I am to take a group — has given the seal of its authority to a myth of unknown dimensions . . . " (1959, pp. 37–38). It is in knowing his own beliefs and emotions that he is moored. Too often such clarity is absent in his devotees, leaving the leaders and groups to flatly rediscover the obvious.
4. Bateson (1972) has described different vantage points as shifts in emphasis in terms of context markers, as postures, actions, or utterances in interactions which give sequences rhythm and pacing. Bateson argues that shifts in this kind of punctuation can change meaning, as in language and music. In a fascinating reanalysis of Sophocles' vs. Freud's versions of the Oedipus story, Galdston (1954) adds quite a different meaning to our appreciation of the psychology of the situation. While Freud emphasizes the parent-child triangle, Galdston underlines the intergenerational chain: parents committing crimes against their children, who then in turn compound them: same story, different emphasis; an original bit of clarity.
5. Examples abound in literature of heroes struggling out of the depths of their immediacy. Balzac's (1835) Eugene finds some dignity and conscience in living through the seamy underbelly of Pere Goriot's boarding house and the family life. Zola's (1885) coalminers became heroes from *inside* the mines. Overcoming the invasiveness of social entanglement can lead to new clarity.

5. Protecting Morale

1. Havens (1988) compares the time-space of the human being to an arrow in flight. Objective-descriptive interviewers ask questions that block the arrow and cause it to fall to the ground. You can learn something about the form of the arrow

lying still on the ground, but you lose a great deal of knowledge about its thrust, direction, power, angle, and so forth. Analytic interviewers sit behind the arrow, from where its direction is well appreciated, but such observers are at the mercy of where the arrow flies. Havens prefers two other positions: alongside the arrow, while placing obstacles in its path to watch the deflections; riding the arrow to feel what the patient feels in his place. These two latter positions are what I recommend for looking for people in surprising landscape, following Havens' lead.

2. In algebraic form: The students get the chance to sink into themselves ($-i$), to meet the challenge of the case (i), to ride it into other worlds ($i+1$, $i+2$, etc.). This means the challenge is taken seriously (i), but loosely held so that it is not overly constraining (this is negative capability).

3. Berger and Kellner (1964) suggest that the marital conversation will be stabilized as long as it is *the final court of judgment* on all *other* conversations: "This process of conversational liquidation is especially powerful because it is one-sided — the husband typically talks with his wife about his friend, but *not* with his friend about his wife. Thus the friend is deprived of the defense of, as it were, counter-defining the relationship" (p. 12). Once other conversations take precedence, the marriage is in trouble. Conversations on other scales can subsume the marital conversation as a component scale, which means the marital conversation gets *used* for purposes not its own. This is often denied by the couple, creating denied coalitions against the other partner (what Haley (1966) called "perverse triangles"). The partner is punished by covert comparison with the ideal third party (Dicks, 1967). This pattern is the chief destroyer of marriages in America.

4. In other words, the sensitivity group conversation (i) falls victim to the preferences for other conversations: to keeping a modicum of good feeling for seminars together in the department ($i+1$), to surviving in the hospital ($i+2$), while retreating into marital conversations ($i-1$) and keeping one's own counsel ($i-2$).

5. The retreat is to mammalian emotion, extraordinarily rich and beautiful in its movements (Hearne, 1986a, b), from the swarming of hierarchical society. Tolstoy (1869) gets back and forth better than anyone between these two lenses, showing the disappearance of the individual in the lens that shows the swarm, showing his reemergence in the lens that shows him in his own self-satisfaction (samodovolnost) (Bayley, 1966).

6. Gogol describes a provincial party in mid-19th century Russia in terms of a swarm of flies:

As he entered the ballroom, Chichikov had for a moment to screw up his eyes, dazzled by the blaze of the candles, the lamps, and the ladies' gowns. Everything was flooded in light. Black frock-coats glided and flitted about singly or in swarms here and there like so many flies on a sparkling white sugar-loaf on a hot July day when the old housekeeper chops and breaks it up into glittering lumps in front of an open window, the children gather round and look on, watching with interest the movements of her rough hands raising and lowering the hammer, while the *serial squadrons of flies* borne on the light breeze, fly in boldly, just as if they owned the place and, taking advantage of the old woman's feeble eyesight and the sunshine that dazzles her eyes, cover the dainty lumps in small groups or in swarms. Already satiated by the abundant summer, which sets up dainty dishes for them on every step, they fly in not so much to eat as to display themselves, to stroll up and down the pile of sugar, to rub their hind legs or their front feet together, or to scratch themselves under their wings, or, stretching out both their front legs, to rub their heads with them, then turn round and fly out again, and again fly in with new tiresome squadrons. (Gogol, pp. 23–4, 1842, my italics)

Henry describes the same tendency in mid-20th century America:

Meanwhile, the orientation of man toward survival, to the exclusion of other considerations, has made society a grim place to live in, and for the most part human society has been a place where, though man has survived physically, he has died emotionally.

This is another reason why, although culture is "for" man, it is also "against" him. And that is why I do not say much about the "good" things in American culture, for I am concerned and deeply worried that unthinking subjection to the primordial impulse to survive is simply producing new varieties of destruction. (Henry, 1963, p. 12)

Both writers will seem excessive to many of our readers. However, I would point out in their defense that the more driven the social organization, the less important become the individual persons who play parts in it (conversely, somewhat inefficient organizations can yield a richness of roles [Barker, 1983] and fun can be allowed to disrupt the drivenness [Henry, 1963, pp. 43–44.]) My own view is that poetic, emotional characters like Gogol and Henry find the commercial swarm unbearable when they discover that their extraordinary moments of speech or teaching count little or briefly with the average person, so that their currency seems enormously devalued: It is as though a great poetry reading were followed by an auction; the book of poems

just read might be bid for $20, at the same level as everything else. This leveling of commercial equivalents is hilariously told by Kurt Vonnegut in his story, "Harrison Bergeron" (1961), which opens as follows:

The year was 2081, and everybody was finally equal. They weren't only equal before God and the law. They were equal every which way. Nobody was smarter than anybody else. Nobody was better looking than anybody else. Nobody was stronger or quicker than anybody else. All this equality was due to the 211th, 212th, and 213th Amendments to the Constitution, and to the unceasing vigilance of agents of the United States Handicapper General.

7. See Ford's story, "Optimists" (1987), about being too close with the neighbors.
8. That is, those who improve their objective self-possession will be freer to enlarge their subjective self-possession (Mann, unpublished) without going too far or too naively forward.

6. Seizing Moments for Transition

1. In Bion's view, the opposing forces were primitive, object-related drive states. He intended to add new information to the working context. As Bateson suggested (1979), a useful transition does this.
2. Ezriel, working with a style which in many ways was similar to Bion's, started with an internal template and focused on the contribution individuals make to the group process. When he became clear about the group tension, he acted to construct for each member "his specific way of coping with this common group tension (and) why he acts in this way . . . with this group problem" (1950, p. 70). As a colleague and contemporary of Bion's, Ezriel shows how differently one can work with a group process model looping the group dynamic back into the individual concern. Though discussed more fully elsewhere in the book, it is worth mentioning here that an internal template can also increase possibilities for movement to levels larger than the group itself (Cooper, 1976).

Whitaker and Lieberman saw movement in the group as a "function of individual differences in the position which each member takes with reference to the immediate (focal conflict)" (1964, p. 61). In describing the relation of the disturbing motive to the reactive motive and the restrictive solution, they underlined the therapist's role in not accepting solutions that close off the conflict. There was a great likelihood that there were continuous reactions to group forces. The therapist's task was to keep equilibria shifting. Bion had his basic assumptions to prevent restrictive closures, Whitaker and Lieberman their triangles of focal conflict. They seized the moment of awareness of unacceptable treatment. The problem inside the doctor was not to be dismissed.
3. Balint's G.P. Groups are interesting to juxtapose here (Bourne, 1976). Here is a method using a wide spectrum of interventions, as Skynner does, in an attempt to make sense of the G.P.'s experience. Balint was also searching for missing pieces—in the doctor-patient relation-

ship, in the group process, in the seminar members' relationship to the group leader, in the fears and worries of the individual physicians. His job was to defuse various bombs and introduce them into the seminar in a way that was growth-producing rather than terrifying. Skynner describes the full boldness of his own family undertaking, but Balint was certainly daring himself in his full and rich use of a seminar format.

4. It needs to be noted that information itself, as Yalom discusses, is one of the curative factors in group psychotherapy. What is being observed by Bach is not the initial intention and/or use of the information, but the fact that, as the group sticks on this direction too long, there is a reversal in the impact of the information on the recipients: Information and feedback become advice, control (dominance-submission struggle), and scapegoating. One must interfere with this process early on if the therapeutic effects of transmitting information are to stay intact. Transitions of various sorts are ways of interrupting the process.

5. Main makes it very clear that group processes, especially in large groups but also in small ones, are riddled with projection and projective identification processes which greatly interfere with the full thinking capacities of individuals. His conclusion is that "at present our best-tested therapeutic technique and most fruitful observations rest on the classic two-body situation. Comparatively little is yet known about multibody psychology and very little about the multibody psychology of large groups" (1975, p. 86). The keys to recovery from large group confusion are group conversations in which the individual can find his "self" and use his faculties for reality-testing. Non-interpretative interventions can serve as well as, if not better than, more abstract interpretations in the therapeutic situations on which he focuses; the idea is to help people rediscover their feelings and thoughts in relation to others. His paper is highly recommended for getting a good feel for large group life. In a classic paper on group process in patient settings, Main (1957) underlines how staff (group) process can be curative by the coordinated efforts of individuals keeping track of themselves in relation to pathology.

6. Surprising resolutions often make the paralysis of the moment stark and the choice to give in inevitable. In a startling play by Durrenmatt (1956), a poverty-stricken town chose sacrificial death of one of its prominent members in greed-driven alliance with a wronged benefactress set on revenge. There was a primitive religious metaphor here, it seemed, choosing human sacrifice of one life to a wrathful god for the survival of the many. The force of the individual interest was overwhelmed, and the clash between the individual and the group—and the inevitable overpowering of the individual—was shockingly exposed.

7. Both Bennis and Shepard (1957) and Mann (1975) write of this kind of forced choice situation, particularly when there is a major chasm in the peer group. These moves and resolutions are interesting to follow in relation to their own central themes about group development.

8. It is clarifying to think about time in Deutsch's terms (Platt, 1970) as a shorthand guide for vertical and horizontal scaling. At the level of the family (peer) group (i) one must take into account the identified patient $(i-1)$ and other family members $(i-1_a...i-1_n)$. When a move must be made on trouble seen at the $i-1$ level, and the i level peer group offers little success, the surrounding group $(i+1)$ might best be next. Broadening the context can occur at levels of *vertical* scaling of ever widening circles of family influence $(i+2$, grandparents; $i+3$, great-grandparents; etc.) or, as in footnote 11, Chapter 3, *horizontal* levels of surrounding groups as they appear at different points in time in the rhythm of the therapy. The algebra helps us see levels we might otherwise miss or not see as clearly.

7. *Free Passage*

1. Of course, the devil himself is free to use the same strategy. See the remarkable adventures in flattery of Chichikov in *Dead Souls* (Gogol, 1842), especially with

Manilov in Chapter 2 and Plyushkin in Chapter 6. See also *The Adventures of Brer Rabbit* (Lester, 1987).

2. Rickman (1951) has a very fine essay about presenting to psychoanalysts in which Freud summarizes the problem most aptly (naturally!): "Freud, by the way, likened verbatim delivery from a manuscript to a person inviting his friend to accompany him into the country, and then he himself rides in a carriage while his friend trudges on foot—it cannot be expected that there will be an easy companionship on such a journey" (p. 229).

3. If you plan to conduct a seminar on nuclear war, you can expect a death-immersion at some point, which is likely to overwhelm the group and wreck its morale for good (Gustafson, unpublished (a)).

4. See Chapter 9 for ample discussion of this problem: what we call the armies of the overpowering, the armies of the oblivious, and the armies of the desperate—none of whom will see much of us. See "The Love Song of J. Alfred Prufrock" (Eliot, 1934) for an unforgettable version of this problem of becoming invisible in someone else's points. This is especially a danger for performers who love to be closely followed. What if you give a splendid lecture and someone gets only one point out of it! Or nullifies the entire effort by finding a single fault and fastening onto it with relish!

5. Our division of labor among the three family team members is as follows:

   1. The lead interviewer opens the interview and closes it with her final message;
   2. The second interviewer has several segments in the middle, alternating with the lead interviewer (about ten minutes per segment).
   3. The third teammate stays entirely behind the mirror. His job is to consult to his two colleagues (especially about dissociated feeling getting into him).

6. Demoralization is very dangerous. See our Chapter 5, Protecting Morale.

7. So many people become operatives in meeting the challenge of the case literally (i), because they lack a larger tradition (i+1) to take perspective from elsewhere (which could give them the freedom of double description), because they lack much expressiveness as an individual voice (i−1). The Bible used to provide that outside perspective (i+1) on secular life (i), while individuality (i−1) could flourish in local color. Now it can all seem but one modern contest after another. Such operating has an enormous potential for being put to evil use, lacking moral cause, lacking individual fulfillment (Lifton, 1986). This is why I try to instill a love of the entire tradition of psychotherapy in my students, why Brodsky proposes the same about the tradition of literature: "If only because the lock and stock of literature is indeed human diversity and perversity, it turns out to be a reliable antidote for any attempt—whether familiar or yet to be invented—toward a total mass solution to the problems of human existence. As a form of moral insurance, at least, literature is much more dependable than a system of beliefs or a philosophical doctrine" (1988b, p. 29). See also our Chapter 6, which is about moving freely by watching for traps at (i−1), (i), and (i+1) levels.

8. The game theorists worked out this distinction between games of a single play and games with many plays: showing how this alteration of the rules provides altogether different possibilities for cooperation. See especially Axelrod and Keohane (1985) and Downs, Rocke, and Siverson (1985).

9. Much more harshly, Brodsky wrote of "suckers for solidity" who think that if the procedure has the right numbers it must be esteemed, who never think to ask if the question studied is worth the procedure. For the latter, you need another tradition from which to judge.

8. *Time and Timing*

1. One would like to press forward, but. . . . if the effort to push forward is not in harmony with the time, a reasonable and resolute man will not expose himself to a personal rebuff, but will retreat with others of like mind. (*I Ching*, 1950, pp. 41–42)

The advice of the *I Ching* suggests a retreat (to a deliberating platform) which could bring "good fortune because he does not needlessly jeopardize himself." Extending the religious metaphor for a moment, Moses discovered that in his prolonged absence the Jews began to worship false gods. The immediate time frame which God felt should guide the true believers was the wait for the holy words Moses was seeking on Sinai. For the Jews, however, the more compelling story of time was the prolonged desertion of Moses. The time scale which revealed the more telling story for the Jews was the past bad treatments and the importance of Moses' saving leadership and desertion (Exodus, Chapter 32). Two different time scales, each dominant on a different holon.

2. Skynner adds a personal note to this kind of timing problem (1986a) when he writes about knowing when it is time to begin to work with his wife as a family therapy team. The crucial event for him is the family members' recovery from one of the mundane and terrible family disputes we all have but often don't bounce back from with as much *savoir faire* as the Skynners. It was as if the family (children included) signaled that it was time to expand the adult partnership; this new idea could be permitted.

3. As discussed by Fenichel (1945), timing has a long tradition as a pivotal facet of psychoanalytic technique. Bad timing can account for negative therapeutic reactions.

9. *Defensible Territory*

1. Such natural history of small groups (i) is not independent of its members (i−1) or of its context (i+1). As Redl (1946) argues, individual members can swing a group for better or for ill. As we have argued (Gustafson, Cooper, et al., 1981), a seminar evolves differently in the Kremlin than at Ohio State. See Chapter 3 concerning Balint Groups for discussion of the dependence of small teaching groups on three to six or seven such levels.

2. Or like "squadrons of flies" in Gogol's *Dead Souls* (1842, p. 24). There Chichikov is perfectly successful in fitting into provincial Russian society by mimicking the correct postures (despite nefarious purposes).

3. Perhaps the most acceptable and beautiful military metaphors for ordering our existence are from Z. Herbert (1968), especially "To Marcus Aurelius," "Elegey for Fortinbras," and "Why the Classics."

4. As with so much in the modern world, the entire advantage lies with those who see what's coming and are more or less prepared. Anticipation is the key virtue. See Gustafson and Cooper (1978) on anticipating "conditions of scarcity" in groups, which makes for mean behavior all around. See Gustafson (unpublished (b)) for anticipating the fast stretches in the river of lived time in the lives of patients.

5. This is not to say that there cannot be

hilarity or spontaneity in such relationships. When the regime is well settled, looseness occurs, without jeopardy. When the regime is in trouble, such occasions become grim and cold. Then watch out, take care, and plan line by line. Colleagues are out to nail each other, if they get an opening.

6. Also this outlook on the social terrain can be seen in modern painters, especially Bosch long before his time (the first painter of the modern contest, like Machiavelli the first author of the modern contest) or more contemporary painters like Francis Bacon in his paintings of Pope Innocent. Bosch and Bacon can show us a world of users and used (fortunately with humor).

7. Nietzsche (1878) shows the characteristic bitterness of having been defeated in such departmental politics, which leads him to denigrate the winners as harshly as possible and to justify himself. This is a position not likely to win friends:

Hence one should consider the teacher, no less than the shopkeeper, a necessary evil, an evil to be kept as small as possible. If the trouble in the German situation today has perhaps its main reason in the fact that too many people live by trade and want to live well (and thus seek to cut the producer's prices as much as possible while at the same time raising the prices as much as possible to the consumer, in order to derive *an advantage from the greatest possible damage to both*) then one can certainly find a main reason for the spiritual troubles in the surplus of teachers: on their account, one learns so little and so badly. (Nietzsche, p. 71, 1954)

. . . For the intermediaries falsify the nourishment almost automatically when they mediate it: then, as a reward for their mediation, they want too much for themselves, which is taken away from the original productive spirits: namely, interest, admiration, time, money and other things.

Better I think to pose the departmental politics as the field "for meeting the challenge of the case" (Winnicott, 1965) (i). You have to win on *this* field, not on some higher field ruled over by the best people in the world or by God himself (i+2, i+n). Once you fight well on this field (i), you can use your tradition (i+1) to augment your forces. As several of my teachers in the department, long before me, discovered, tradition (i+1) alone will not get an opening unless it is led by someone who will arrange to win the political fight. This is how tradition (i+1) gets lost, putting in its last appearance in someone's speech elsewhere about what should have been.

8. If you stand back far enough from a department of psychiatry in a medical school (to the distance of a sociologist or of an ecologist), you are no longer surprised that it should be a field on which the crudest struggles for power should take place: for where else can a man (women have a poorer chance to win here) get paid tens of thousands for teaching a few hours a week and tens of thousands for administering (arranging his own way when he can) and tens of thousands for seeing patients who come readily to him as a professor. We would expect a certain ferocity to hold onto such a privileged waterhole. When it is quiet here (as Foucault argues), it must mean that some regime has got the place running smoothly for its interests — until the next outbreak of another group contesting its hegemony. Not only songbirds but man himself "hotly contest(s) territories with the most abundant resources" (Marks, 1987). Darwin would expect no less.

9. Skillful teachers have to be very careful about unchecked giving. The difficulty is more complicated than an imbalance of giving by the teacher, which is met by irresponsibility from the students, although that is commonplace enough. *That* problem can be managed by fair trade; if I am going to provide such and such a seminar, your matching responsibilities (if you want to be allowed to be included) are such and such work. Then the defaulting can be met by the "tit for tat" strategy described later in this chapter. More complicated than this fair trade is the likelihood that the teacher's devotion to the subject will be met by a lesser devotion because the students have seven other priorities of equal force — after all, they mostly have not or will not decide to give their very lives to the subject like their teacher. This means that the fair trade that is arranged for the occasion of the seminar will not carry over very far beyond the seminar: A mutual commitment for the seminar makes it appear (as illusion) that mutual delight might last. This is apt to be a great letdown for the teacher who has not anticipated the lack of carryover: Once they finish the seminar, their hierarchy of interests will show itself to be entirely different from the teacher's hierarchy of interests. Psychotherapy may be number seven on their lists, while first on his. Thus, they may make few sacrifices to learn more about it beyond the seminar (delighted as they appeared to be in the seminar event). The teacher will be less pained if he sees his great delight has a commercial equivalence for them with all the other currencies of the department. This is like Lewis Carroll being the equivalent of an author of a horse story for my eight-year-old daughter. I can get used to these points of view, once I anticipate how different they are from my own (the shape of our interests in psychotherapy may look similar but their sizes are very different).

Even more troubling than being the commercial equivalent of certain other subjects is to be looked down upon as less than them! The most interesting work routinely faces this threat, for profoundly simple reasons well explained by Newton (1981) in his discussion of why C. Wright Mills (1959) is neglected altogether in sociology: "Now quoting Mills stimulates little beyond a look of dumb perplexity, at most a dim presentiment of danger on the faces of indentured graduate students; their mentors, of course, are too busy writing renewal grants even to consider Mills's remark." The teacher of writers such as Mills should be ready for the "dim presentiment of danger" leading directly to attempts to disqualify the writer in question. Two huge mistakes are likely here: (1) If you allow them to run on unchecked (as I described concerning Jung's dream work), they will run you off the road with the force of their contempt; (2) but if you down their objections, you will run them off the road into dejection. This is what Haley (1966) called a "perverse triangle": either you or they are the ousted third party. The best recourse is to back their doubts, which enlivens them, while putting them in place as valid points in a larger picture. Mutuality defeats the perverse triangle.

10. Mark McGwire got a hard time from a columnist in the San Francisco Chronicle for finally chasing a pitcher who tried to bean him. So long as he was a perfect unflappable gentleman when pitchers tried to terrorize him away from home plate, then he was esteemed. I witnessed a similar event in a psychotherapy meeting, when a colleague to my right on a panel was asked from the audience, "Why aren't you free like _____ (sitting to my left) to use your own associations along with those of the patient about the dream?" My colleague to the right first replied matter of factly why he went strictly with the patient's associations. Ten minutes later (finally spilling over with rage) he must have realized that he had not parried the disqualifications that he was uptight compared to our colleague on the left (in California a serious charge!). Bringing this up he got the audience to laugh. But then he lost it (his rage) and went on to attack the disqualifier for her hostility, disqualifying himself as the Big Man attacking a poor student. The colleague on the left finished him off humorously by saying, "Who would like to ask a question now?" The audience roared at the expense of my col-

league on the right, who had failed to be a gentleman.

11. Sometimes it is enough to avoid getting hung by such people: William Carlos Williams gives an example of surviving by one's wits: "Scogan [famous court buffoon attached to the household of Edward IV] ordered to be hanged, but allowed the privilege of choosing the tree, escaped hanging by being unable to find a tree to his liking . . . " (1925, p. 80).

12. As Horowitz and Arthur (in press) argue, it is crucial to learn to refrain from driving a boss who thrives on intimidating rages (especially out of some sense of injustice)—when you've got a point about his injustice, he will thunder worse and worse, hoping to drown it in you by sheer intimidation. There is a famous psychotherapist who excels in this tactic when challenged, taking half-hours to reply in heat.

13. Adroit skill such as possessed by my friend will not always avail. Two votes swung in response to his stratagem, but four longstanding debts were collected by his opponent. As Bourdieu (1977) has so marvelously shown, local, provincial power depends on gifts, benefits, advantages, which build up a "symbolic capital" of indebtedness, which may be called in at any crisis. Justice, deserts, letters from the most prestigious (i+1), are less powerful than local debts (i), which is what ultimately defends local privilege against being invaded, judged and snared. Local privilege can be in the service of the "dead hand of the past," as in this instance, but it may start a remarkable tradition. Symbolic capital will defend either. I wrote my friend to say just this and to comfort him with the words of Josiah Royce: "The cause can no longer be served in the old way, and must be the object of new efforts, and so of some new form of devotion . . . human loyalty can never be perfected without such sorrow. Regard defeat and bereavement, therefore, as loyalty's opportunity" (Royce, p. 294, 1936). Losing causes sometimes inspire the greatest devotion. I hoped this injustice to him would be built into a greater triumph.

11. Gathering Strength

1. The Polish poet Zbigniew Herbert (1968) shows us an attitude to emulate in Thucy-

dides, who took his minor part in the Peloponnesian War for just that, something to say in passing. "The lesson," as John Bailey (1987, p. 219) wrote, "is for art." Herbert writes:

the Greek colony Amphipolis
fell into the hands of Brasidos
because Thucydides was late with relief

for this he paid his native city
with lifelong exile

exiles of all times
know what price that is

. . .

Thucydides says only
that he had seven ships
it was winter
and he sailed quickly

Better to be perfunctory about what hardly deserves mention.

2. Contests are neither intrinsically helpful nor harmful. The Greeks (Nietzsche, 1872, "Homer's Contest") made fruitful use of them for art and for sports, while the IK (Turnbull, 1972) have lowered themselves to the most degraded, cold, mean contests for mere survival. We seem to range somewhere in between. It seems that a certain amount of wealth and prosperity helps to keep us out of degraded "conditions of scarcity" (Gustafson and Cooper, 1978). As Cavafy warned E. M. Forster: "Never forget about the Greeks, Forster. Never forget we are bankrupt . . . Pray that you — you English with your capacity for adventure — never lose your capital. Otherwise you will resemble us, restless, shiftless, liars" (Annan, 1988).

3. I find insinuation to be the most deadly weapon to beware of in situations which purport to be art and science (civility), but actually provide occasions for disqualifying the speaker (oneself): viz., when I show videotapes to large gatherings interested, supposedly, in what I can show them about brief psychotherapy (Gustafson, 1986). Most come to learn, but some come to unseat me in favor of themselves or the god of their school. I recall one such occasion, where I was brought to a large city by a team of people mostly devoted to the work of another kind of doctor of brief therapy, their leader being the exception. He was interested in my work as a way for himself out of the narrows of this god. I knew I would find myself in the crossfire. Sure enough, it was not long before they started in on me for not being as vigorous in challenging the patient as their doctor would be sure to be doing by now. But the challenges came in the form of insinuations, such as, "Wouldn't it be more helpful to the patient if you didn't let that pass?" Of course, what they meant was that the therapy was hopelessly weak. Therefore, I chose not to tackle the literal question, but to state the full disqualification of myself that lay under that literal surface. Also, I refrained from quarreling with these people, who would have had great interest in extended skirmishes, which would take me away from my large audience. Therefore, I said, "I'd like to pose these interesting challenges for the discussion of everyone in a little while. Let's make a list of them on the blackboard, starting with: 'Weak Doctor.'" Nearly everyone burst out laughing. But I did come back to their disqualifications, as something worthy of discussion. I did not want to use my dominance to humiliate them, only to keep them from disqualifying me and the day's work.

4. My children and I have always loved stories about this sneaky realm. My youngest and I especially relish *The Tales of Uncle Remus* (Lester, 1987). Brer Rabbit is ingenious, outrageous, playful. No objections from him about how the world is organized! He takes full advantage.

5. Another great advantage of dwelling in the interior compartments, while peering into the outer compartments, is that you will not be gotten down by long stretches of nothing happening! This is why senators take work with them to the Senate, occasionally lending an ear to what a colleague says, but mostly tuning them out.

6. "Ulysses" puts this problem in grand, 19th century writing:

It little profits that an idle king,
By this still hearth, among these barren crags,
Matched with an aged wife, I mete and dole
Unequal laws unto a savage race,
That hoard, and sleep, and feed, and know not me . . .

How dull it is to pause, to make an end,
To rest unburnished, not to shine in use! . . .
Come, my friends,
Tis not too late to seek a new world.
Push off, and sitting well in order smite
The sounding furrows; for my purpose holds

To sail beyond the sunset, and baths
Of all the western stars, until I die . .
(Tennyson, 1833)

See the end of Conrad's Nigger of the Narcissus (1987, p. 171) for a moving end of such a voyage, even of the entire seagoing 19th century epic.

7. Every man, woman and child has his or her own inscapes (Margulies, 1989). I have borrowed many of them, like going to sea with Melville (1851), or Conrad (1900), or aboard the King's Ship (Bayley, 1981; Shakespeare) or in Lawrence's little ark (1959, pp. 138–140), like going to war with Zbigniew Herbert's (1968) generals, Marcus Aurelius, Thucydides, and Fortinbras, like riding the long trains into the west of Sherwood Anderson (Fleming, 1976). We all borrow and invent our own.

8. Finishing this book, I dreamt I got out my motorcycle from a parking place behind my father's Ford dealership which was a two-dimensional large sheet of cardboard. The surprise of the onlookers to see me pull a three-dimensional motorcycle out of a two-dimensional cardboard was very pleasant. It reminds me of the playing cards in the Queen of Hearts (Carroll, 1862). With her around, having two dimensions was your best refuge, unless you could be fully at home in the world. Even then, look out! The subject of self-possession, so marvelously opened by David Mann in his new essay (unpublished), allows a direct extension of this book into the realm of psychotherapy. For now, I can no more than hint at the subject. Some are self-possessed in the subjective sense, like the learned Smelfungus, who lacks all sense of how he comes across objectively:

Sterne further assailed the ill-tempered physician:

'The learned Smelfungus travelled from Boulogne to Paris—from Paris to Rome—and so on—but he set out with the spleen and jaundice, and every object he pass'd by was discoloured or distorted—He wrote an account of them, but 't was nothing but the account of his miserable feelings. . . .

'I popp'd upon Smelfungus again at Turin, in his return home; and a sad tale of sorrowful adventures he had to tell, 'wherein he spoke of moving accidents by flood and field, and of the cannibals which each other eat: the Anthropophagi'—he had been flay'd alive, and bedevil'd, and used worse than St. Bartholomew, at every stage he had come at—

'—I'll tell it, cried Smelfungus, to the world. You had better tell it, said I, to your physician.' ("In the Street—Calais.") (Sterne, 1767, p. 629)

Some are self-possessed in the objective sense of contesting well with the world, but do not know what they feel, imagine or believe in (Bateson, 1971). Conversely, some are at home with themselves and in the world, being fully with themselves in danger (where the world is but a background), being fully with the swarming of the world (where they have put a part to play, to move with the swarming). How we get patients from the lack of self-possession to being at home with themselves and with the world is a nice subject for future description. It is a class of problems in the modern contest.

12. *An Attitude For All Seasons*

1. Realizing one's powerlessness can be the direct road to the solution. A useful attitude in the face of powerlessness holds trenchant belief that something can (eventually) be done (somewhere), but loose holding about any particular battle or campaign. There is a sense of commitment to the contest and to the excitement of discovering anew how the battles are to be fought. There can be no falseness about the intensity of the involvement. Tolstoy describes beautifully (when talking about the works of Guy de Maupassant) that there must be a "moral relation" of the author to his subject; the artist must care about his subject dearly and know what and whom he loves and hates. Without this, there is charming pretension, superficial and wasteful use of artistic skills. One part of the experience of powerlessness is the awareness of what one cares about as the author of one's own participation. The solution to the question of powerlessness is sometimes stark realization of what we were trying to accomplish. The uncrossable river makes clear the sincerity of the pursuit of the trail.

II. The Practical Systemic Guide

W<small>E HAVE LIMITED</small> ourselves to about twelve reading recommendations on each practical discipline which can be utilized with the extended cases in our text to provide full semester courses on seven practical subjects: (A) individual psychotherapy; (B) teaching; (C) group therapy; (D) group relations (group analysis, participant observation, sensitivity); (E) family therapy; (F) organizational management and consultation; (G) global problems. Following the reading list for each subject is the *pagination of the text* that bears on the subject.

(A) INDIVIDUAL PSYCHOTHERAPY

1. The concept that patients fall prey to extremely powerful patterns like obsessionalism, hysteria, schizophrenia, alcoholism, and so forth, is a truism of psychiatry. But the conventional thinking is to call them "disorders" and then prescribe a simple (linear) antidote (antipsychotic, antidepressant, etc.). Sullivan (1954, 1956) was the first to take them seriously as huge patterns (dynamisms he called them), which, when recognized, could be played into, or broken out of. The first step was overcoming selective inattention to their extreme redundancy (the patient characteristically and suavely ignores this by saying to himself, "Isn't it amazing that such and such happened" (again)).

2. But this clarity about the pattern that connects and defeats the patient must be gotten while backing the patient as a going concern (an extremely strong distinction between the pattern and the person caught in it is necessary). Havens (1986) wonderfully carries out this individuation of the patient, "letting him speak," like Dennison (1969) did in *The Lives of Children*, like Tolstoy did in *War and Peace* (1869), as do the poets in Vendler's contemporary collection (1985). This discovery and backing of the individual locate what Tolstoy called his "self satisfaction" or "samodovolnost" (Bayley, 1966). Vendler's introduction (1985) is all about this subject as well. It is what I call "the territory outside the neurosis," which can provide the place from which leverage can be exerted.

3. Patients nearly always present their problem on a field of certain size (as of the family, as of individual identity, as of their biochemistry!). Meeting the challenge of the case (Winnicott, 1965) means dealing adequately with the problem on the field in question. This is the "convention of the single field," by far the most prevalent psychotherapy practiced (Gustafson, 1987). The alternative is to track the problem from this field onto neighboring fields, whereby will be found "a pattern that connects" them all (Bateson, 1979). But to see these neighboring fields, very small to very large, one needs a set of lenses to bring them into view (Gustafson, 1989b). This is the "convention of the pattern that connects," which

extends previous versions of this like Reich's concept of the constant attitude, or Sullivan's concept of the security operation, or Selvini Palazzoli's concept of the family game (Gustafson, 1986).

4. Once the enormous redundancy (and power) of this pattern that connects is seen, the challenge is to discover what leads back into its suction, versus what reliably leads out. Sullivan (1954, 1956) was superb at this, as is Michael White (1983, 1984, 1988). As White describes so well, once the exit moves are mapped, there are always painful or frightening "transitional problems" (Winnicott, 1965, 1971; Gustafson, 1986) to be reckoned with.

5. The extreme power of the constant attitude (security operation, family game) has to do with *fit* between life in the family and life in the world: the two are likely to drive each other enormously—when the family pattern gives certain advantages in the commercial world, when the commercial pattern gives certain advantages in the family. This is most vividly shown in Freud's Rat Man Case (1909), where everything is imagined as a degraded activity of rats. I differ from previous writers about this much discussed case in emphasizing that Freud located this man's fervent honesty (Pattern B) as territory outside the degraded pattern (Pattern A) and traced the edge of this degradation everywhere, including its considerable temptations. Nothing less could allow the patient to feel free of its sly grasp. Once the family and the commercial world are greatly in collusion like this, the individual needs much help to locate the edge (over and over again) which divides being sucked back into its sway (A), versus standing outside in different territory (B). Gogol (1835, 1836, 1842) vividly describes this problem. So does George Eliot (1871).

6. The pathological pattern may take over nearly the entire life of the person, such that the only deliverance may come from recognizing being totally defeated by it: viz., the Western drivenness of exerting tremendous willpower, which requires periodic breaks into drunkenness, pain, etc. (Bateson, 1971). Such a pattern is extremely simple, but extremely likely to continue because of its fit with commercial culture, and many family cultures.

7. Yet once territory outside the terrible grinding pattern can be located, the patient is delighted to find his own self satisfaction. This is a kind of white area. The patient usually leads immediately into a grey area, where such delight is threatened: viz., a patient of mine who felt entirely secure as a boss in volunteer activities, but easily disrespected by her secretary at work. Then there are always black areas where the patient feels utterly lost (transitions must help patients not to get lost in these—Sullivan was especially good at it, as were Winnicott and Balint (Gustafson, 1986, Chapters 6, 7, 8)).

8. Even if the awful pattern leads into enormous unsuspected difficulties in the modern contest (which can be finally anticipated by the patient), it is also extremely important that the patient feel entirely comfortable with him or herself alone, for his or her own couch is the final refuge of every day. Thus, the work with dreams is extremely important (Erikson, 1954; Freud, 1900; Gustafson, unpublished (b); Jung, 1933; Kuper and Stone, 1982; Margulies, 1989), both to secure this territory and to foresee new difficulties in the modern contest (as Jung (1933) put it, the night watchman sees different troubles from the day watchman).

9. The schools of psychotherapy ought to come into view as simply as the twelve

philosophers studying the King's elephant: viz., namely in terms of each's field of vision for a part of the pattern that connects (in terms of each's available lenses). See Gustafson (1989b) for working this out for the schools of brief psychotherapy; see Friedman (1988) for this concerning the current analytic field; see Gustafson (1986, 1987) and Havens (1986) for the range and depth of methods to be included.

10, 11, 12. It is difficult to propose in outline form what will take an entire next book to explicate. I leave off here for now in this sketch of my present procedure with individual patients. The astute reader may have recognized already that I have outlined postures for the individual psychotherapist which take care of bearings (help and fierce advantage are usually confused), organizing (the pattern as the common antagonist, vertical and horizontal readiness for all the fields on which the pattern will recur), reading situations (clarity about the edge of the pattern, protection of morale by readiness for expectable defeats in the thin world of the modern contest), moving freely (transitions above all are the great skill of the individual psychotherapist), counterposing (to get out of the rule to the exception) and complex counterposing (finding what is invaluable, setting compartments between this inside, and adapting to the conditions of the contest outside). All of this means helping the patient with subjective and objective self-possession (Mann, unpublished).

(B) Teaching

1. Rice (1969) is helpful for clarifying boundaries of a teaching event, which can protect it against the invasions of concerns from smaller (individual, family, friends) and larger (department, work services, publications) systems. Without clear, sharp, defendable expectations, most teaching events will be pulled apart.

2. But sharp boundaries can pull for didactic lessons from the professor, which put students into what Freire (1970) calls a "culture of silence." Freire is very useful for showing how to "pose problems," a process which brings out the "generative language" that is the students' own (as opposed to the "banking method" of education, which makes "deposits" in the students).

3. Vendler (1985) poses this crucial distinction in teaching in terms of the capabilities of poetic language, which can defend local expressiveness from "the anonymous census of history," from language which is forgotten so soon as it is spoken or written, being designed to leave behind its "deposit" of information like a glacier.

4. Yet the poetic capacity is no call for lack of discipline. Hearne (1986a, b) shows how the two are the same, in the right hands. The nature of the animal cannot be called out without the greatest discipline.

5. Another way of saying this is that education without talent, form, sincerity and moral purpose (Tolstoy, no date) is worth little.

6. Seminar teaching can evoke the great childhood pleasures of the peer group (Stevenson, 1892).

7. Yet seminars need to be drawn in more tightly at times, not to diverge too much from their shared purpose (Gosling, 1979).

8. Also, the pull of the modern contest into winners and losers has to be carefully watched for (Mann, 1975).

9. There are many possible struggles between subgroups for their desired working conditions in the group (Gustafson, Cooper, et al., 1981).
10. The pulls of the student culture can have crushing effects (Redl, 1946, Mizrahi, 1985a, b).
11. Structural coupling can be expected to be extremely powerful in setting patterns (Maturana and Varela, 1980; Gustafson, 1986, Chapters 17 and 23), of which the leader may want to stand clear (the so-called "strange loops" of Cronen, Johnson and Lannamann (1982)).
12. Bateson (1979) shows how to reach in teaching into the "pattern that connects." Rice (1986) offers a good intellectual exercise in changing and staying the same in the academic profession.

(C) Group Therapy

1. Bateson (1972) sets the stage for thinking of individuals in their social context. He makes it clear that group work takes on the individual *in context*, and may be the treatment of choice for certain difficult cases.
2. Rice (1969) shows the virtues of formality in securing the initial organization of the group.
3. Yalom (1975) presents and defends the curative virtues of cohesiveness. His clarity and good organization shouldn't be passed up. He also lends some empirical steadiness to issues of selection. When the journey from point A to point B has relatively clear terrain, Yalom is an invaluable guide. Rutan and Stone (1984) also give a useful overview of the group therapy landscape.
4. Bion (1959) is extraordinary in using his sense of duty to get involved in the group process, yet staying dispassionate enough to observe tremendous freshness and make a lot of sense of it. Bion is an ever-surprising personal model for the group therapist, to say nothing of the considerable utility of his theories.
5. Mann (1975) follows Bion's tradition, and points to a very powerful group theme, winner-losers, while giving the group therapist a handle on how to experience oneself in a group and learn from it. Mann describes the capacity to be open to the experience and to see it from different observing postures.
6. Balint (1954) is clear about the importance of attitude in letting the "otherness of others" merge. Gustafson and Cooper (1978) also strive to describe this kind of attitude. An attitude which opens up and evokes individuals' participation in the effort is crucial for group therapists to struggle with, rather than assuming that people in pain will do it all on their own.
7. Laing (1961), working with a metaphor of collusion and relying heavily on Genet (1958), gives meaning to the power of peer interaction. He makes a convincing argument that collusion is a dimension which group therapists must also watch for in themselves.
8. Sillitoe (1967), as well as any technical writer and more enjoyably than most, describes the group members' tension between being committed to their own needs and plans and following the plans of peers and authorities for them. A group therapist must monitor both levels of this tension, which is at the crux of much group drama.
9. Gosling (1979) helps us be aware as group therapists that being right is less important than being able to stand back, make corrections, and play, in a

Winnicott sense, with group culture and atmosphere. He also presents a useful model for a survival attitude for members.

10. Hughes (1964) and Hearne (1986a, b) remind us of our responsibility as group therapists that there is more than one story that ties together group events, and that plausibility and respect for the others should be our guides. And we can always change the story when the weight of data shifts.

11. Havens (1965) warns us that the hardest part of our job in therapy in general, and group therapy is no different, is enduring the pain of our patients.

12. Skynner (1987) helps the group therapist with the search for the right attitude — for long-range survival with buoyancy.

(D) GROUP RELATIONS

1. Freud (1921) is a solid foot on the ground of understanding group life from a drive point of view. He suggests a view of the psychological connection between the individual and the group and introduces the stormy underbelly which the student of self-study should enter with open eyes.

2. Bion (1959) presents a model of self-study from a leader point of view, which both makes Freud's picture more complete and offers the student of groups a way of evoking data about group dynamics and group development.

3. Rice (1965) was one of the seminal thinkers who transferred Bion's method into a self-study organization at the Tavistock Institute for Applied Social Research, the Group Relations Conference. Rioch (1970) summarizes his methods, which involve self-study in a variety of carefully designed exercises, focusing on leadership and authority in groups.

4. Some of the political implications of self-study organizations, as well as a broader sense of the learning potential in self-study are discussed by Palmer (1985) and Gustafson and Cooper (1978a).

5. DeLoach (1988) offers a primer for working with and leading (consulting, in Tavistock jargon) a small self-study group.

6. Mann (1975), Slater (1966), and Bennis and Shepard (1956) each give their own version of the intellectual evocativeness of self-study in a time-limited, classroom setting.

7. Balint (1954) and Freire (1970) give self-study tremendous range by taking group analysis into the difficult contests of worlds as different as medicine and political consciousness.

8. Bennis, Berlew, Schein, and Steele (1973) and Lewin (1945) come to the task of self-observation in groups from another point of view and lay the cornerstones for the sensitivity approach (of the National Training Laboratories' T-Groups). The history of cross-fertilization between the NTL and Tavistock methods suggests that these methods are attending to different aspects of group life with similar ideals about the outcome of self-study.

9. Klein and Astrachan (1971) offer a formal starting point for comparing the NTL and Tavistock approaches to self-study. Sometimes a good guide is worth using on a complicated journey on which, constrained by time, one doesn't have the luxury of getting lost.

10. Where can self-study be useful? Lofgren (1976) and Menzies (1960) describe applications of the Tavistock method of self-study in hospitals. They stand out

in a context of many health-related and mental health-related uses of this meth-od.

11. Klein, Thomas, and Bellis (1971) offer an exciting social application of group analysis to vital social issues. Colman and Geller's (1985) *Group Relations Reader* is a good reference to other social-focused applications.

12. Main (1975), Turquet (1975) and Skynner (1975) offer a window into the challenge of large group analysis. All three of these articles are large challenges in and of themselves.

13. Parsons and Shils (1951), Mills (1967), and Edelson (1970) give excellent background for the use of systems theory from a sociological perspective.

(E) FAMILY THERAPY (MILAN TRADITION)

1. Selvini Palazzoli et al. (1978) are poetic, terse, evocative, taking many readings like a lyric poem to comprehend very complex thinking.

2. Selvini Palazzoli (1980), Selvini Palazzoli et al. (1978, 1989), and Selvini Palazzoli and Prata (1982) have crucial technical ideas you will find nowhere else in this literature.

3. Selvini Palazzoli's recent writings (1985, 1986, 1988) are crucial to understanding the latest phase of her work. Best of all is Selvini Palazzoli, Cirillo, Selvini and Sorrentino (1989).

4. Selvini Palazzoli (1988) conducts the reader through all three or four phases of the twenty-year scientific journey.

5. This journey is summarized well by Gustafson (1986, 1989a).

6. The divergent, but complementary, path taken from the original Milan team by two of its original members, Boscolo and Cecchin, can be followed in their earliest paper (Boscolo and Cecchin, 1982) to their recent book (Boscolo, Cecchin, Hoffman, and Penn, 1987).

7. Tomm (1984, 1987, 1988) has explicated the technical capacities of the Milan teams so well, that his essays are invaluable — indispensable in fact — to any team that wants to match some of their work.

8. De Shazer's little essay (1987) is extremely important to show how to get out of strange loops (Cronen, Johnson, and Lannamann, 1982) that will destroy the therapeutic relationship. If the maximal strategies for doing this are to be understood, this minimalist strategy must be mastered.

9. The many levels of the marital conversation which bear upon its ultimate success or failure are well conveyed by Dicks (1967), Berger and Kellner (1964), and Wamboldt and Wolin (in press).

10. The ability to work with biological psychiatry and to do systems consultations to other helping professionals was taught to us with great élan by the Birmingham Team (Burnham and Harris, 1985; Harris and Burnham, 1985; Burnham, 1986).

11. Havens (1986) has been indispensable to us for handling relationships with individual members of families, to keep them on the field (a subject passed over by the literature in this tradition, but of the greatest practical importance).

12. The work of the Madison team is best conveyed by chapters in this book, especially Chapters 3 and 7. Anticipations of this work can be found in Gustafson (1987) and Gustafson's review of the entire twenty-year journey of Selvini Palazzoli (1989a).

13. The sound work of Stierlin and Weber (1989) on anorexia shows this family pattern and how to get out of it.
14. Michael White (1983, 1984, 1988) and White and Epson (in press) provide extremely clear thinking and practice about posing junctures which lead back into the suction of the great patterns of family pathology, versus out of them.

(F) Organizational Consultation and Management

1. It takes some time to really know what one is getting involved in when facing the modern contest on an organizational battleground. Weber (Gerth and Mills, 1946) puts the modern organization in context and lays out critical operating principles of bureaucracies.
2. Miller and Rice (1967) offer a systems analysis of organizations, which stands (for these authors) at the corner of one solid approach to consultation and management. They present an open system theory view with examples of intervening within this framework.
3. In showing the gears of the organizational "mind," how it actually works, Steinbruner (1974) considers decision-making in bureaucracy and gives a good feel for why certain things do and don't happen when it comes to organizational planning. The intervener can feel securely humble.
4. Miller, Galanter, and Pribram (1960) also have an idea about how planning occurs. They get a psychology of the organization broader than the cognitive/political angle of Steinbruner.
5. Schumacher (1973) and Tuan (1980) put the organization in *its* larger cultural context. As with Bateson (1979), this dimension gives the intervener a useful platform for standing back.
6. Terkel (1972) provides a window into the workers' perspective. Though informal, it is very informative. Reed (1976) offers a formal method for discovering people's niches in their organization, as well as a method for answering the challenge of what to do about it: a fine and clear case example is by Berry and Tate (1988).
7. Caplan (1970) was a pioneer in a particular style of mental health consultation. His model is still very generically useful for organizational interventions and is widely practiced.
8. Cooper and Gustafson (1981) approach systems consultation with a family metaphor. Even with a systems approach, one needs a useful metaphor to capture the experience of being in the organization.
9. Selvini Palazzoli et al. (1986) take their systems view of families as the metaphor, and present well their intervention style.
10. Kerr (1963) is one among a class of books about running major organizations written by the top person in the organization. Very illuminating, at times wise, about the enormity of the job. Again, helps secure the humility of the intervener.
11. Jones (1986) represents a class of writings sensitizing the intervener and manager to the issues of minority and the third world groups.
12. Sarason (1971), in a school setting, describes a sensible approach to planful change with considerable respect for the system's integrity. A useful discussion of the problem of change vs. no change.

13. Berry and Tate (1988) show how consultation can help a person survive in a grinding organization.

(G) Global Problems

1. The best and richest collection is the book edited and organized by Calhoun with 162 contributors (1983).
2. Forrester (1971) is the best introduction to the interaction of major global problems in non-linear, non-intuitive, non-imagined ways.
3. Keen and Deutsch (1986) concerns the reorganizing capacities of large-scale organizations. They mention the benefits, but not the disasters.
4. For the disastrous side of the reorganizing capacity, see Lifton (1986) and Solzhenitsyn (1973).
5. The problems of power are best handled by Bourdieu (1977), Foucault (1980), and Galbraith (1983).
6. Steinbruner (1974) is clearer than anyone on the limitations of large-scale organizations: the inability to handle tradeoffs, except as a linear sequence of decisions.
7. Dyson (1984) is the most eloquent, clear, comprehensive writer on the subject of nuclear war.
8. Steinbruner (1987) shows how the nuclear trigger works: relatively off or relatively on. No one else has disclosed the crucial organizational problems of decision about using or not using the nuclear end of the world.
9. We find Fanon (1963) gets across the race problems better than anyone from the side of the black and poor and colonized peoples of the world.
10. The overwhelming educational problems right in this country are well conveyed by Kozel (1985) and Herndon (1965), Bernstein (1973) for the English lower class, Freire (1970) for the peasants and city poor of Latin America.
11. Economics on the global scale can be introduced by Schumacher (1973), Greider (1987), and Galbraith (1983, 1986a). Ehrlich and Ehrlich (1986 and the *Lancet* editorial (1987) pose the grave problems which are related: namely, overpopulation and hunger.
12. Somehow it is still possible to be hopeful. After all, the Soviets have decided as a matter of policy to defeat us by taking away our image of the enemy as *them*. Perhaps, there will be a great new unifying idea for mankind again (Commager, 1985).

III. The Intellectual Systemic Guide

A BROAD SOCIAL THEORY will draw from many disciplines of knowledge, selecting according to the interests of the writer (Habermas, 1971). Therefore, no two writers are likely to have the same reading lists, although they may overlap, where knowledge-constitutive interests, traditions, education and history coincide. We divide and outline crucial readings for the theoretical disciplines, which have provided the scaffolding for the construction of our book, into the following categories (some writers will *not* be divided so neatly, but we have put them in one or another place): (A) cybernetic systems theory; (B) sociology, anthropology, political science, history, and economics; (C) studies in the prevention of nuclear war; (D) studies in social class; (E) ecology, biology, and philosophy of science; (F) literature and religion; (G) individual psychotherapy, psychiatry and psychology; (H) group dynamics; (I) systemic family therapy and theory; (J) methodology in social science. Then we outline the crucial concepts and readings for the constructions of each of our 12 chapters.

(A) CYBERNETIC SYSTEMS THEORY

1. Ashby (1970) tackles the problem of tradeoffs between simplicity and complexity, discussed by Steinbruner (1974), Gustafson (1987), and Selvini Palazzoli (1980).
2. Coleman (1971) discusses role-holding in systems as relatively independent of persons.
3. Deutsch (1966) constructs systems with hierarchical ordering of feedback loops, discussed later by Mills (1967) for small groups and Keen and Deutsch (1986) for very large groups.
4. Forrester (1971) discusses non-linear consequences of systems which are counter-intuitive to images of the situations.
5. Lewin (1945, 1947) portrays groups as systems with "gates," "channels," "gate-keepers," etc. to capture the very uneven importance from region to region.
6. Platt (1970) describes sudden changes in systems, especially "Deutsch's theorem," which show how an entity may undergo a shift in identity (i) when there is an oscillation between its most powerful component $(i-1)$ and the surrounding context $(i+1)$.
7. Steinbruner (1974) discusses how very large systems set up decision-making as a *sequence* of standard operating procedures (like the sequence of postures in this book).

(B) Sociology, Anthropology, Political Science, History and Economics

1. Aristotle (1943) opens the discussion of struggle between factions.
2. Bloch (1953) poses the difference between poor and skillful history in terms of the capacity to handle the existing "testimony" (the "tracks" of the past, as in a courtroom).
3. Bourdieu (1977, 1984) proposes the replication of societies in terms of embodied practices of trade in material and symbolic capital, often disguised by euphemism. The later work, concerning the formal requirements of popular culture, is invaluable.
4. Fisher (1935) gives a history of Europe organized by and against the waves of invasion, first from the East, recently from the West.
5. Freire (1970) shows the "culture of silence" of rural and city poor who adopt the "director culture" (language, gestures) of the powerful, but who may break out by discovery of their own "generative" words, language. Lloyd (1972) summarizes Freire well.
6. Foucault (1980) shows the strategies of power since the middle ages in many fields, especially the ability to characterize, define, label. Dreyfus and Rabinow (1982) summarize and interview Foucault well.
7. Habermas (1971, 1973) describes the knowledge-constitutive interests and the places where political systems come apart.
8. Henry (1963, 1973) proposes that sociology study not the downfall from terrible systems, but the remarkable exceptions that somehow come through the sham, through the "vulnerability systems."
9. Hughes (1964) discusses the battle over method in history, giving a fine introduction to Bloch (1953).
10. Levi-Strauss (Charbonnier, 1969) is remarkable on many subjects, including society as hot or cold engine.
11. Machiavelli (1527) lays out the practice of power (so close to Bourdieu (1977) about practice).
12. Marx (1967) explains, among so much, the expropriation of the "surplus value" of labor.
13. Ollman (1971) shows the way in which Marx's concepts fit together so that any term is a pars pro toto.
14. Schumacher (1973) shows how economic systems on the small scale can conserve long-term interests, while meeting the challenge of the present.
15. Sennett (1979) shows how managers use euphemism to secure large advantages over subordinates.
16. Weber (Gerth and Mills, 1946) characterizes the structure of authority, especially the engines of modern bureaucratic authority.
17. Commager (1985), however, sees the loss of the great unifying ideas of the past: The City of God, The Brotherhood of Man.
18. Tuan (1980) poses a segmented, modern world, later (1986) resolves some of the strain with a perspective on enduring civilization.
19. Voltaire (1759) sees trouble at every turn, once you leave your garden.
20. Galbraith (1981, 1983, 1986a) is master of the euphemisms of power. He enjoys showing the sacrifices and who makes them.

21. Greider (1987) places the Federal Reserve Board in the center of the board.
22. Heilbroner (1989) clarifies the victory of capitalism over state socialism, which has become obvious in the eighties, leading to powerful new trends in East-West relations.

(C) STUDIES IN THE PREVENTION OF NUCLEAR WAR

1. Baker (1982): Would you trust experts who advised a 30-story pile of shingles on your house?
2. Barnett (1987) places nuclearism among the other great objectives of American foreign policy.
3. Boyer (1984) shows public interest in nuclear weapons occurring only in crises, such as the Cuban missile crisis or the Reagan build-up.
4. Downs, Rocke and Siverson (1985), and Axelrod and Keohane (1985) tackle possible nuclear cooperation as a problem for game theory.
5. Dyson (1984) is the best writer to encompass so many aspects of the subject: scientific, military, historical, personal and political.
6. Fischer (1984) shows that actual strength is the capacity to stay out of nuclear war, which calls for neither hawkish nor dovish policy.
7. Frank (1982) is most eloquent about "the image of the enemy."
8. Gustafson (unpublished [a]) discusses why most organizations have no depth of field in their perception of nuclear war as a threat. Janis (1967) tells of the pitfalls of group decision-making at high levels of government.
9. Kaplan (1983) traces the strange line of policy about nuclear weapons from its series of expert sources.
10. Kull (1982) utilizes a concept from Wall Street to comprehend "the greater fool market of nuclear weapons."
11. Lifton and Falk (1982) explore the "deformation" of attitudes about these weapons which occur through "images" of security and danger.
12. Rathjens (1986) points us toward the greatest danger of local theaters of war getting out of control.
13. Russett (1983) gives the clearest explication of the game theory of the Prisoners' Dilemma as a model for cooperation versus defection from nuclear agreements. Searles (1977) gives a highly individualized appreciation of our (self) destructiveness.
14. Sherwin (1977) tells the story of Hiroshima policy in terms of our using the bomb as "the master card of diplomacy."
15. Steinbruner (1987) shows the central control problems of the firing of nuclear weapons: especially depending on whether the entire system is dampened or on alert.
16. White (1986) edits the best collection of essays of experts from all quarters on this subject.

(D) STUDIES IN SOCIAL CLASS

1. Bach (1954): The "peer court" of group therapy has never been better described: middle class miseries.
2. Bernstein (1973): The "restrictive code" cuts off the possibilities of the "elaborated code" needed for success in the modern world.

3. Bourdieu (1977): See (B). Complementary to Bernstein.
4. Burawoy (1979): "Making out on the shop floor" is a kind of restricted code for workers which leads to being co-opted.
5. Editorial (1987). Hunger is now a problem of distribution, of "conditions of trade stacked against poor countries."
6. Ehrlich and Ehrlich (1986): The coming disasters of over-population are graphically described.
7. Fanon (1963): "Because it is a systematic negation of the other person and a furious determination to deny the other person all attributes of humanity, colonialism forces the people it dominates to ask themselves the question constantly: 'Who am I'?" (p. 250). And so forth: an eloquent evoking of the terrors of being caught up in a colonialist war, by a skillful black psychiatrist.
8. Herndon (1965): The "restrictive code" of black kids in junior high proves formidable to a struggling white teacher.
9. Freire (1982): The "director culture" of the city people makes them poor, blank and dumb, while their own "generative words" bring them alive. Complementary to Fanon and Herndon. Klein, Thomas and Bellis (1971) warn of the stand-off between the protectors of privilege and the disadvantaged.
10. Kozol, J. (1985). "A third of the nation cannot read these words," Kozol begins.
11. Lifton (1986): God protect us from such apparatuses as Lifton describes. Complementary to Solzhenitsyn: see below.
12. Terkel (1972) interviews a gamut of people about their working lives: only a few relish their working days.

(E) ECOLOGY, BIOLOGY, AND PHILOSOPHY OF SCIENCE

1. Allen and Starr (1982) probably have more parallels to this book than any other: especially helpful about hierarchy as a strategy, vertical and horizontal scaling, perturbations, filters. Allen, O'Neill and Hoekstra (1984) is about finding one's way between fields of different scale through the common phenomenon.
2. Bateson (1979) concerns the "pattern that connects," from very small to very large, in living systems.
3. Botez (1983) poses the "over-complexity syndrome" and characterizes its recurrent features.
4. Calhoun (1983) is one of the first attempts to pose the researchable problems of the planet earth in our time, as well as to see how they fit together, via contributions of 162 leading thinkers in biology, social science, and many other related disciplines.
5. Colinvaux (1983) discusses *niche* for human beings, which may be broad or very narrow.
6. Edelman (1979, 1982, 1985) poses a "selection theory" of the brain, that vertical hierarchical pathways get selected by being used (the patterns that connect).
7. Gould (1987) and Eliade (1954) show how history enters into evolution, so that structures used for a given function may be taken over or co-opted later for other functions.
8. Kuhn (1962) distinguishes "normal science" from "revolutionary science" by the

tendency to follow strict sets of rules, until the anomalies build up to such an extent that a new paradigm is proposed to restructure the field.

9. Lakatos (1970) proposes a more gradualist tendency of a series of models which better fit the testimony (more like Bloch about history).

10. Maturana (1980) proposes two great biological laws of conservation: the law of the conservation of organization and the law of the conservation of accommodation. Together these characterize the phenomenon of "structural coupling" between organisms.

11. Popper (1957) contributes the concept of "piece-meal social engineering" as a practical consequence of our position of only being able to "interpret" social reality by the light of our own interests moving into an unknown darkness: like rebuilding a ship as it plunges ahead. Magee (1973) has the best summary of Popper's opus.

12. Rosenfeld (1985, 1986) summarizes Edelman and Geschwind very well about higher brain coordination.

(F) LITERATURE AND RELIGION

1. Bayley (1981) shows the surprising landscape of Shakespeare, the unforgettable walk on the Dover Cliffs of Edgar and Gloucester, secret freedoms suddenly appearing in such places. He also throws open the doors to the fascinating writers of Central Europe (1987), including Brodsky, Herbert and Milosz, to Tolstoy (1966) and to the short story (1988).

2. Balzac (1835) presents the power of the civilized capital over the young and the old: how the hope to win draws us on, losing though we must at certain hopeless games. This is similar to Bourdieu (1977). Here is the center panel of the modern world as it emerged in the early 19th century: where the old civility met the frantic contest.

3. Berry's letter (1982) is eloquent counsel against pride in knowing so much.

4. Borges draws out so sympathetically what fools we become for importance (1979), for overcoming boredom (1962): the downside of Stevenson's story (1892) of secret society when it is drawn into the public realm.

5. Brodsky (1986, 1987, 1988) writes about eluding the hounds of the State, "the mass police entertainment," the "cliche as engine of history," through language.

6. Camus (1967) shows how a man can be destroyed by his best acts, which offend both sides of the revolution.

7. Crane (1969) gives us the pulling together of "The Open Boat," dissolving as the shore is in sight, very much as in Conrad (1897). The appeal, Conrad writes, " . . . is to bring the light of magic suggestiveness . . to play for an evanescent instant over the commonplace surfaces of words: of the old, old words, worn thin, defaced by ages of careless usage" (p. 27) . . . to the subtle but invincible conviction of solidarity that knits together the loneliness of innumerable hearts . . . its effect endures forever (p. 26).

8. Casty (1967) delineates what his title suggests, "The Shape of Fiction and the Cage of Form," followed by his selection of short stories.

9. Dante (1314) is unforgettable about the surprising landscape discovered by those forgetting God: the levels of hell fitting the pursuit.

10. Eliot (1871) shows two passionate young people underestimating the power of commercial rural society to draw them into hellish situations: Dorothea and Dr. Lydgate.

11. Gass (1983) writes of man as the "measurer" of all things, lost in the simpler uses, thereby reduced, losing the most interesting measures such as metaphor, which depend on the "angle" between the terms compared. Gass (1988) turns Nietzsche's method upon Nietzsche himself, but fairly and sympathetically, showing pretensions driven by vulnerability to the modern commercial culture. Annan (1988) uses Forster's *Howard's End* to show how we need the commercial winners.

12. Gogol's wild satires (1835, 1836, 1842) vividly picture the human tendency to be carried to destruction by the social origins of commerce. See an astute summary of his aims in the introduction to *Dead Souls* (p. 10, 1842).

13. Hearne (1986a, b) is especially memorable about the epic space of training horses, the domestic space of the straight lines of cats.

14. Herbert (1968): For me the most eloquent poems are: "To Marcus Aurelius," "Elegy of Fortinbras," and "Why the Classics?": all conversations with great generals.

15. The *I Ching* (1950): the ancient Chinese reckoning of practice, for the conduct of lives, governments, families, and so forth, which attempts to propose different postures for different seasons, so to speak.

16. Lester (1987): The confusion of help (fierce taking of advantage) may be greatly enjoyed in this new version of *The Adventures of Brer Rabbit*. Unlike the modern contest, this farce takes stable forms which allow the caricature. Similar in both subject and form to de Moliere (1666, 1669). The modern contest is less funny, partly as its pace *defies* our mastery through humor. We are always trying to stay caught up with it.

17. Orwell (1946) proposes how language may be used to show or to hide.

18. Richards (1922): "Words are astonishingly like people. They have characters . . . " and so forth.

19. Sontag (1966): Surface, momentum and direct address may protect writing from interpretation (being taken over by the hot engines).

20. Sterne (1767): "The learned Smellfungus traveled from Boulogne to Paris . . . but he set out with the spleen and jaundice, and every object he pass'd by was discoloured or distorted — He wrote an account of them, but t'was nothing but an account of his miserable feelings" (f., p. 629). This footnote quotes another book by Sterne, which gives the briefest version of the comic genius which takes a drawn-out form in *Tristram Shandy*.

21. Stevenson (1892): "His life from without may seem but a rude mound of mud; there will be some golden chamber at the heart of it, in which he dwells delighted" (p. 216).

22. Tolstoy (1894): Talent, form, sincerity, moral purpose: Lacking one of the four, the writer's work falls (in Bayley, 1966, p. 852).

23. Vendler (1985) contrasts the great realms of the modern lyrical poem where we may be delivered to ourselves from a modern context in which we are likely to disappear.

24. Whitman (1881–1882): "Aside from the pulling and the hauling stands what I am. Stands amused, complacent, compassionating, idle, unitary."

(G) INDIVIDUAL PSYCHOTHERAPY, PSYCHIATRY AND PSYCHOLOGY

1. Beahrs (1986): The circularity of bio-, psycho- and social patterns means that "focal points" that are useful in any one will affect the other two realms: a realization of Engel's (1980) biopsychosocial model.
2. A hint of the enormous power of correct reckoning of the social world can be found in Bennett (1985).
3. Freud (1900), Jung (1933), Erikson (1954), Kuper and Stone (1982), Margulies (1989) and Gustafson (unpublished (b)): The night watchman of the dream complements the day watchman to tell us about ourselves in relation to the world: another set of bearings is provided.
4. Friedman (1988) shows the "hard lens" vs. the "soft lens" in current analytic work, which quite lays open the current analytic field of controversy to simple inspection.
5. Gustafson (1986, 1987a, 1987b, in press): Different fields of perspective on helping individual patients vary from very small (intrapsychic) to very large (systemic organization), from very fast (gesture) to very slow (relatively constant attitudes).
6. Havens (1973, 1986): Different languages of the different schools of psychiatry open up different worlds.
7. Marks (1987): Darwinian perspective finally comes full scale into thinking about the problems of patients.
8. Janis (1967), Milgram (1973) and Asch (1955): Group-think, submission to command, and distortion of perception to fit into a group are cleverly shown by experiment.
9. Lifton (1986): The killing machine is studied from many complementary angles: an unprecedented courageous research.
10. Sashin (1985) and Callahan and Sashin (in press): Remarkable visualization of complex spaces generated by more than a few crucial variables in the lives of patients: ten-dimensional, non-linear, topological models.
11. Sullivan (1954, 1956): "Selective inattention" to the patterns that suck us in is the great subject of psychotherapy according to Sullivan, since we can learn to correct this inattention. See also Havens on Sullivan (1976) and Gustafson on Sullivan (1986, Chapter 6).

(H) GROUP DYNAMICS

1. Balint (1954, 1957): The cardinal principles of non-intrusion and non-abandonment allow groups "the courage of their own stupidity," especially "Balint Groups" for doctors, also ably described by Bourne (1976) and Gosling and Turquet (1967).
2. Bennis and Shepherd (1956): The expectable crises of small groups turn around subgroups with opposite inclinations for working conditions: the dependents

and independents, later the close and the distant. This classic is located in a useful compendium: Gibbard, Hartman and Mann (1974).

3. Bion (1959) was a daring pioneer of extrapolation from his own "experiences" as a group consultant to the "basic assumptions" implicit in the climate of the group. See Pines (1985) for the continuation of the line of work, a set of essays dedicated to Bion.

4. Cooper (1976, 1977) and Gustafson (1979a, 1981), Gustafson (1976a, 1976b, 1978a, 1983), Gustafson and Cooper (1978a, 1978b, 1979, 1983, 1985), and Gustafson, Cooper, Lathrop, Ringler, Seldin and Wright (1981), tackle the unsolved problems in the Tavistock tradition generated by Bion for helping small groups to study their own working.

5. Main (1975), Skynner (1975) and Turquet (1973) show the peculiar working of large groups of town-meeting size, in the most useful collection of essays on this subject (Kreeger, 1975).

6. Mann (1975): The struggle of winners and losers in subgroups in self-analytic groups has many phases, ups, downs, search parties, and implications for leaders and for teachers in classrooms and seminars.

7. Bach (1954): The severity of the "peer court" at work in passing judgment on one another leaves an angle of entry for a leader to use this primitive practice for access to deeper discussion.

8. Gosling (1979) is one of the most evocative essays ever written about small groups.

9. Mills (1967) is one of the first, most successful attempts to show a hierarchy of purposes (strategies) in small groups.

10. Palmer (1979, 1985) and Reed (1976) clarify levels of learning in self analytic groups according to Bateson's distinction between Level I, Level II and Level III learning, then organize their learning projects accordingly. McCaughan and Palmer (unpublished) recently have developed a new event: "Systems Thinking for Harassed Managers."

11. Rice (1965, 1969) and Miller and Rice (1967) exploit the concept of leadership as control of boundaries and as utilization of latent emotionality. One of the most useful ideas: "They have also to be able to accept that they will never be paragons . . . that making mistakes, as they will, is less important than the ability to recover from them" (Rice, 1965, p. 49).

12. Skynner (1986b) is the most cogent of the English group therapists about attitude, responsibility and where to bear down and where to watch. He fulfills what Foulkes (1964) proposed as the group-analytic method of group therapy.

13. Slater (1966) gave mythological depth to self-analytic groups in fascinating explications.

14. Yalom (1975) has dominated the American scene of group therapy for several decades because his clear and simple directions are like those for a basketball coach: one, set up a situation which has good players, good practice routines and practically runs itself; two, watch the process for how it gets hung up and call a time out to discuss the problem at hand. He augments this with his large list of "therapeutic factors" which makes him popular with American psychologists who are thus supplied with a research agenda. Rutan and Stone (1984) follow in Yalom's tradition of clear dedication to good routines.

(I) SYSTEMIC FAMILY THERAPY AND THEORY

1. Pearce and Cronen (1980), Cronen, Johnson and Lannamann (1982) show how the recursive "strange loop" described by Hofstadter (1979) occurs between levels in the family hierarchy.
2. Selvini Palazzoli, Boscolo, Cecchin and Prata (1978), Selvini Palazzoli, Cirillo, Selvini and Sorrentino (1989), Selvini Palazzoli (1980, 1985, 1986, 1988), Boscolo, Cecchin, Hoffman and Penn (1987), Cecchin (1987) work out how to map the family game in terms of "positive connotation" which wins acceptance ("euphemism," Bordieu, 1977), while implicitly challenging the win–lose pattern (Gustafson, 1989a).
3. Skynner (1981, 1987) and Skynner and Cleese (1983) show how families hide their developmental deficits, how they may be looked for under the cover-up, how they may be handled by being given to the therapist himself as dilemmas.
4. Stierlin (1988) is wonderfully clear about systemic thinking as having possibilities for undue optimism, or pessimism: like Californian therapy, or French sociology. Stierlin and Weber (1989) balance the two well.
5. Tomm (1984, 1987, 1988) works out the logic of the Milan teams as a series of *postures* (circularity, neutrality, hypothesizing, strategizing) in the service of an interested, curious intention. We have found this *posture* concept extremely important for describing a sequence for action readiness as we descend into the valley of the surprising landscape (orienting, organizing, reading, moving freely, counterproposing, complex counterproposing). Indeed, his four postures and our last four postures could be said to overlap a great deal in their implications for action.
6. White (1983, 1984, 1988) is unparalleled in his clarity about what perpetuates suction back into family-destroying patterns, versus what steps lead out of them. White and Epson (in press) puts this marvelously in political and literary terms.

(J) METHODOLOGY IN SOCIAL SCIENCE

1. As Gould (1988) argues so eloquently, there are two fundamental styles of science. One is what he calls Athenian science, which is concerned with a search for underlying unity and simplification in "laws of nature," such as has been so successful in physics. The other is what he calls Manchesterian science, which is concerned with "explaining the inordinately complex particulars that never occur twice in nature's intricacy." (p. 32) We believe our subject lies in the latter realm. As Allen and Starr (1982) argue, the first kind of (Athenian) science works well in systems with very small numbers of objects, such as the mechanics of colliding bodies for which calculus is sufficient, and for very large numbers of objects, such as huge populations of consumers, for which statistics (and recently recursive functions (Gleick, 1988)) are sufficient. For systems with middle numbers of objects (like ecological systems), a different kind of (Manchesterian) science seems most promising, which relies upon hierarchical models (Bateson, 1971; Maturana and Varela, 1980; Gustafson, 1986).
2. Like ecology, evolutionary science and history, we look for better ways to organize the "testimony" (Bloch, 1953). Interpretations which fail to include available

findings are inadequate. We prefer briefer explanations over longer ones. These are "rules of evidence," as important to these sciences as to a court of law (Bloch, 1953; Hughes, 1964).

3. But we seek also to explain phenomena which are still unfolding, "cascading down channels" little known to us, to use Gould's phrase, where a small jot can make a huge difference: "Humans are here because *Pikaia* (the first chordate) survived the great winnowing of the earth's first multicellular fauna, because one odd group of early fishes had forelimbs that could be modified to support a body under terrestrial gravity, because dinosaurs died and mammals prevailed . . . " etc. (p. 32). For guiding us in such a dark, we also need "rules of relevance," for finding what Bateson (1979) called "the difference that makes a difference."

4. When a social project founders, it is often not obvious which part of the social machinery needs tinkering. Such projects are like ships at sea: they must keep sailing, while being overhauled in some few respects (Popper, 1957). We seek "rules for revising," so that second chances can be better run than first chances (Berry, 1987), for what Popper (1957) calls "piecemeal social engineering." Always, there are trade-offs to reckon with: viz. The bombardier beetle is heavily armored, but awfully slow (Marks, 1987); less prey vigilance time for a bird may allow more feeding, but run undue risks (Marks, 1987). We prefer (with Stierlin, 1988) consideration of trade-offs which range freely between "systemic optimism" ("better trade-offs can be found") and "systemic pessimism"? ("this can only get worse on the present course").

5. But revising is dangerous in the midst of formidable adversaries, like the sea, or like groups of men. Therefore, we follow Bateson's (1979) distinction between structures that are adapted to fast occasions versus those structures that are susceptible to change only very slowly. Following Karl Tomm (1984, 1987, 1988), we have utilized the concept of "posture" for meeting difficulties, and invented our own array of postures, from very slow to very fast. In the slow postures, we entertain our subject very conservatively, being very reluctant to change tradition that has been invaluable. In the faster postures, we'll switch a great deal to fit fast changing circumstances.

6. Revising is also dangerous with an inadequate view of the relevant fields and relevant timing of events. You won't see what's coming. Therefore, we believe that a range of lenses (Gustafson, 1989b) is indispensable, to bring into focus neighboring fields (which have their own grain and extent), from very small to very large. Also, we believe that we must be tuned to the different frequencies in which events arrive, some continually, some once in a century, and so forth. We have borrowed these crucial concepts of vertical and horizontal scaling from Allen and Starr (1982).

7. The extraordinary complexity of man the evolving social creature in the forms of the modern contest can lead to unwieldly discourses, which are quite unsuited to the practical lives we lead in our practical disciplines. Thus, we look for parsimony of explanation, in the form of what Bateson (1979) called "the pattern that connects:" We like to assume that the 12 philosophers may all have partial views of the same form (such as an "elephant"). Yet, we balance this, carefully, for no two of those creatures are quite alike, and the individual differences seem to delight both the creatures and ourselves.

8. Location (Bourdieu, 1984, and Edelman, 1989) has an enormous effect on what happens to an object in a system. This must not be left out of our science.

Chapter 1. The Modern Territory.

1. The importance of loyalty to the inside route in social worlds of all sizes became most clear to us from Dante (Alighieri, 1314) Royce (1936), Selvini Palazzoli et al. (1978) and Bourdieu (1977).
2. The confusion over help (and taking advantage) only comes into focus if you are looking for it, because the official gloss of most social organizations is to separate the world of help (inside) from the world of harm (outside). All the interesting problems of this book come from opening up this center panel *between* the left panel of help and the right panel of outright battle. Even when persons *intend* to be helpful, they often find that what is helpful for themselves is exactly what makes the other person(s) feel inferior, unimportant or stupid. Any interest can work perversely on one's partners (what Haley (1967) called a "perverse triangle" or "denied coalition against"). Since partners in any enterprise have third interests on other levels, both smaller and larger in scope, mutual relations are continually challenged with this perversity. Selvini Palazzoli et al. (1989) recognize this in the family field as the central phenomenon (to be managed well or badly, with huge consequences). We propose it as central for the entire modern territory (for competence in managing oneself in these fluid worlds) (for what Mann (unpublished) calls "objective self possession").
3. The importance of meeting the crude challenge of the case good naturedly came across to us most clearly from Winnicott (1965) and Skynner (1987) and Bourdieu (1984) and the importance of diversification in the biosocial world came across to us from Allen and Starr (1982). We learned to see individuals as victims of patterns from Selvini Palazzoli et al. (1978, 1989) and White (1983, 1984, 1988). The possibility of working the crude horizontal while moving vertically into smaller and larger perspectives puts all three of these difficult lessons into a single practice.

Chapter 2. Us and Them

The common antagonist is our descriptor of a stage upon which are many theoretical players, most central of which include:

1. Freud (1921, 1930) who in his biological metaphor paints onto our understanding of the social canvas the antagonisms and struggles between a "civilized" veneer and drive states. From an ethological perspective, Lorenz (1952) underlines the same social struggle.
2. The systemic focus on authority and boundaries was helpful in making it clear how important clarity is in securing the organization and work of the group. Rice (1969), Newton (1988; Newton and Levinson, 1973), and Lofgren (1976) make their contribution at a theoretical and practical level simultaneously.

3. Frank (1982) added a useful piece in emphasizing the dynamism of the "image of the enemy." It lent a vivid image to Erikson (1966) and Durkin (1981), and suggested the controllability—for better or worse—of where, when, and how groups choose to do battle.

4. Through the vigorous presentation of negative consequences to certain kinds of cohesive situations, Janis (1967) and Lifton (1986) underline the embattled nature of group life to keep itself "honest" and accomplish its mission. This was about as directly as anyone has spoken to the nonlinearity of cohesiveness in describing natural groups; it is broader than the simple dichotomy of success-failure.

5. Yalom (1985), perhaps more than any other group therapy writer, speaks of the simple and profound benefits of a "cohesiveness" that stays linear.

6. Selvini Palazzoli et al. (1978, 1986, 1989) were clear in having a method which takes on the problem of entry into family systems in the face of strong coherence. We have taken some of their thinking into the general group world as it helps us think about entry, the "otherness of others," and the underlying unity of systems.

Other critical images came from writers outside our own disciplines. Some of the most helpful ones were as follows:

7. Brodsky (1986) shows the liberating as well as the imprisoning impact of standing against a stark enemy (especially in one's own culture) armed primarily with language.

8. Galbraith (1986a) builds on Brodsky in the sense of showing how standing back with good humor and sharp senses can help one appreciate very vicious antagonists, defanging them, making drawing closer less dangerous. The view of the antagonist changes radically depending on the distance of the observer.

9. Authors like Stevenson (1892) use language so well to create a feeling of being on the inside, inside the tent, and from this posture why there can be so much to defend. Like Galsworthy (1916), an insider's view of being inside; like Miller (1950), the fragility of our sense of control of our social world.

10. Forrester (1971) helped me with the image of being on the inside of tents of tremendously varying sizes, each with its own needs for and forms of protection, and all inevitably inter-connected.

Other authors utilized in this chapter include: Gosling (1979), Blum and Rosenberg (1968), Kerr (1963), Kozol (1967), Jaques (1974), Menzies (1960), Klein (1959), Caplan (1970), and Sarason (1971). All have an interest in complexity of being in or out of the tent, negotiating across the entry, and the impact on a group's common mission of forces varying over a field as broad as the individuals' unconscious to the national political context.

CHAPTER 3. VERTICAL AND HORIZONTAL READINESS

Vertical and horizontal readiness is deeply and widely implied, but hardly spelled out anywhere before this chapter. The theoretical sources which we have relied upon to come to this perspective include:

1. Gosling (1979) discusses the difference between tight and loose holding of situations. This essay is transitional because tight holding keeps you in the challenge of the present situation on the field in which the challenge is posed, while loose holding opens up different fields and different times to awareness.
2. Winnicott (1965) is clearest about "meeting the challenge of the case" at hand: another crucial, transitional idea, because moving afield is hazardous without taking care of the adaptive challenge that is upon us.
3. Bateson (1979) distinguishes between these fast adaptive challenges and the slow patterns that connect and hold together, in the temporal perspective, while showing the many different hierarchical structures of living systems, in a spatial perspective.
4. Most family therapists borrow something from Bateson, but the Milan teams (Selvini Palazzoli et al., 1978, 1989, Boscolo et al., 1987, Tomm, 1984, 1987) show the greatest inventiveness in the use of timing and spacing in relation to the family (Gustafson, 1986; 1989a).
5. The group and organizational field has seen little systemic thinking about timing and spacing, except for Mills (1967) and Selvini Palazzoli et al. (1986).
6. Gustafson (1986) shows how individual psychotherapy has evolved by enlarging the field of perspective from intrapsychic to character-analytic to interpersonal to systemic fields of consideration. Sashin (1985) and Callahan and Sashin (in press) show the complex spaces generated by more than a few variables in individual patients. Gustafson (1987) shows how the great simplifying conventions of brief psychotherapy takes similar slices of this 10- or 12-dimensional space. Gustafson (1989b) proposes a set of lenses which allow us to see fields from very small to very large.
7. Platt (1970) introduces Deutsch's theorem, which shows one way in which sudden transformations of a given space are prepared by strong interaction between a component of that space and the context that surrounds the given space.
8. Vertical and horizontal scaling were invented by Allen and Starr (1982) to show or model the phenomena of ecology, where fields of different scope and different timing have such crucial interactions. We have transferred their thinking over into the social, human world.

The authors utilized in this chapter to allude to vertical and horizontal readiness are Gribbin (1977), Reich (1933), Leopold (1949), Auerbach (1986), Horkheimer (1972), Klein (1959), Freire (1970), Sennett (1979), Bernstein (1973), Popper (1957), and Browne (1682). All show an interest in phenomena governed by interactions between fields of different scope and tempo.

It could be said that all poems, dramas and novels explore exactly this subject. The literacy critics who I find most helpful in showing how these explorations are carried out are:

9. Richards (1922) discusses the character of words, which like those of people, can have drastic consequences.
10. Orwell (1946) shows how words can be used to show or to hide relations.
11. Frye (1957) shows the descent of the hero from godly to sub-human space, from leisurely, countless variations to sudden epiphany, in the evolution of Western literature.

12. Percy (1975) explains metaphor's thrill as the distance traveled between the subjects compared.
13. Gass (1983) poses metaphor as the most complex measuring device for man the measurer of all things. He emphasizes the "angle" between the subjects compared.
14. Vendler (1985) describes how we are local beings who depend upon language to keep us from disappearing into the anonymity of social hierarchy, of history.
15. Bayley (1966, 1981, 1987, 1988): See (F) Literature and Religion.

CASE EXAMPLES

A. The organization of the Brief Psychotherapy Clinic has been discussed before by Gustafson (1986, especially Parts IV and V).
B. Balint Group strategy is outlined by Balint (1954) and Bourne (1976), illustrated extensively by Balint (1957), and applied to work with medical students and medical residents by Gustafson (1978, 1981). The complex predicaments of the medical resident are vividly presented by Mizrahi (1984A, B).
C. Milan family therapy team strategy is a large subject presented in outline in The Practical Systemic Guide (E).

CHAPTER 4. GAINING AND RENEWING CLARITY

Staying in a mode of active pursuit of understanding, while at the same time being clear about what one does appreciate, is the central (theoretical) tension of this piece of territory. Our sources here tend to imply one facet and be more explicit about the other:

1. Bion (1959), Slater (1966), Redl (1946), and Gibbard and Hartman (1973) are central amongst authors who saw a cohering thread which read authority and leadership in terms of drives.
2. Bennis and Shepard (1956) and Tuckman (1965) built coherent developmental models, combining peer and leadership foci.
3. Mann (1975) was pivotal in providing a fascinating focus for understanding and an emphasis on active pursuit from a variety of social levels.
4. Skynner (1981, 1987) sensitizes us to the surprise of discovery and a way (his way) of waiting, watching, and moving.
5. Freire's (1970) problem posing to remove the oppressiveness of the director culture, is central in clarifying an important evocative method. A good description of generativity being discovered through the day-to-day language of the members.
6. Deutsch (in Platt, 1970) and Simon (1977) are the clearest for us in how to think ecologically about roaming over fields of greatly varying size or pursue understanding — especially in complex organizations.
7. Gosling (1979) showed the importance of changing directions, being able to see the importance of reversing positions to opening up new perspectives and possibilities for information on different fields, in group life.
8. Weiss & Sampson (1986) helped us be clear on how important enactments are, even in a pursuit (of individual psychotherapy) which has classically overempha-

sized verbal interchange. Miller, Galanter, and Pribram (1960) further suggest the decisions to enact could be unconscious.

9. Hearne (1986a, 1986b) was eloquent in properly focusing our responsibility as interveners on understanding others in *their* terms, presented within the metaphor of animal training. Her articles are witty and well written as well as useful, especially for animal lovers.

10. Since language is our central tool much of the time, Orwell (1946), and Pearce and Cronen (1980) are invaluable guides in how to use it and receive it in a way that fosters understanding, not obscurity, falseness, and "strange loops".

11. Balzac (1835) and Conrad (1897), amongst many other authors, give a literary window into the pain of trying to grasp and hold onto an understanding of social life under shifting conditions. A reminder that the social ecology is terrifyingly unstable, and stable, often at the same time but at a different grain and extent.

Here again the available field of information is widened. From outside our disciplines, the following were particularly helpful: Calhoun (1983), Erikson (1950), Freud (1921), Hughes (1964), Gould (1987), Gustafson (1987), Kerr (1963), Miller (1978). All roam a broad terrain pursuing a coherent picture of our life as social creatures. Each has his unique and useful perspective.

CHAPTER 5. PROTECTING MORALE

It is all too easy to go wrong on this subject, which takes a great deal of balance. Underestimation of foul ups gets you hurt. Overestimation is very unattractive. Who wants to listen to a bitter person? We want to listen to a guide who is very astute about where trouble comes from, but who helps us take it in stride.

What knowledge is required for such guiding? We break down the components as follows:

1. Some categories of disappointment: such as nothing happening, rude surprises, glossing over. This categorizing has to be close or evocative of daily experience in the modern world. Literary sources have been most helpful to us for evoking disappointment: especially Brodsky (1980, 1986), Gogol (1835, 1836), and Voltaire (1759). We rely upon Edelman's concept of knowledge as adequate categorizing (1982).

2. Some explanation of the dominant human preoccupation: Here there is broad agreement between writers as diverse as Levi-Strauss (Charbonnier, 1969), Galbraith (1981, 1983, 1986), and Foucault (1980), Gogol (1835, 1836, 1842), Balzac (1835), Moliere (1666, 1669), and Gass (1983, 1988): Man is chiefly engaged in measuring everything for profit. This knowledge-constitutive interest is often blind to other interests, which then get fouled up or lost in the mill. The "modern contest" sacrifices many other concerns, such as presence, justice and self-defense.

3. This "commercial" picture of man ought to jibe with his worse possibilities, which are predatory, as described by Darwin (1899), Marks (1987), Gould (1987), Havens (1986), Brodsky (1986), Gogol (1835, 1836, 1842), etc.

4. Yet we must not lose sight of the defense of civilization, of language, of humor, of love, or our knowledge is pointless. The knowledge of the bad must be subsumed by the knowledge of the good. Before the modern period, a writer would say that the knowledge of God is more important than knowledge of the world, as Dante Alighieri (1314) shows most vividly. In the modern period, this is still very important in the oratory of Martin Luther King or Desmond Tutu. The newer form depends upon humour, something which you will hear in Tutu's sermons as well. John Bayley summarizes this humour as follows: "Civilization, in their context, is an affair of basic humour, a humour which is naturally present in every aspect of their being and their works, like salt in sea water" (p. 205, 1987). Every hard disappointment can be bathed in this sea water. If you don't, you'll be in trouble with yourself. Robin Skynner (1986A, 1986B, 1987; Skynner and Cleese, 1983) gives our favorite examples of this perspective in our own field of psychiatry.

5. But this humour has to be elusive not to be pinned to the wall. Once you accept the need for elusiveness, in yourself and in others, you are prepared for the difficulties of finding other people. Brodsky (1986) and Gass (1983) and Havens (1986) are our favorite writers on this subject. We have been especially helped by Haven's Grand Rounds Lecture at the University of Wisconsin in April, 1988, in which he compared the individual being to an invisible arrow moving through space-time, which can be tracked as in the cloud-chamber of a physicist, by placing small objects of conversation in its path to watch for its deflection.

6. The concept of scale from Allen and Starr (1982) is indispensable, because people switch scale so adroitly. This concept is crucial to follow presence, to comprehend gross misuse of any social body, to seeing through gloss. Without such thinking, the "ceremony of innocence," to use Yeat's (1920) phrase, will surely be drowned.

7. When we are *sufficiently* removed, the suction of overwhelming patterns becomes farcical, as in de Moliere (1666, 1669), Sullivan (1954, 1956), Selvini-Palazzoli et al. (1978), or Lester (1987).

CHAPTER 6. SEIZING MOMENTS FOR TRANSITION

The great challenge in this part of the group landscape is how to get off the train in a way that stays connected to the journey, when one is about to be lulled or constrained into unacceptable stupor. Theory which connected for us here set up a double description (see Bateson below) contrasting actively chosen movement and just being carried along blindly. We have tried to learn how to live with both, without being trapped by either.

1. Sullivan (1954) speaks to the heart of the matter in describing abrupt, accepted, and smooth transitions, in *Psychiatric Interview*, Chapter 10. In his (1965) *Clinical Studies in Psychiatry*, Chapter 12 on Obsessionalism, he gives a picture of what we are up against when communication is made out of fly-paper. Havens (1965, 1986) is almost a companion piece to Sullivan in giving encour-

agement to take the worst of others' pain, staying live and active with it. Neither take on the group field directly, but seem nonetheless invaluable for the intense conversationalist of any stripe.

2. Bion (1959) and Whitaker and Lieberman (1964) show us the view through their particularly fertile lenses, Bion especially moving so vividly back and forth between the two levels of group life, work and basic assumption, which he saw so clearly. There are many summaries of his work, but we must recommend that the reader stick with the original, the summaries miss Bion's freshness and agility when he makes transitions.

3. Skynner (1987), a daring warrior in Bion's style, covers remarkable range of internal ground with family groups and describes his own process of intervening in a very useful technical way. He encourages surprise and freshness.

4. Palmer (1979), in the context of group relations work offers a useful heuristic for self-examination of the state of the group in trying to imagine how he would present the group to outsiders (in his case, to his staff colleagues). A clear thinker in general, Palmer's concern with meeting his group members at their level is a good model for moving in concert.

5. Balint (1954) gives a good description of working back and forth between opposing currents of patient needs and physician. Working opposing currents is one way the issue of pacing and direction got underlined for us. Also refer to Ringler, Whitman, Gustafson and Coleman (1971), and Jerse, Whitman and Gustafson (1984) for working with opposing currents in leading cancer patient groups.

6. In some ways, even more basic than Balint is Bateson's (1979) double description, how to take advantage of two sources of information perceived simultaneously — as in binocular vision. Given the prominence of single-focus theories. Bateson helped us see the value of a more complex level of learning for finding our way out of labyrinthine group situations.

7. Some of the seminal works in social psychology helped us appreciate how enslaving group participation can be, how compelling it is for us to lose movement. Goffman (1961) and Milgram (1973) are two among many examples in the tradition of conformity research. To some extent, we can all be slaves to our own single-theory, i.e., being accepted by the group. Galbraith (1986) sees this same entrapment from his sardonic platform overlooking our culture as a whole.

8. Literature relates to this kind of problem in many places. Conrad (in *Typhoon*, 1912) and Genet (in *The Balcony*, 1958), give a taste for the disaster of being caged by our limitations or desires. Borges (1979) and Anderson (1957) insist we break out before it is too late.

9. Once again, Deutsch (in Platt, 1970) is invaluable. This time in suggesting possibilities for movement vertically within an organization and generally being clear minded about surrounding sources of influence. Aldrich (1971) presents the organizational terrain in formal terms. Gustafson's (1986) discussion of his brief therapy "method of methods" was useful in combination with Deutsch, in suggesting the importance of being clear about the domain of usefulness of a single-focus theory or a single level in a vertical structure. We were encouraged to formulate our "method of methods" here as including the capacity to look at a situation from different platforms or points of view.

CHAPTER 7. FREE PASSAGE

This subject divides into getting into and getting out of cages.

A. Getting In
  1. From Berger and Kellner (1964) and Wamboldt and Wolin (unpublished) we borrowed the concept of the "marital conversation" which judges all other conversations as a kind of supreme, final court. Wamboldt and Wolin (unpublished) elaborate Berger and Kellner (1964), who, in turn, developed the idea from a paragraph by Nietzsche (1878, p. 59).
  2. Once you consider that fields of any size or scope (Allen and Starr, 1982) can have their conversations, then you may imagine that any one of them can be dominant over the others (not just the marital conversation over the others).
  3. Block (1953) and Hughes (1964) discuss this for the conversation of historians, by analogy to the courtroom, suggesting that there are better and worse "rules for testimony."
  4. We elaborated our own "grammar of cages," borrowing the concept of the "loose end" from Selvini-Palazzoli (1985) (Gustafson, 1986), the crucial "locution" from Kuhn (1970), the "wall" between inside and outside from Klein (1959). The "ceiling" is implied in Havens (1986) but not named as such, the "tilt of the board" utilized in Selvini-Palazzoli (1988) but not named as such. The "floor" is our own invention.

B. Getting Out
  1. The Tavistock and Group-Analytic traditions for study of groups by participant observation have been a fertile source for studying traps and exits in large groups. See Rice (1965) for a description of how to set up such a study of a large group of fifty persons or even more. The best essays on this subject are collected in a book devoted to the large group by Kreeger (1975). We both spent over ten years as consultants to these events, which were extremely useful in arranging difficult situations to find one's way out of on an experimental basis.
  2. Turquet (1975), Main (1975) and Skynner (1975) write most persuasively about the situations one can get trapped in, what they have found most useful to get out, in ways that may be constructive for the entire group.
  3. Lifton (1986) extends what we call "the perfunctory impasses" of everyday life into a full description of the totalitarian nightmare, allowing an extremely useful comparison of the differences between the two: some way down the road and fully down the road of evil.
  4. The use of adequate levels of observation to keep from being trapped into a disturbing interaction ("strange loop") develops from Bateson (1972, 1979), Pearce and Cronen (1980), Cronen, Johnson and Lannaman (1982), Selvini-Palazzoli et al. (1978), Gustafson (1986), and Selvini-Palazzoli et al. (1986, 1988).
  5. Simpler exit strategies are described by de Shazer (1987) with families and Steinbruner with large organizations (1974).
  6. Michael White (1983, 1984, 1988) has discovered exit strategies for most of the major problems seen in family therapy.

CHAPTER 8. TIME AND TIMING

The writers whose work provided the underpinning for our discussion of time cluster in two groups: more linear and more non-linear. The more linear writers suggested finding the right time, giving time for interactional process to develop, and attending to staying connected. The more non-linear writers took a multidimensional view of the system and drew our attention to time scales as one way of differentiating and making parallels across a larger field.

A. More Linear
1. Balint (1954) and Skynner (1981, 1987) both move slowly and use time to make strategic decisions: Balint moves to maximize safety, watching to neither abandon nor intrude; Skynner takes time to become part of the system and then moves to defuse family bombs. Whitaker and Lieberman (1978) represent a tradition of waiting for a specific moment to emerge (depending on theoretical platform).
2. Prominent views of group development, represented by the likes of Bennis and Shepard (1956), Slater, (1966), and Tuckman (1965), tend to view time in group life as more linear, going through specific phases from beginning to end.
3. Greenson (1967) and Fenichel (1945) offer windows into the importance of time in a psychoanalytic context. Also a more linear view, they focus on finding (or waiting for) the right moment to intervene to move forward a process of unfolding and insight.
4. Many places in literature offer the richness of possibilities in the straight line of time. Andreyev (1918) and de Maupassant (1885), for instance, draw our attention to time as it moves forward in lives, encompassing events and circumstances and having inevitable outcomes—as certain as day following night; the morality of the black and white truths.

B. More Non-Linear
1. Most pivotal here is Gould (1987) whose major contribution to our thinking was the notion that we could usefully think of two kinds of time as operating simultaneously: time's arrow and time's cycle. Appreciating the fruitfulness of their interaction added to our sense of how groups developed over long time sweeps. Selvini-Palazzoli (1988) brings the same message closer to home in describing the same kind of complexity with considerable clarity in family life and family therapy.
2. Allen and Starr (1982) in their hierarchical model, note time as it occurs in different ecological levels. In using their model in our group territory, we discovered an escape from constraint through operating with a natural frequency either faster than the neighboring holon or slower, e.g., by being quicker than a family to read its circularity or using a much longer time frame to see its circularity as part of an operation of many generations—thereby we are not taken over by them. The risk here in escaping constraint is non-relation, or intrusion or abandonment. So ecology, the arrow and cycle of time, must be considered together. In Platt (1970), Deutsch takes on a hierarchical model, emphasizing the potential for influence across many levels

in the political and educational ecology. Implied are the advantages of strategic retreats in evaluating time from different positions.

3. Fisher (1935), Carey (1986), Koshland (1986) and Westheimer (1987) give incisive, if brief, pictures of the warp of time depending on observing position. These contributions make very clear how significant one's platform is, because subsequent actions can have profoundly disastrous results over time.

4. Literary windows are many. Galsworthy (1916) in "The Apple Tree," Conrad (1912) in "Typhoon," and Melville (1856) in "Bartleby" juxtapose sharply contrasting time frames, revealing just how deep certain social chasms can be.

Chapter 9. Defensible Terrain

A military metaphor for daily struggles in groups is likely to seem overdrawn to some readers, unless they already feel themselves to be in some kind of social war. Certainly, everyone feels the heat of the countless contests that seem to comprise America. Some may be privileged to live in entirely civilized territory. For the latter, this subject may be unnecessary.

A. The Field in Question:
   1. Machiavelli (1527) has a bad reputation for advocating ruthless, utterly cold uses of princely power. For that, he deserves ill will. But his writing it all out, in such unforgettable terms, helps his readers to defend themselves from exactly what he proposed. There is no dishonor in able defense. The most pleasant of characters is he who refrains from hurting others, but who will *not* allow himself to be hurt either (Fischer, 1984, pp. 31–32). Thus, we feel that Machiavelli can be put to splendid use, not in the service of a prince, but in the service of defense of modest ventures.
   2. Weber (Gerth and Mills, 1946) still provides the best description of the modern instruments of power: bureaucratic human machines.
   3. Galbraith (1983) shows how the field of power is altered by the extreme diversity of players, but also by the concentration of powers in the military-industrial complex: the music is "mass cacophony" over an extremely powerful ground bass.
   4. Foucault (1980) shows the extension of bureaucratic measuring and comparing and categorizing into every field: making the modern contest omnipresent.
   5. Brodsky (1986, 1988A, 1988B), Bayley (1987), Gass (1983, 1988), and Vendler (1985) are the best literary guides to defending local territory from the vast powers of generalization.

B. The Armies of the Oblivious:
   The game theorists (Russett, 1983; Axelrod, 1985; Downs, Rocke and Siverson, 1985) offer the best strategies, for the antagonists are totally impersonal.

C. The Armies of the Desperate:
   The problem of "roving contempt" is our own construction. Havens (1986) is the

best writer about "shaking assumptions" as a superior, more mobile strategy than "confrontation."

D. The Armies of the Overpowering:
 Machiavelli (1527), Galbraith (1983), and Brodsky (1986, 1988A, 1988B) have been our chief advisers about these engines.

Chapter 10. Changing and Staying the Same

The underpinning to changing or staying the same is the willingness and ability to appreciate the value of tradition, the importance of regulated renewal, and a platform for seeing both. If there is a single character to the readings in this section, it was the wisdom of this tripartite perspective.

1. Bateson, particularly in his (1979) discussion of the U.C. Regents, gave an intellectual view of the territory, built on his (1972) notions of "double-bind" and levels of learning. Lewin is no less useful in posing individual vs. group. Both were crucial figures in their own group-focused disciplines.
2. Bion (1959) showed how having an alternative way of thinking is part of the fiber of a successful small group worker. Taking the data of immediate experience and placing it alongside his sense of duty, revealed his key. In so doing, Bion showed how his double description was so tied to action (intervention). Here is a vivid example of Bateson's *caveat* that "the evolutionary process must depend upon . . . double increments of information" (1979, p. 21).
3. Skynner (1981, 1987) is a master at derailing tradition without derailing the individuals involved. He models the boldness it takes to confront group (family) ritual.
4. Selvini-Palazzoli (1988) and her colleagues provide a counterpiece to Skynner, coming at the change process from the view of positive connotation, i.e., how things got how they are and shouldn't be radically tampered with. Also, Palazzoli and the Milan school point to the value of constancies in breaking up strange loops (in part) by using double descriptions embedded in different levels of time.
5. If there are too many fragments or segments, better find the constancies. Literature at the cusp of major cultural shifts helps us with this, as Howells (1885), De Maupassant (1885), and Zola (1885).
6. Forrester (1971) and Keen and Deutsch (1986) put Bateson in a wider cultural context, and made us consider fast changes, anti-tradition, and the consequent loss of constancies. We realized that political and organizational planning must take this double description into account: long term reckoning *and* quickness of adaptation.
7. Bly (1982) suggested we can take some parts of tradition apart without dismantling the whole thing. Steele (1988) shows how to do that in thinking about the complexity of race relations.
8. Gould (1987) and Eliade (1954) showed how the complement of linear and circular time enrich each other. The big lesson here was "eschew false dichotomies" which can be both limiting and deadening.

CHAPTER 11. GATHERING STRENGTH

The concept of placing a series of compartments between oneself and the world is ancient. What is new is its multiplication and the particular forms that have evolved between religious and secular space: what we call the middle compartments.

A. A Six Deep Structure:
   1. Winnicott (1971) opened this possibility up for us with his concept of "transitional space" half way between inside and outside.
   2. Bateson (1972) showed us how complicated hierarchical structures, such as formidable antagonists, cannot be mapped without one more level of structure than the antagonist, just as a globe cannot be comprehended on a flat piece of paper.
   3. Pearce and Cronen (1980) and Cronen, Johnson and Lannamann (1982) taught us how the *lack* of a level of structure external to the field in question draws you into the "strange loops" of the field.
   4. The Milan Team (Selvini-Palazzoli et al., 1978, 1986, 1988) gave us the best practical demonstrations of five levels of hierarchy used to comprehend four or less. See Gustafson (1989a; 1986, Chapter 10) for explaining this practice we have borrowed.

B. War:
   1. Colinvaux (1983) is most clear about the place of war in securing niches.
   2. Levi-Strauss (Charbonnier, 1969) is most clear about the place of inequality ("whether we call it slavery, serfdom or class distinctions is not of any fundamental importance" p. 33) in social (hot) engines.
   3. The literary writers I have loved most on this subject are George Eliot (1871), Yeats (1920) and Herbert (1968).
   4. The historian who takes this theme most vividly for me is Fisher (1936).

C. Contests:
   1. Foucault (1980) sharpened the modern contest most for me.
   2. The Milan team (Selvini Palazzoli et al., 1978, 1986, 1989) plays most ably.

D. The Center Compartment of the Modern World:
   This is our own construct. See Chapter 1.

E. Civility:
   1. The concept is borrowed from Tuan (1986).
   2. The "rules of evidence" come from Bloch (1953).

F. Play:
   1. Winnicott's (1971) chief contribution is about the crucial playful use of this "transitional space."
   2. Stevenson (1892) captures it unforgettably.
   3. Tennyson (1833) and Conrad (1912) show its serious nature in adults.

G. Solitude:
   To last in this world, one must have a place where one is alone with one's maker,

or mountain, or inner sanctum, for along the way there may be no friend at hand in the middle of the night, for in the end one has to die alone. Slater's groups (1966) play with this religious space as part of their art, by removing the expected classroom contest. Slater shows how god, the mountain and one's little local (unmovable) rock dissolve into each other. An unmovable group leader evokes all of this. Writers who evoke such places for us include:

1. Blumenthal (1980)
2. Ammons (1987)
3. Bayley (1981)
4. Lawrence (1959)
5. Royce (1936)
6. Frost (in Ellmann, 1976)

CHAPTER 12. AN ATTITUDE FOR ALL SEASONS

One can come at the challenge of a survival attitude from many angles. I have proposed three facets of posture which keeps me connected to my group work as it goes from peak to valley and back up again: having perspective on winning, lasting the long haul, and taking on oneself.

Having an intellectual preparation, as presented in Chapters 1–11, is essential to keeping one's bearings. But how to have an emotional platform is the challenge of Chapter 12.

1. *Perspective on winning* is akin to a survivor attitude. Real survivors have been a big help here. Brodsky (1988a), for instance, has much to offer as a social commentator, and also about how to survive the oppressiveness of social life by being prepared for exile.
2. Bateson (1979) is the clearest about living in two worlds of time simultaneously for purposes of survival in organizations: immediate time of fast adaptation and the longer time of slow change and evaluation.
3. Among the many writers in our field who demonstrated *determination*, Mann (1975), Skynner (1987), and Bion (1959) are helpful models for how to stick with a point of view under fire, play the game strictly by the rules.
4. Certain works of literature are particularly good at portraying standing against exploitation, *being clear about one's own course*, for better or worse. Sillitoe (1967), Conrad (1912), and De Maupassant (1975) number amongst these. They raise many useful questions for us as social operators: Where is the line drawn between commitment to self vs. commitment to others? Where does determination become stubbornness and stupidity? What are the implications of moral relation to an immoral social course? The excitement was of discovering and shaping our own one-man revolution (Frost, 1936).
5. And humor musn't be forgotten in social life. Bayley (1987) and Bermel (1982) remind us how to keep it all in perspective if we are to be able to make the inner adjustments (Gass, 1988) needed to survive for the long haul.

Bibliography

Aldrich, H. (1971). Organizational boundaries and inter-organizational conflict. *Human relations, 24,* 279–293.

Alexander, F., & French, T. M. (1946). *Psychoanalytic therapy, principles and applications.* New York: Ronald Press.

Alighieri, Dante (1314). *Inferno.* Translated by John Ciardi. New York: New American Library, 1954.

Allen, T. F. H., O'Neill, R. V., & Hoekstra, T. W. (1984). Interlevel relations in ecological research and management: Some working principles from hierarchy theory. *USDA Forest Service General Technical Report RM-110,* July, 1984.

Allen, T. F. H., & Starr, T. B. (1982). *Hierarchy, Perspectives for Ecological Complexity.* Chicago: University of Chicago Press.

Almond, R. (1974). *The healing community: dynamics of the therapeutic milieu.* New York: Jason Aronson.

Almond, R., & Astrachan, B. (1969). Social system training for psychiatric residents. *Psychiatry, 32,* 277–291.

Alvarez, A. (1988). Witness. Review of Czeslaw Milosz: *The collected poems, 1931–1987. New York Review of Books,* June 2, 1988, 21–22.

Ammons, A. R. (1987). *Sumerian vistas.* Poems. New York: W. W. Norton.

Anderson, S. (1957). Unlighted Lamps. In Wallace and Mary Stegner (Eds.). *Great American short stories,* New York: Dell, 287–308.

Andreyev, L. (1918). *The seven that were hanged.* New York: Boni and Liveright.

Annan, N. (1988). Gentlemen and players. *New York Review of Books,* September 29, 1988.

Arendt, H. (1958). What was authority? In Friedrich, J. (Ed.), *Authority.* Cambridge: Harvard University Press.

Aristophanes (413 BC). *Lysistrata.* San Francisco: Chandler Publishing Co., 1959.

Aristotle (330 BC). *Politics.* Translated by Benjamin Jowett. New York: Modern Library, 1943.

Asch, S. E. (1955). Opinions and social pressure. *Scientific American, 193,* 31–35.

Ashby, W. Ross (1970). *An introduction to cybernetics.* London: Chapman and Hall.

Auerbach, R. (1986). Celtics. *Capital Times,* May 13, 1986, Madison, Wisconsin.

Axelrod, R., & Keohane, R. O. (1985). Achieving cooperation under an anarchy: Strategies and institutions. *World Politics, 38,* 226–254.

Bach, G. (1954). *Intensive group psychotherapy.* New York: Ronald Press.

Baker, R. (1982). Nuclear experts not all that smart. December 9, 1982, *Milwaukee Journal* (*New York Times*).

Baker, R. (1989). A low-ranked ball can ruin a person. January 20, 1989, *Wisconsin State Journal* (*New York Times*).

Balint, M. (1952). New beginning and the paranoid and the depressive syndromes. *International Journal of Psychoanalysis, 33,* 214. Reprinted in Balint, M. (1953). *Primary love and psychoanalytic technique.* New York: Liveright.

Balint, M. (1954). Method and technique in the teaching of medical psychology. II. Training general practitioners in psychotherapy. *British Journal of Medical Psychology, 27,* 37–41.

Balint, M. (1957). *The doctor, his patient, and the illness.* New York: Internaitonal Universities Press.

Balzac, H. de (1835). *Pere Goriot.* New York: The Modern Library, 1946.

Barker, R. G. (1983). The threat of efficiency. In J. B. Calhoun (Ed.), *Environment and population,* New York: Praeger.

Barnett, R. J. (1987). The four pillars. *The New Yorker,* March 9, 1987, 76–89.

Bateson, G. (1971). The cybernetics of "self:" a theory of alcoholism. *Psychiatry, 34,* 1–18. Also reprinted in Bateson (1972).

Bateson, G. (1972). The logical categories of learning and communication. In *Steps to an ecology of mind.* New York: Ballantine Books, 279–308.

Bateson, G. (1972). Style, grace and information in primitive art. In Bateson, G., *Steps to an ecology of mind,* New York: Ballantine.

Bateson, G. (1972). *Steps towards an ecology of mind.* New York: Ballantine.

Bateson, G. (1979). *Mind and nature: a necessary unity.* New York: Dutton.

Bayley, J. (1966). *Tolstoy and the novel.* London, Chatto and Windus. Reprinted 1988, Chicago: University of Chicago Press.

Bayley, J. (1981). *Shakespeare and tragedy.* London: Routledge and Kegan Paul.

Bayley, J. (1987). *The order of battle at Trafalgar and other essays.* New York: Weidenfeld and Nicolson.

Bayley, J. (1988). *The short story, Henry James to Elizabeth Bowen.* New York: St. Martin's Press.

Beahrs, J. O. (1986). *Limits of scientific psychiatry. The role of uncertainty in mental health.* New York: Brunner/Mazel.

Bennett, M. J. (1985). Focal behavorial psychotherapy for acute narcissistic injury: De Mopes—report of a case. *American Journal of Psychotherapy, 39,* 126–133.

Bennis, W. (1988). Mr. "Right Stuff" tricks search panel. *The Washington Times,* page C2, April 28.

Bennis, W. G., & Shepard, H. A. (1956). A theory of group development. *Human Relations, 9,* 415–437. Reprinted in Gibbard, G. S., Hartman, J. J., & Mann, R. D. (Eds.), *Analysis of groups,* San Francisco: Jossey Bass, 1974.

Bennis, W.G., Berlew, D. E., Schein, E. H., & Steele, F. I. (1973). *Interpersonal dynamics. Essays and readings on human interaction.* Third Edition. Homewood, Illinois: Dorsey Press.

Berger, P. L., & Kellner, H. (1964). Marriage and the construction of reality: An exercise in the microsociology of knowledge. *Diogenes, 46,* 1–24.

Bermel, A. (1982). Farce. New York: Simon and Schuster.

Bernstein, B. (1973). *Class, codes and control. Volume I: Theoretical studies towards a sociology of language.* St. Albin, Herts: Paladin.

Berry, T., & Tate, D. (1988). Success in a new task—a role consultation. *Management Education and Development, 19,* 215–226.

Berry, W. (1987). Letter to Wes Jackson. In W. Berry. *Home economics, fourteen essays by Wendell Berry,* 3–5. Berkeley: Northpoint Press.

Bion, W. R. (1959). *Experiences in groups.* New York: Basic Books, Inc.

Bloch, M. (1953). *The historian's craft.* Translated by Peter Putnam. New York.

Blum, A. F., & Rosenberg, L. (1968). Some problems involved in professionalizing social interactions: The case of psychotherapeutic training. *Journal of Health and Social Behavior, 9,* 72–85.

Blumenthal, M. (1980). *Days we would rather know. Poems by Michael Blumenthal.* New York: Penguin Books.

Bly, C. (1982). Quietly thinking over things at Christmas. In *Letters from the country.* 51–58, New York: Penguin Books.

Borges, J. L. (1962). The lottery in Babylon. In *Labyrinths. Selected stories and other writings.* New York: New Directions Publ. Co., 51–59.

Borges, J. L. (1979). *The book of sand.* Middlesex, England: Penguin Books Ltd.

Boscolo, L., & Cecchin, G. (1982). Training in systemic therapy at the Milan Center. In R. Whiffen & J. Byng-Hall (Eds.), *Family therapy supervision: Recent developmetns in practice,* London: Academic Press.

Boscolo, L., Cecchin, G., Hoffman, L., & Penn, P. (1987). *Milan Systemic Family Therapy: Conversations in Theory and Practice.* New York: Basic Books.

Boszormenyi-Nagy, I., & Spark, G. (1984). *Invisible loyalties,* New York: Brunner/Mazel.

Botez, M. C. (1983). Overcomplexity syndrome: A therapeutic approach. In J. B. Calhoun (Ed.), *Environment and population,* New York: Praeger.

Bourdieu, P. (1977). *Outline of a theory of practice.* Translated by Richard Nice. Cambridge, England: Cambridge University Press.

Bourdieu, P. (1984). *Distinction. A social critique of the judgment of taste.* Translated by Richard Nice. Cambridge: Harvard University Press.

Bourne, S. (1976). Balint groups: G. P. seminars and the doctor-patient relationship. *Psychiatria fennica,* 339–347.

Bowen, M. (1978) *Family therapy in clinical practice.* New York: Jason Aronson.

Boyer, P. (1984). From activism to apathy: Americans and the nuclear issue, 1963–1980. *Bulletin of the Atomic Scientists, 40,* 14–23.

Brenman, M. (1952). On teasing and being teased: And the problem of "moral masochism." *The Psychoanalytic Study of the Child,* 7: 264–285.

Brodsky, J. (1980). *A part of speech.* New York: Farrar, Straus & Giroux.

Brodsky, J. (1986). *Less than one. Selected essays.* New York: Farrar, Straus, Giroux.

Brodsky, J. (1988a). The condition we call exile. *New York Review of Books,* February 4, 16–20.

Brodsky, J. (1988b). Uncommon visage. The Nobel lecture. *New Republic,* January 4 and 11, 27–32.

Browne, T. (1682). *Religio medici,* eighth edition. In A. M. Witherspoon, & F. J. Warnke (Eds.), *Seventeenth-century prose and poetry.* New York: Harcourt, Brace and World, 1929.

Bruner, J. (1967). *Toward a theory of instruction.* Cambridge: Harvard University Press.

Burnham, J. B. (1986). *Family therapy. First steps toward a systemic approach.* London and New York: Tavistock Publications.

Burnham, J., & Harris, Q. (1985). Therapy, supervision, consultation. Different levels of system. In D. Campbell and R. Draper (Eds.), *Applications of systemic family therapy*: The Milan approach. London: Academic Press.

Buroway, M. (1979). *Making out on the shop floor: Changes in the labor process under monopoly capitalism.* Chicago: University of Chicago Press.

Buruma, I. (1986). Us and others. Review of *War without mercy: Race and power in the Pacific war* by J. Dower in *New York Review of Books,* August 14, pp. 23–25.

Calhoun, J. B. (1983). *Environment and population. Problems of adaptation. An expermental book integrating statements by 162 contributors.* New York: Praeger.

Callahan, J., & Sashin, J. I. (in press). Models of affect-response and anorexia nervosa. *Annals of the New York Academy of Sciences.*

Camus, A. (1967). The guest. In A. Casty (Ed.), *The shape of fiction.* Lexington, MA: D. C. Heath.

Caplan, G. (1970). *The theory of practice of mental health consultation.* New York: Basic Books.

Carey, W. D. (1986). On institutional memory. *Science, 234,* 9 (editorial).

Carroll, L. (1862). *The annotated Alilce. Alice's adventures in wonderland and through the looking glass.* New York: Clarkson N. Potter, Inc., 1960.

Casty, A. (1967). *The shape of fiction.* Lexington, Mass.: D. C. Heath.

Cecchin, G. (1987). Hypothesizing, circularity, and neutrality revisited: An invitation to curiosity. *Family Process, 26,* 405–413.

Charbonnier, G. (1969). *Conversations with Claude Levi-Strauss.* Translated by John and Doreen Weightman. London: Jonathan Cape.

Chatwin, B. (1989). The song lines quartet, *New York Review of Books,* January 19.

Coleman, J. S. (1971). Social systems. In P. A. Weiss (Ed.), *Hierarchically organized systems in theory and practice.* New York: Hafner.

Colinvaux, P. (1983). Human history: A consequence of plastic niche but fixed breeding strategy. In J. B. Calhoun (Ed.), *Environment and population,* New York: Praeger.

Collins, R. (1979). *The credential society. A historical sociology of education and stratification.* New York: Academic Press.

Colman, A. D., & Geller, M. H. (Eds.) (1985). *Group Relations Reader 2.* Washington, D.C.: A. K. Rice Institute.

Commager, H. S. (1985). Science, nationalism and the academy. *Academe: Bulletin of the American Association of University Professors, 71,* November-December, 9–13.

Conrad, J. (1897). *The nigger of the 'Narcissus'*. London: Penguin Books, 1963.
Conrad, J. (1900). *Lord Jim*. New York: Viking Penguin, 1957.
Conrad, J. (1912). *The secret sharer*. From *The shadow line and two other tales* (Typhoon and the secret sharer). New York: Doubleday Anchor, 1959.
Cooper, L. (1976). Co-therapy relationships in groups. *Small Group Behavior, 7*, 473–497.
Cooper, L. (1977). Mirroring: One vehicle to organizational clarity. *International Journal of Social Psychiatry, 22*, 288–296.
Cooper, L., & Gustafson, J. P. (1979a). Planning and mastery in group therapy: A contribution to theory and technique. *Human Relations, 32*, 689–703.
Cooper, L., & Gustafson, J. P. (1979b). Towards a general theory of group therapy. *Human Relations, 32*, 967–981.
Cooper, L., & Gustafson, J. P. (1981). Family-group development: Planning in organizations. *Human Relations, 34*, 705–730.
Crane, S. (1898). The open boat. In J. Katz (Ed.), *The portable Stephen Crane*, 1969. Middlesex, Endland: Penguin Books, 360–386.
Cronen, V. E., Johnson, K. M., & Lannamann, J. W. (1982). Paradoxes, double binds, and reflexive loops: An alternative theoretical perspective. *Family Process, 21*, 91–112.
Crossley-Holland, K. (1985). *The fox and the cat. Animal tales from Grimm*. New York: Lothrop, Lee and Shephard Books.
Darwin, C. (1899). *The expression of the emotions in man and animals*. New York: Appleton.
DeLoach, S. S. (1988). *Study group consultancy. Elements of the task*. New Orleans, LA: S. S. DeLoach.
De Shazer, S. (1985). *Keys to solution in brief therapy*. New York: Norton.
De Shazer, S. (1987). Minimal elegance. *Family Therapy Networker*, October, 1987, 57–60.
De Tocqueville, A. (1835). *Democracy in America*. Edited by R. D. Heffner. New York: Mentor Books, 1956.
Dennison, G. (1969). *The lives of children. The story of the first street school*. New York: Vintage.
Deutsch, K. W. (1966). *The nerves of government*. New York: The Free Press.
Dicks, H. V. (1967). *Marital tensions*. New York: Basic Books.
Downs, G. W., Rocke, D. M., & Siverson, R. M. (1985). Arms races and cooperation. *World Politics, 38*, 118–146.
Dreyfus, H. L., & Rabinow, P. (1982). *Michel Foucault: Beyond structuralism and hermeneutics*. Chicago: University of Chicago Press.
Durkin, J. (Ed.) (1981). *Living systems: Group psychotherapy and general systems theory*. New York: Brunner/Mazel.
Durrenmatt, F. (1956). *The visit*. New York: Grove Press.
Dyson, F. (1984). *Weapons and hope*. New York: Harper & Row.
Edelman, G. M. (1979). Group selection and phasic reentrant signaling: A theroy of higher brain function. In G. M. Edelman & V. B. Mountcastle (Eds.), *The mindful brain*, Cambridge, MA: MIT Press, 51–100.
Edelman, G. M. (1982). Through a computer darkly: Group selection and higher brain function. *Bulletin of the American Academy of Arts and Sciences, 36*, 20–49.
Edelman, G. M. (1985). Neural Darwinism: Population thinking and higher brain function. In M. Shafto (Ed.), *How we know*, San Francisco: Harper and Row, 1–30.
Edelman, G. M. (1989). *Topobiology: An introduction to molecular embryology*. New York: Basic Books.
Edelson, M. (1970). *Sociotherapy and psychotherapy*. Chicago: University of Chicago Press.
Editorial (1987). Poverty, malnutrition, and world food supplies. *The Lancet*, August 29, 1987, 487–488.
Ehrlich, P. R., & Ehrlich, A. H. (1986). World population crisis. *Bulletin of the Atomic Scientists*, April, 13–17.
Eliade, M. (1954). *The myth of the eternal return*. Princeton: Princeton University Press.
Eliot, G. (1871). *Middlemarch*. Harmondsworth, Middlesex, England: Penguin, 1965.
Eliot, T. S. (1934). The love song of J. Alfred Prufrock. In T. S. Eliot, *The waste land and other poems*. New York: Harcourt, Brace and Company.
Ellmann, R. (Ed.) (1976). *The new Oxford book of American verse*. New York: Oxford University Press.

Engel, G. L. (1980). The clinical application of the biopsychosocial model. *American Journal of Psychiatry, 137,* 535–544.

Erikson, E. H. (1950). *Childhood and society.* New York: Norton.

Erikson, E. H. (1954). The dream specimen of psychoanalysis. *Journal of the American Psychoanalytical Association, 2,* 5–56.

Erikson, K. (1966). *Wayward puritans. A study in the sociology of deviance.* New York: John Wiley & Sons.

Ezriel, H. (1950). A psycho-analytic approach to group treatment. *British Journal of Medical Psychology, 23,* 59–74.

Fanon, F. (1963). *The wretched of the earth.* Translated by Constance Farrington. New York: Grove Press.

Fenichel, O. (1945). *The psychoanalytic theory of neurosis.* New York: Norton.

Fisher, H. A. L. (1935). *A history of Europe. Volume 1.* London: Eyre & Spottiswoode.

Fischer, D. (1984). *Preventing war in the nuclear age.* Totowa, NJ: Rowman and Allanheld.

Fleming, A. (Ed.) (1976). *America is not all traffic lights. Poems of the midwest.* Boston: Little, Brown.

Ford, R. (1987). Optimists. *The New Yorker,* March 30, pp. 28–36.

Forrester, J. W. (1971). Behavior of social systems. In P. A. Weiss, (Ed.), *Hierarchically organized systems in theory and practice.* New York: Hafner, 81–122.

Forster, E. M. (1941). *Howards end.* Harmondsworth, Middlesex, England: Penguin Books.

Foucault, M. (1973). *Madness and civilization. A history of insanity in the age of reason.* Richard Howard (Tr.). New York: Vintage Books.

Foucault, M. (1980). *Power/knowledge. Selected interviews and other writings.* C. Gordon (Ed.). New York: Pantheon Books.

Foulkes, S. H. (1964). *Therapeutic group analysis.* London: Allen and Unwin.

Frank, J. (1971). *Persuasion and healing.* Baltimore: Johns Hopkins University Press.

Frank, J. (1982). *Sanity and survival in the nuclear age, psychological aspects of war and peace.* New York: Random House, 115–137.

Freire, P. (1970). *Pedagogy of the oppressed.* New York: Herder and Herder.

Freud, S. (1900). The interpretation of dreams. *The standard edition of the complete psychological works of Sigmund Freud, 4.* J. Strachey (Ed. and tr.). New York: Norton.

Freud, S. (1909). Notes upon a case of obsessional neurosis. *Standard edition, 10,* 153–318. New York: Norton.

Freud, S. (1921). Group psychology and the analysis of the ego. *Standard edition, 18.* New York: Norton.

Freud, S. (1930). *Civilization and its discontents. Standard edition, 21.* New York: Norton.

Freud, S. (1932). Why war? *Standard Edition, 22,* 195–218. New York: Norton.

Friedman, L. (1988). The clinical popularity of object relations concepts. *Psychoanalytic Quarterly. LVII,* 667–691.

Frost, R. (1936). Building soil: A political pastoral. In E. Connery Lathern (Ed.), *The poetry of Robert Frost.* New York: Holt, Rinehart and Winston, 1969.

Frye, N. (1957). *Anatomy of criticism. Four essays.* Princeton, New Jersey: Princeton University Press.

Galbraith, J. K. (1981). *A life in our times. Memoirs.* Boston: Houghton Mifflin Company.

Galbraith, J. K. (1983). *The anatomy of power.* Boston: Houghton Mifflin Company.

Galbraith, J. K. (1986a). *A view from the stands.* Boston: Houghton Mifflin Co.

Galbraith, J. K. (1986b). Lecture to inaugurate The Madison Foundation, Madison Wisconsin.

Galdston, I. (1954). Sophocles contra Freud: A reassessment of the Oedipus Complex. *Bulletin New York Academy Medicine, 30,* 803–817.

Galsworthy, J. (1916). *Caravan. The assembled tales of John Galsworthy.* New York: Charles Scribner's Sons, 263–313, 1926.

Gass, W. H. (1983). Groping for trouts: On metaphor. *The Salmagundi Reader,* 421–433.

Gass, W. H. (1988). The polemical philosopher. *New York Review of Books,* February 4, 1988, 35–41.

Genet, J. (1958). *The balcony.* New York: Grove Press, Inc.

Gerth, H. H., & Mills, C. W. (1946). *From Max Weber: Essays in sociology.* New York: Oxford University Press.

Gibbard, G. S., & Hartman, J. J. (1973). The Oedipal paradigm in group development. A clinical and empirical study. *Small Group Behavior, 4*, 305-354.

Gibbard, G. S., Hartmann, J. J., & Mann, R. D. (1974). *Analysis of groups*. San Francisco: Jossey-Bass.

Gleick, J. (1988). *Chaos. Making a new science*. London, Heinemann.

Goffman, E. (1961). *Asylums*. Garden City, New York: Doubleday.

Gogol, N. (1835). Nevsky Prospect. In L. J. Kent (Ed.), *The complete tales of Nikolai Gogol*. Chicago: University of Chicago Press, vol. 1, 207-238, 1985.

Gogol, N. (1836). The nose. In L. J. Kent (Ed.), *The complete tales of Nikolai Gogol. vol. 2*, Chicago: University of Chicago Press, 215-239, 1985.

Gogol, N. (1842). *Dead souls*. New York: Viking Penguin, 1961.

Gosling, R. H. (1979). Another source of conservatism in groups. In W. G. Lawrence (Ed.), *Exploring individual and organizational boundaries, A Tavistock open systems approach*. New York: John Wiley and Sons.

Gosling, R. H., & Turquet, P. M. (1967). The training of general practitioners. In R. H. Gosling, D. H. Miller, D. Woodhouse, & P. M. Turquet (Eds.), *The use of small groups in training*. London: Codicote Press.

Gould, S. J. (1986). Cardboard Darwinism. *New York Review of Books*, September 25, 47-54.

Gould, S. J. (1987). *Times's arrow, time's cycle*. Cambridge: Harvard University Press.

Gould, S. J. (1988). Mighty Manchester. *New York Review of Books*, October 27, 1988.

Gramsci, A. (1957). *The modern prince and other writings*. New York: International Publishers.

Gramsci, A. (1973). *Letters from prison*. Translated by L. Lawner. New York: Harper & Row.

Greenson, R. R. (1967). *The technique and practice of psychoanalysis. Volume I*. New York: International Universities Press, Inc.

Greider, W. (1987). Annals of finance. The price of money. I. Temple secrets. II. Full faith and credit. III. The hardest choice. *The New Yorker*, November 9, 16 and 23, 49-104, 68-113 and 49-104.

Gribbin, J. (1977). *White Holes: Cosmic Gushers in the Universe*. New York: Dell.

The Grubb Institute (1981). *Working papers on organizational role analysis*.

Gustafson, J. P. (1976a). The passive small group: Working concepts. *Human Relations, 29*, 793-803.

Gustafson, J. P. (1976b). The pseudo-mutual small group or organization. *Human Relations, 29*. 989-997. Reprinted in G. Lawrence (Ed.), *Exploring boundaries*. New York: Plenum Press.

Gustafson, J. P. (1978a). Schismatic groups. *Human Relations, 31*, 139-154.

Gustafson, J. P. (1978b). The work of the student doctor: A pilot project. *British Journal of Medical Education, 12* , 300-305.

Gustafson, J. P. (1981). The control and mastery of aggression by doctors: A focal problem for the Balint Group with medical residents. In L. Wolberg & M. Aronson (Eds.), *Group and Family Therapy 1981*. New York: Brunner/Mazel.

Gustafson, J. P. (1983). Repression in small working groups. In J. Calhoun (Ed.), *Problems of adaptation*. New York: Praeger.

Gustafson, J. P. (1986). *The complex secret of brief psychotherapy*. New York: Norton.

Gustafson, J. P. (1987). The neighboring field of brief individual psychotherapy. *Journal of Marital and Family Therapy, 13*, 409-422.

Gustafson, J. P. (1989a). A scientific journey of twenty years. *Journal of Strategic and Systemic Therapies*, July, 1989.

Gustafson, J. P. (1989b). The great simplifying conventions of brief psychotherapy. In J. Zeig & S. Gilligan (Eds.), *Brief therapy: Myths, methods and metaphors*. New York: Brunner/Mazel.

Gustafson, J. P. (unpublished manuscript (a)). One-eyed organizations in the world of nuclear weapons. Address to the Annual Meeting of the A. K. Rice Institute, April, 1985.

Gustafson, J. P. (Unpublished manuscript (b)). Finding and going forward: The two great challenges of long-term psychotherapy, 1988.

Gustafson, J. P., & Cooper, L. (1978a). Toward the study of society in microcosm: Critical problems of group relations conferences. *Human Relations, 31*, 843-862.

Gustafson, J. P., & Cooper, L. (1978b). Collaboration in small groups: Theory and technique for the study of small group processes. *Human Relations, 31*, 155–171.

Gustafson, J. P., & Cooper, L. (1979). Unconscious planning in small groups. *Human Relations, 32*, 1039–1064.

Gustafson, J. P., & Cooper, L. (1983). The divergent problems of brief groups. In L. Wolberg & M. Aronson (Eds.), *Group and family therapy 1983*. New York: Brunner/Mazel.

Gustafson, J. P., & Cooper, L. (1985). After basic assumptions: On holding a specialized versus a general theory of small groups. In M. Pines (Ed.), *Bion and group psychotherapy*, London: Routledge and Kegan Paul.

Gustafson, J. P., Cooper, L., Lathrop N., Ringler, K., Seldin, F., & Wright, M. K. (1981). Cooperative and clashing interests in small groups, Part I. *Human Relations, 34*, 315–337. Part II. *Human Relations, 34*, 367–368.

Habermas, J. (1971). *Knowledge and human interests*. Jeremy J. Shapiro (Tr.). Boston: Beacon Press.

Habermas, J. (1973). *Legitimation crisis*. Thomas McCarthy (Tr.). Boston: Beacon Press.

Haley, J. (1967). Toward a theory of pathological systems. In G. N. Zuk & I. Boszormenyi-Nagy (Eds.) *Family therapy and disturbed families*. Palo Alto: Science and Behavior Books.

Hanauske-Abel, H. M. (1986). From Nazi holocaust to nuclear holocaust: A lesson to learn. *The Lancet*, August 2, 271–273.

Harris, Q., & Burnham, J. (1985). A training programme in systemic therapy: The problem of the institutional context. In R. Draper (Ed.), *Systemic family therapy*. London: Academic Press.

Havens, L. (1965). The anatomy of a suicide. *New England Journal of Medicine, 272*, 401–406.

Havens, L. L. (1973). *Approaches to the mind*. Boston: Little, Brown. Reprinted by Harvard University Press, 1988.

Havens, L. L. (1976). *Participant observation*. New York: Aronson.

Havens, L. (1986). *Making contact, Uses of language in psychotherapy*. Cambridge, Massachusetts: Harvard University Press.

Havens, L. L. (1988). Talking with difficult patients. Grand Rounds, Department of Psychiatry, University of Wisconsin, March 2, 1988.

Havens, L. L. (unpublished manuscript). The possibilities of human existence.

Hawthorne, N. (1851). *The house of the seven gables*. New York: Bantam Books, 1981.

Hearne, V. (1986a). Reflections. Questions about language. I. Horses. *The New Yorker*, August 18, 33–57.

Hearne, V. (1986b). Reflections. Questions about language. II. Cats. *The New Yorker*, August 25, 78–89.

Heilbroner, R. (1989). The triumph of capitalism. *The New Yorker*, January 23, 1989, pp. 98–109.

Henry, J. (1963). *Culture against man*. New York: Vintage Books.

Henry, J. (1973). *On sham, vulnerability and other forms of self-destruction*. New York: Random House.

Herbert, Z. (1968). *Selected poems*. Trnaslated by Czeslaw Milosz and Peter Dale Scott. New York: Ecco Press, 1986.

Herndon, J. (1965). *The way it spozed to be*. New York: Simon and Schuster.

Hesse, H. (1943). *Magister Ludi (the glass bead game)*. R. and C. Winston (Tr.). New York: Bantam, 1970.

Hobbes, T. (1651). *Leviathan, or, the matter, form, and power of a commonwealth, ecclesiastical and civil*.

Hofstadter, D. R. (1979). *Godel, Escher, Bach*. New York: Basic Books.

Holmes, O. W. (1858). *The autocrat of the breakfast table*. New York: Heritage Press, 1955.

Homer. *The Odyssey*. Robert Fitzgerald (Tr.). New York: Anchor Books, 1963.

Hopkins, G. M. (1953). *A Hopkins reader*. John Pick (Ed.). New York: Oxford University Press.

Horkheimer, M. (1972). Authority and the family. In *Critical theory, selected essays*. New York: Seabury Press, 47–128.

Horowitz, M. J., & Arthur, R. J. (in press). Narcissistic rage in leaders: The intersection of individual dynamics and group process. *International Journal of Social Psychiatry*.

Howells, W. D. (1885). *The rise of Silas Lapham*. New York: New American Library of World Literature, 1963.

Hughes, H. S. (1964). *History as art and as science*. New York: Harper & Row.

(The) I Ching or Book of Changes. Richard Willhelm (Tr.). Princeton, NJ: Princeton University Press, 1950.

Illich, I. (1970). *Deschooling society*. New York: Harper & Row.

Jacobson, E. (1953). Contribution to the metapsychology of cyclothymic depression. In P. Greenacre (Ed.), *The affective disorders*. New York: International Universities Press, pp. 49–83.

Jaques, E. (1974). Social systems as a defense against persecutory and depressive society. In Gibbard, G. S., Hartmann, J. J., & Mann, R. D. (Eds.), *Analysis of groups*. San Francisco: Jossey-Bass.

Janis, I. L. (1967). *Victims of group think*. Boston: Houghton Mifflin.

Jerse, M. A., Whitman, H. H., & Gustafson, J. P. (1984). Cancer in adults. In H. Roback (Ed.), *Helping patients and their families cope with medical problems*, Chapter 10, 251–284. San Francisco: Josssey-Bass.

Jones, E. W. (1986). Black managers: The dream deferred. *Harvard Business Review*, May–June, 84–92.

Jung, C. G. (1933). Dream-analysis in its practical application. In C. G. Jung, *Modern man in search of a soul*. W. S. Dell & Cary F. Baynes (Tr.). New York: Harcourt, Brace.

Kaplan, F. (1983). *The wizards of Armageddon*. New York: Simon and Schuster.

Keats, J. (1817). Letter to George and Thomas Keats. In M. H. Abrams (Ed.), *The Norton anthology of English literature*, New York: Norton, 1986, Volume 2, pp. 862–863.

Keen, J. P., & Deutsch, K. W. (1986). Societal learning, political systems and education: Some prospects and priorities for the future. *Systems Research, 3,* 89–96.

Kerr, C. (1963). *The uses of the university*. New York: Harper & Row.

Klein, E. B., & Astrachan, B. M. (1971). Learning in groups: A comparison of study groups and T groups. *Journal of Applied Behavioral Science, 7,* 659–683.

Klein, E. B., Thomas C. S., & Bellis, E. C. (1971). When warring groups meet: The use of a group approach in police-black community relations. *Social Psychiatry, 6,* 93–99.

Klein, M. (1959). Our adult world and its roots in infancy. In M. Klein, *Envy and gratitude and other works*, 1946–1963. New York: Dell, 1975.

Koshland, D. E. (1986). Spanking, reason, and the environment. *Science, 234,* 409 (editorial).

Kozol, J. (1967). *Death at an early age*. New York: Bantam Books.

Kozol, J. (1985). *Illiterate America*. New York: Anchor Press/Doubleday.

Kramer, J. (1986). A letter from Europe. *The New Yorker*. June 30, 65–77.

Kreeger, L. (Ed.) (1975). *The large group, dynamics and therapy*. London: Constable.

Kuhn, T. S. (1962). *The structure of scientific revolutions, Second Edition*. Chicago: University of Chicago Press.

Kuhn, T. S. (1970). Logic of discovery or psychology of research. In I. Lakatos & A. Musgrave (Eds.), *Criticism and the growth of knowledge*. Cambridge, England: Cambridge University Press.

Kull, S. (1985). Nuclear nonsense. *Foreign Policy,* Spring, 1985, 28–52.

Kuper, A., & Stone, A. A. (1982). The dream of Irma's injection: A structural analysis. *American Journal of Psychiatry, 139 ,* 1225–1234.

Laing, R. D. (1959). *The divided self*. An existential study in sanity and madness. London: Tavistock Press.

Laing, R. D. (1961). *Self and others*. Middlesex, England: Penguin Books.

Laing, R. D., & Cooper, D. G. (1964). *Reason and violence: A decade of Sartre's philosophy 1950-1960*. New York: Vintage, 1971.

Lakatos, I. (1970). Falsification and the methodology of scientific research programmes. In I. Lakatos & A. Musgrave (Eds.), *Criticism and the growth of knowledge*. Cambridge, England: Cambridge University Press.

Lawrence, D. H. (1959). *Selected poems*. New York: Viking Press.

Lear, E. (1871). The jumblies. In E. Lear, *Nonsense songs, stories, botany, and alphabets*. London: Robert P. Bush.

Leopold, A. (1949). *A Sand County Almanac*. New York: Oxford University Press.

Lester, J. (1987). *The tales of Uncle Remus. The adventures of Brer Rabbit.* New York: Dial Books.

Lewin, K. (1945). The research center for group dynamics of the Massachusetts Institute for Technology. *Sociometry, 2,* 126–136.

Lewin, K. (1947). Frontiers in group dynamics. II. Channels of group life; social planning and action research. *Human Relations, 1,* 143–147.

Lifton, R. J. (1986). *The Nazi doctors.* New York: Basic Books.

Lifton, R. J., & Falk, R. (1982). *Indefensible weapons. The political and psychological case against nuclearism.* New York: Basic.

Lloyd, A. S. (1972). Freire, conscientization, and adult education. *Adult Education, 23,* 3–20.

Lobel, A. (1988). *The turnaround wind.* New York: Harper & Row.

Lofgren, L. B. (1976). Organizational design and therapeutic effect. In E. J. Miller (Ed.), *Task and organization.* New York: John Wiley, 235–242.

Lorenz, K. (1952). *King Solomon's ring.* New York: Thomas Y. Crowell Co.

Lowell, R. (1985). Epilogue. In H. Vendler (Ed.), *The Harvard book of contemporary American poetry.* Cambridge, Massachusetts: Harvard University Press, p. 112.

MacArthur, R. (1972). Strong, or weak, interactions? *Transactions Connecticut Academy of Arts and Sciences, 44,* 177–188.

Machiavelli, N. (1527). *The prince and the discourses.* New York: Modern Library, 1950.

Madison, J. (1787). The Federalist, numbers 10 and 15, 1787. In R. Hofstadter (Ed.), *Great issues in American history, A documentary record.* New York: Vintage Books, 1958.

Magee, B. (1973). *Karl Popper.* New York: Viking Press.

Mailer, N. (1968). *The armies of the night.* New York: Signet Books.

Main, T. F. (1957). The ailment. *British Journal of Medical Psychology, 30,* 129–145.

Main, T. F. (1975). Some psychodynamics of large groups. In L. Kreeger (Ed.), *The large group. Dynamics and therapy.* London: Constable, 57–86.

Mann, D. W. (unpublished). A simple theory of the self.

Mann, R. D. (1975). Winners, losers and the search for equality in groups. In C. Cooper (Ed.), *Theories of group processes.* London: Wiley.

Margulies, A. (1989). *The empathic imagination.* New York: W. W. Norton.

Marks, I. (1987). *Fears, phobias, and rituals, The nature of anxiety and panic disorders.* New York: Oxford University Press.

Marx, K. (1967). *Capital. A critique of political economy. Volume 1. The Process of Capitalist Production.* Translated by Samuel Moore and Edward Aveling. F. Engels (Ed.). New York: International Publishers.

Maturana, H. F., & Varela, F. J. (1980). *Autopoiesis and cognition. The realization of the living.* Boston: D. Reidel.

Maupassant, G. de (1885). *Bel-Ami.* Harmondsworth, Middlesex, England: Penguin Books, 1975.

McCaughan, N., & Palmer, B. (unpublished). Systems thinking for harassed managers.

McGrath, J. (1987). In this corner: It's only fitting that Indiana won. *The Capital Times,* Madison, Wisconsin, Tuesday, March 31.

Melville, H. (1851). *Moby-Dick or, the whale.* Edited with an Introduction by Alfred Kazin. Boston: Houghton Mifflin, 1956.

Melville, H. (1856). *Billy Budd and other tales.* New York: Signet Classic (1961).

Menzies, I. E. P. (1960). A case-study in the functioning of social systems as a defense against anxiety. A report on the nursing service of a general hospital. *Human Relations, 13,* 95–121.

Milgram, S. (1973). Behavioral study of obedience. In W. G. Bennis et al. (Eds.), *Interpersonal Dynamics.* Homewood, Illinois: Dorsey Press, 60–72.

Miller, J. G. (1978). *Living systems.* New York: McGraw-Hill.

Mills, C. W. (1959). *The sociological imagination.* New York: Oxford University Press.

Mills, T. (1967). *The sociology of small groups.* Englewood Cliffs, N.J.: Prentice-Hall.

Miller, A. (1950). *Death of a salesman.* New York: The Viking Press.

Miller, E. J., & Rice, A. K. (1967). *Systems of organization.* London: Tavistock Publications.

Miller, G. A., Galanter, E., & Pribram, K. H. (1960). *Plans and the structure of behavior.* Holt, Rinehart & Winston, Inc.

Milosz, C. (1988). *Czeslaw Milosz: The collected poems, 1931–1987.* New York: Ecco Press.

Mitscherlich, A. (1978). Group psychology and the analysis of the ego—a lifetime later. *Psychoanalytic Quarterly, 47,* 1–23.

Mizrahi, T. (1984a). Managing medical mistakes: Ideology, insularity and accountability among internists-in-training. *Social Science Medicine, 19,* 135–146.

Mizrahi, T. (1984b). The outpatient clinic: The crucible of the physician-patient relationship in graduate medical training. *Journal of Ambulatory Care Management,* May, 1984, 51–68.

Moliere, J. B. P. de (1666, 1669). *The misanthrope and Tartuffe.* Translated into English Verse by Richard Wilbur. New York: Harcourt, Brace, Jovanovich, 1954.

Morris, W., & Morris, M. (1977). *Morris dictionary of word and phrase origins.* New York: Harper & Row.

Newton, P. M. (1981, winter). *Who among us still hopes to learn about the nature of man?* University Publishing.

Newton, P. M. (1988). Free association and the division of labor in psychoanalytic treatment. *Psychoanalytic Psychology, 6,* 31–46.

Newton, P. M., & Levinson, D. J. (1973). The work group within the organization: A sociopsychological approach. *Psychiatry, 36,* 115–142.

Nietzsche, F. (1872). Homer's Contest. In W. Kaufman (Ed), *The portable Nietzsche.* W. Kaufman (Ed), New York: Viking Press, 1954, pp. 32–39.

Nietzsche, F. (1878). Human, all too human. In W. Kaufman (Ed.), *The portable Nietzsche.* New York: Viking Press, 1954.

Ollman, B. (1971). *Alienation, Marx's conception of man in capitalist society.* Cambridge, England: Cambridge Universitiy Press.

Orwell, G. (1946). The politics of the English language. In G. Orwell, *A collection of essays by George Orwell.* New York: Harcourt, Brace, Jovanovich.

Palmer, B. W. M. (1979). Learning and the group experience. In Lawrence, W. G. (Ed.), *Exploring individual and organizational boundaries,* Chapter 12, 169–192. New York: Wiley.

Palmer, B. W. M. (1985). Ambiguity and paradox in group relations conferences. In M. Pines (Ed.), *Bion and group psychotherapy.* London: Routledge & Kegan Paul, 274–305.

Parsons, T., & Shils, E. A. (Eds.) (1951). *Toward a general theory of action.* New York: Harper & Row.

Pearce, W. B., & Cronen, V. S. (1980). *Communication, action and meaning, the creation of social realities.* New York: Praeger Publishers.

Percy, W. (1975). Metaphor as mistake. In W. Percy, *The message in the bottle.* New York: Farrar, Straus, and Giroux.

Pines, M. (Ed.) (1985). *Bion and group psychotherapy.* London: Routledge and Kegan Paul.

Platt, J. (1970). Hierarchical restructuring. *Bulletin of Atomic Scientist,* November 2–4, 46–48. Reprinted in *General Systems,* 15 (1970).

Popper, K. (1957). *The poverty of historicism.* Second Rev. Ed. New York: Basic Books, 1966.

Porter, K. A. (1935). Theft. In R. V. Cassill (Ed.), *The Norton anthology of short fiction, Third edition.* New York: Norton, 1986.

Potok, C. (1967). *The chosen.* New York: Fawcett Crest.

Rathjens, G. W. (1986). The strategic dimension. *Disarmament, 9,* 27–46.

Redl, F. (1946). Group emotion and leadership. *Psychiatry, 5, 573–596.*

Reed, B. D. (1976). Organizational role analysis. In C. L. Cooper (Ed.), *Developing social skills in managers.* London: Macmillan.

Reich, W. (1933). *Character analysis.* New York: Farrar, Straus and Giroux, 1949.

Reider, N. (1953). A type of transference to institutions. *Bulletin of the Menninger Clinic, 17,* 58–73.

Renoir, J. (1974). The grand illusionist turns 80. *New York Times,* September 15, 1974, Film.

Rice, A. K. (1965). *Learning for leadership. Interpersonal and intergroup relations.* London: Tavistock Publications.

Rice, A. K. (1969). Individual, group and intergroup processes. *Human Relations, 22,* 565–584. Reprinted in E. J. Miller (Ed.), *Task and organization.* London: John Wiley and Sons, 1976.

Rice, E. R., & Austin, A. E. (1988). High faculty morale. *Change,* March/April, 51–58.

Rice, E. R. (1986). The academic profession in transition: Toward a new social fiction. *Teaching Sociology, 14*, 12–23.

Richards, I. A. (1922). Introduction to *Roget's pocket thesaurus*. New York: Simon and Schuster, 1946.

Rickman, J. (1951). Reflections on the function and organization of a psychoanalytical society. *International Journal of Psychoanalysis, 32*, 218–237.

Ringler, K., Whitman, H. H., Gustafson, J. P., & Coleman, F. (1981). Technical advances in leading a cancer patients' group. *International Journal of Group Psychotherapy, 31*, 329–344.

Rioch, M. J. (1970). Group relations: Rationale and technique. *International Journal of Group Psychotherapy, 20*, 340–355.

Rosenfield, I. (1985). A hero of the brain. *New York Review of Books, 32*, November 21, 1985, 49.

Rosenfield, I. (1986). Neural Darwinism: A new approach to memory and perception. *New York Review of Books*, October 9, 1986, 21–27.

Rosenhan, D. L. (1973). On being sane in insane places. *Science, 179*, 250–258.

Royce, J. (1936). *The philosophy of loyalty*. New York: MacMillan.

Russett, B. (1983). *The prisoners of insecurity*. San Francisco: W. H. Freeman.

Rutan, J. S., & Stone, W. N. (1984). *Psychodynamic group psychotherapy*. Lexington, Mass.: Collamore Press.

Saint Exupery, A. de (1943). *The little prince*. Translated from the French by Katherine Woods. New York: Harcourt, Brace, Jovanovich.

Sarason, S. B. (1971). *The culture of the school and the problem of change*. Boston: Allyn and Bacon.

Sarason, S. B., & Klaber, M. (1985). The school as a social situation. *Annual Review of Psychology, 36*, 115–140.

Sashin, J. I. (1985). Affect tolerance: A model of affect-response using catastrophe theory. *Journal of Social and Biological Structure, 8*, 175–202.

Schaeffer, S. F. (1974). *Anya*. New York: Avon Books.

Schafer, R. (1959). Generative empathy in the treatmetn situation. *The Psychoanalytic Quarterly, 28*, 342–374.

Scheim, D. E. (1988). *Contract on America, The Mafia murder of President John F. Kennedy*. New York: Schapolsky Publishers.

Schilder, P. (1940). Introductory remarks on groups. *The Journal of Social Psychology, 12*, 83–100.

Schilder, P. (1951). *Psychoanalysis, man, and society*. New York: Norton, 268–287.

Schumacher, E. F. (1973). *Small is beautiful, economics as if people mattered*. New York: Harper & Row.

Searles, H. F. (1972). Unconscious processes in relation to the environmental crisis. *Psychoanalytic Review, 59*, 361–374.

Selvini Palazzoli, M. (1980). Why a long interval between sessions. Therapist control of the family-therapist suprasystem. In M. Andolfi & I. Zwerling (Eds.), *Dimensions of family therapy*. New York: Guilford Press.

Selvini Palazzoli, M. (1985). The problem of the sibling as referring person. *Journal of Marital and Family Therapy, 11*, 21–34.

Selvini Palazzoli, M. (1986). Towards a general model of psychotic family games. *Journal of Marital and Family Therapy, 12*, 339–349.

Selvini Palazzoli, M. (1988). *The work of Mara Selvini-Palazzoli*. M. Selvini (Ed.), Northvale, New Jersey: Jason Aronson, Inc.

Selvini Palazzoli, M., Anolli, L., DiBlasio, P., Giossi, L., Pisano, I., Ricci, C., Sacchi, M., & Ugazio, V. (1986). *The hidden games of organizations*. New York: Pantheon Books.

Selvini Palazzoli, M., Boscolo, L., Cecchin, G. F., & Prata, G. (1977). Family rituals: A powerful tool in family therapy. *Family Process, 16*, 445–453.

Selvini Palazzoli, M., Boscolo, L., Cecchin, G. F., & Prata, G. (1978). *Paradox and counterparadox: A new model in the therapy of the family in schizophrenic transactions*. New York: Aronson.

Selvini Palazzoli, M., & Prata, G. (1982). Snares in family therapy. *Journal of Marital and Family Therapy, 8*, 443–450.

Selvini Palazzoli, M., Cirillo, S., Selvini, M., & Sorrentino, A. M. (1989). *Family games, general models of psychotic processes in the family*. New York: W. W. Norton.

Selvini Palazzoli, M., & Viaro, M. (1988). The anorectic process in the family: A six-stage model as a guide for individual therapy. *Family Process, 27*, 129–148.

Sennett, R. (1979). The boss's new clothes. *New York Review of Books, 26*, 42–46.

Shakespeare, W. *Complete works*. Baltimore, Maryland: Penguin Books, 1969.

Sherwin, M. J. (1977). *A world destroyed. The atomic bomb and the grand alliance*. New York: Vintage.

Sillitoe, A. (1949). The loneliness of the long distance runner. In A. Casty, *The shape of fiction*. Lexington, Mass: D. C. Heath and Co., 296–326 (1967).

Simon, H. A. (1977). *Models of discovery*. Boston: D. Reidel Publishing Co.

Skynner, A. C. R. (1975). The large group in training. In L. Kreeger (Ed.), *The large group, dynamics and therapy*. London: Constable, 227–251.

Skynner, A. C. R. (1981). An open system, group-analytic approach to family therapy. In A. Gurman, & D. Kniskern (Eds.), *Handbook of family and marital therapy*. New York: Brunner/Mazel.

Skynner, R. (1983). Make sure to feed the goose that lays the golden egg: A discussion on the myth of altruism. *Journal of Psychohistory, 10*, 389–395.

Skynner, R. (1986a). The psychotherapy teacher–getting older. Narrowing down or opening out? *Bulletin of the Royal College of Psychiatrists, 10*, 341–345.

Skynner, R. (1986b). What is effective in group psychotherapy? *Group Analysis, 19*, 5–24.

Skynner, R. (1987). *Explorations with families, group analysis and family therapy*. John R. Schlapoborsky (Ed.). London: Methuen.

Skynner, R., & Cleese, J. (1983). *Families and how to survive them*. London: Methuen.

Slater, P. E. (1966). *Microcosm, structural, psychological and religious evolution in groups*. New York: John Wiley & Sons.

Solzhenitsyn, A. (1973). *The Gulag Archipelago*. New York: Harper & Row.

Sontag, S. (1966). *Against interpretation*. New York: Farrar, Strauss and Giroux.

Steele, S. (1988). I'm black, you're white, who's innocent? *Harper's*, June 45–53.

Steig, W. (1982). *Doctor De Soto*. New York: Scholastic Inc.

Steig, W. (1984). *Rotten island*. Boston: David R. Godine.

Steinbruner, J. D. (1974). *The cybernetic theory of decision. New dimensions of political analysis*. Princeton, NJ: Princeton University Press.

Steinbruner, J. D. (1987). Choices and trade offs. In A. B. Carter, J. D. Steinbruner, and C. A. Zraket (Eds.), *Managing Nuclear Operations*. Washington, D.C.: Brookings, Chapter 16, 535–554.

Stendhal (1830). *The red and the black*. Charles Tergie (Tr.). New York: Collier Books, 1961.

Sterne, L. (1767). *Tristram Shandy*. New York: Odyssey Press, 1940.

Stevenson, R. L. (1892). The lantern-bearers. In *Across the Plains*. London: Chatto and Windus, Piccadilly.

Stierlin, H. (1988). Systemic optimism, systemic pessimism. *Family Process, 27*, 121–127.

Stierlin, H., & Weber, G. (1989). *Unlocking the family door: A systemic approach to the understanding and treatment of anorexia nervosa*. New York: Brunner/Mazel.

Sullivan, H. S. (1954). *The psychiatric interview*. New York: W. W. Norton & Co.

Sullivan, H. S. (1956). *Clinical studies in psychiatry*. New York: W. W. Norton & Co.

Tennyson, A. (1833). Ulysses. In M. H. Abrams (Ed.), *The Norton anthology of English literature*, Fifth Edition, Volume 2. New York: Norton, pp. 1108–1110, 1986.

Terkel, S. (1972). *Working*. New York: Avon.

Tolstoy, L. (1894). Introduction to the works of Guy de Maupassant. In J. Bayley (Ed.), *The portable Tolstoy*. New York: Viking Press.

Tolstoy, L. (1869). *War and peace*. Translated by C. Garnett. New York: Random House.

Tomm, K. (1984). One perspective on the Milan systemic approach: Part I. Overview of development, theory and practice. Part II. Description of session format, interviewing style and interventions. *Journal of Marital and Family Therapy, 10*, 113–125 and 253–271.

Tomm, K. (1987). Interventive interviewing. Part I. Strategizing as a fourth guideline for the therapist. Part I. Reflexive questioning as a means to enable self-healing. *Family Process, 26*, 113–125 and 167–183.

Tomm, K. (1988). Interventive interviewing: Part III. Intending to ask lineal, circular, strategic, or reflexive questions? *Family Process, 27*, 1–15.
Tower, J., Muskie, E., & Scowcroft, B. (1987). *The Tower commission report*. New York: Bantam Books.
Trevelyan, G. M. (1942). *A shortened history of England*. London: Penguin, 1959.
Tuan, Y. (1980). *Segmented worlds and self*. University of Minnesota Press.
Tuan, Y. (1986). *The good life*. Madison: University of Wisconsin Press.
Tuan, Y. (1989). Letter to colleagues, May 15, 1989 (Volume 4, Number 17).
Tuckman, B. W. (1965). Developmental sequence in small groups. *Psychological Bulletin, 63*, 384–399.
Turnbull, C. M. (1972). *The mountain people*. New York: Simon and Schuster.
Turquet, P. M., & Gosling, R. (1965). Appendix. Illustration of a general practitioners' seminar at work. In Gosling, R., Turquet, P. M., Miller, D. H., and Woodehouse, D. (Eds.), *The use of small groups in training*. Hitchen, Herefordshire: Codicote Press, 114–144.
Turquet, P. M. (1975). Threats to identity in the large group. In L. Kreeger (Ed.), *The large group, dynamics and therapy*. London: Constable, 87–144.
Tutu, D. (1988). Lecture to the University of Wisconsin, Field House, Madison, Wisconsin, May, 1988.
Vendler, H. (1985). *The Harvard book of contemporary American verse*. Cambridge, Massachusetts: Harvard University Press.
Vendler, H. (1988). Review of Ammons' *Sumerian vistas*. New Yorker: February 15, 1988.
Voltaire (1759). *Candide*. In B. R. Redman (Ed.), *The Portable Voltaire*. New York: Viking Press, 1949.
Von Foerster, H. (1973). On constructing a reality. In F. E. Preiser (Ed.), *Environmental design research*, Volume 2. Stroudberg: Dowden, Hutchinson and Ross, 288–308.
Vonnegut, K., Jr. (1961). Harrison Bergeron. In A. Casty (Ed.), *The shape of fiction*. Lexington, Massachusetts: D. C. Heath, 376–380, 1967, 1975.
Vosnesensky, A. (1966). *Antiworlds. Poetry by Andrei Vosnesensky*. Translated by Patricia Blake and Max Hayward. New York: Basic.
Wamboldt, F. S., & Wolin, S. J. (unpublished). Reality and myth in family life: Changes across generations.
Watzlawick, P., Weakland, J., & Fisch, R. (1974). *Change, principles of problem formation and problem resolution*. New York: Norton & Co., Inc.
Weber, M. (1968). *On charisma and institution building*. Chicago: University of Chicago Press.
Weiss, J., & Sampson, H. (1986). *The psychoanalytic process. Theory, clinical observations, and empirical research*. New York: Guilford Press.
Westheimer, F. H. (1987). Are our universities rotten at the "core"? *Science, 236*, 1165–1166.
Whitaker, D. S., & Lieberman, M. A. (1964). *Psychotherapy and the group process*. Chicago: Aldine Publishing Co.
Whitaker, D. S., & Lieberman, M. A. (1978). Strategy, position and power. In Gibbard, G. S., Hartman, J. J., & Mann, R. D. (Eds.). *Analysis of groups*. San Francisco: Jossey-Bass, 372–386.
White, M. (1983). Anorexia nervosa: A transgenerational system perspective. *Family Process, 22*, 255–273.
White, M. (1984). Marital therapy — practical approaches to longstanding problems. *Australian Journal of Family Therapy, 5*, 27–41.
White, M. (1988). Family therapy and schizophrenia: Addressing the "in-the-corner lifestyle." *Dulwich Centre Newsletter*.
White, M., & Epson, D. (in press). *Literate means to therapeutic ends*. New York: W. W. Norton.
White, R. K. (Ed.) (1986). *Psychology and the prevention of nuclear war*. New York: New York University Press.
Whitman, W. (1881–1882). Song of myself. In R. Ellmann (Ed.), *The new Oxford book of American verse*. New York: Oxford University Press, 1976.
Williams, W. C. (1925). *In the American grain*. New York: New Directions.
Winnicott, D. W. (1947). Hate in the countertransference. In D. W. Winnicott, *Through pediatrics to psycho-analysis*. New York: Basic Books, 1975.

Winnicott, D. W. (1965). The use of the term therapeutic consultation. Outline for a course given by Winnicott in September, 1985, provided by Robin Skynner.

Winnicott, D. W. (1971). *Playing and reality*. London: Tavistock Publications.

Yalom, I. D. (1975). *Theory and practice of group psychotherapy*, second edition. New York: Basic Books, Inc.

Yeats, W. B. (1920). The second coming. In *Selected poems and two plays of William Butler Yeats*. M. L. Rosenthal (Ed.), New York: Collier Books, 1962, p. 91.

Zola, E. (1885). *Germinal*. Middlesex, England: Penguin Books, 1954.

Press. Reprinted with permission from the publisher. Colinvaux, P. (1983). Human history: A consequence of plastic niche but fixed breeding strategy. In J. B. Calhoun (Ed.), *Environment and Population*. New York: Praeger. Charbonnier, G. (1969). *Conversations with Claude Levi-Strauss*. Translation by John and Doreen Weightman. London: Jonathan Cape. Reprinted with permission from the publisher. Fisher, H. A. L. (1935). *A history of Europe. Volume I*. London: Eyre & Spottiswoode. Vosnesensky, A. (1966). "Antiworlds". Poetry by Andrei Vosnesensky. Translated by Patricia Blake and Max Hayward. New York: Basic Books. Heilbroner, R. (1989). The triumph of capitalism. *The New Yorker*, January 23, 1989, pp. 98–109. Reprinted by permission; © 1989 Robert Heilbroner. Henry, J. (1963). *Culture against man*. New York: Vintage Books. *(The) I-Ching or Book of Change*, (1950), the Richard Wilhelm translation rendered into English by Cary F. Baynes. Bollingen Series XIX. Copyright 1950, © 1967, © renewed 1977 by Princeton University Press. Reprinted with permission from the publisher. The I-Ching, in *The Shape of Fiction* (1975), edited by Alan H. Casty. 2nd ed. Lexington, MA: D. C. Heath. Reprinted with permission from the publisher. Mill, T. (1967). *The Sociology of Small Groups*. Englewood Cliff, NJ: Prentice-Hall. *Roget's Pocket Thesaurus*, (1964) p. vi. New York: Harper & Row.

Index